Roman Britain's
Missing Legion

By the same author:

Sea Eagles of Empire
Empire State: How the Roman Military Built an Empire
Septimius Severus in Scotland
Roman Legionaries: Soldiers of Empire
Ragstone to Riches
Julius Caesar: Rome's Greatest Warlord
Old Testament Warriors
Pertinax: The Son of a Slave Who Became Roman Emperor

Roman Britain's Missing Legion

What Really Happened to IX Hispana?

Simon Elliott

Pen & Sword
MILITARY

First published in Great Britain in 2021 and reprinted in 2021 by
Pen & Sword Military
An imprint of
Pen & Sword Books Ltd
Yorkshire – Philadelphia

ISBN 978 1 52676 572 7

A CIP catalogue record for this book is
available from the British Library.

Printed and bound in the UK by CPI Group (UK) Ltd, Croydon, CR0 4YY.

Pen & Sword Books Limited incorporates the imprints of Atlas, Archaeology,
Aviation, Discovery, Family History, Fiction, History, Maritime, Military, Military
Classics, Politics, Select, Transport, True Crime, Air World, Frontline Publishing,
Leo Cooper, Remember When, Seaforth Publishing, The Praetorian Press,
Wharncliffe Local History, Wharncliffe Transport, Wharncliffe True Crime and
White Owl.

For a complete list of Pen & Sword titles please contact

PEN & SWORD BOOKS LIMITED
47 Church Street, Barnsley, South Yorkshire, S70 2AS, England
E-mail: enquiries@pen-and-sword.co.uk
Website: www.pen-and-sword.co.uk

Or
PEN AND SWORD BOOKS
1950 Lawrence Rd, Havertown, PA 19083, USA
E-mail: Uspen-and-sword@casematepublishers.com
Website: www.penandswordbooks.com

Contents

This book is dedicated to three individuals who all, in their own ways, have inspired my passion for classics and archaeology, and encouraged me throughout my academic and writing career. These are Professor Andrew Lambert of King's College London, Dr Andrew Gardner of University College London, and Dr Steve Willis of the University of Kent. Thank you all.

Ut Veniant Omnes!

Introduction

This book is an historical detective story concerning the mysterious disappearance of the 5,500 men of *legio* IX *Hispana*, one of Rome's most famous military units. Uniquely among the Roman legions, of which there were over time more than sixty (and at any one time in the Empire a maximum of thirty-three), we have no idea what happened to it. It simply disappears from history.

This historical conundrum has grabbed the attention of academics, scholars and the wider public for hundreds of years. One of the first to write on the subject was British antiquarian John Horsley who published his *Britannia Romana* or the *Roman Antiquities of Britain* in 1732. In this work he detailed when each Roman legion arrived and left Britain. However, he noted that there was no leaving date for *legio* IX *Hispana*, a fact he found difficult to explain. Then, in the 1850s, the renowned German scholar Theodor Mommsen published his multi-volume *The History of Rome*. In this he speculated that the IXth legion had been the subject of an uprising by the Brigantes tribe of northern Britain around AD 117/118, it being wiped out in its legionary fortress at York (Roman *Eboracum*). Mommsen speculated it was this event that prompted the new Emperor Hadrian to later visit Britain in AD 122 and initiate the construction of Hadrian's Wall.

Such was Mommsen's reputation that his theory became the received wisdom regarding the legion's fate well into the twentieth century AD, when it was then popularized by a number of historical fiction works. One above all others cemented the fate of *legio* IX *Hispana* in the popular imagination. This was *The Eagle of the Ninth*, the seminal work published by children's author Rosemary Sutcliff in 1954. Her second book, this told the story of her hero Marcus Flavius Aquila who travelled north of Hadrian's Wall to track down the fate his father's legion, *legio* IX *Hispana*. Her conceit was that the IXth legion had been annihilated in the far north of Britain, beyond the northern border rather than in York, during yet another uprising. This novel proved as popular with adults as with children, capturing the imagination of an entire generation, and is still a best seller to this day. It inspired numerous subsequent works, including Karl Edward Wagner's 1976 *Legion from the Shadows* and Amanda Cockrell's 1979 *The Legions of the Mist*. The story of the IXth legion also became the subject of an eponymous BBC TV series in 1977, and later received the attentions of Hollywood with blockbusters such as 2010's *Centurion* and 2011's *The Eagle*. It was even the focus of a *Dr Who* episode in 2017.

Such mention of these various antiquarian and modern references and treatments leads elegantly to a wider description of the sources used in this book. Firstly, given the long chronology within which the story of the IXth legion sits, we are lucky to have multiple ancient sources available. These always come with the usual health warnings regarding their variable accuracy and reliability, but are nevertheless valuable.

An important early source in the story of the first IXth legion (that detailed in this book is actually the second to exist) is Julius Caesar himself in his own *The Conquest of Gaul* and *Civil War*, together with his contemporaries Cicero with his letters and various works and Sallust with his *Catiline's Conspiracy*, and also Caesar's legate Aulus Hirtius who added a chapter to *The Gallic War* and may have edited *On the African War* and *On the Spanish War* (both narrating Caesar's activities there). Moving onto the wider story of *legio* IX *Hispana*, other key ancient sources include Marcus Velleius Paterculus and his late first century BC/early first century AD *Roman History*, Plutarch with his early second century AD *Lives*, Cornelius Tacitus with his *Annals, Histories* and *Agricola* (mid-late first century AD to early second century), Suetonius with his *Twelve Caesars*, and Appian with his *Roman History* written in the mid-second century AD. Also of use are Cassius Dio with his *Roman History*, and Herodian with his *History of the Roman Empire*. Another key source is the now anonymous *Historia Augusta*, a collection of biographies of Roman Emperors, junior colleagues, designated heirs and usurpers from the accession of Hadrian in AD 117 to the accession of Diocletian in AD 284. Written towards the end of the fourth century AD in Latin, modern scholars believe it was based on a single work dating to the period of Dio and Herodian. The leading twentieth-century historian and classicist Sir Ronald Syme believed the author to be an individual he dubbed 'Ignotus', while others favour a lost work by the Senator and historian Marius Maximus, at least for part of it. The *Historia Augusta* is thought particularly unreliable, and frequently reads as though the author is more interested in entertaining his audience than reporting historical fact (Pausche, 2009, 115). To the *Historia Augusta* we can also add the works of the later Latin chroniclers Flavius Eutropius, Aurelius Victor and Paulus Orosius. The first two (and given their use as sources by the third, that too by default) likely used as a major source the so-called 'Kaisergeschichte' hypothetical set of short histories now lost. Burgess (1993, 491) argues this was written between AD 337 and AD 340. Again, these sources should be considered with care, especially given the length of time between the events they describe and the date they were written (particularly relevant given the focus here on the fate of *legio* IX *Hispana*).

In terms of modern sources, the various works of Anthony R. Birley have been most useful, particularly his definitive 2005 edition of *The Roman Government of Britain*, while as ever David Mattingly's 2006 *An Imperial Possession: Britain in the Roman Empire* has proved invaluable. Other key modern works have included Patricia Southern's 2013 *Roman Britain*, Sam Moorhead and David Stuttard's 2012 *The Romans Who Shaped Britain*, and Duncan B. Campbell's 2018 *The Fate of the Ninth*.

Meanwhile, the many works on the Roman military of Adrian Goldsworthy and Ross Cowan have provided much of the vital detail needed when considering the daily lives of the legionaries of the IXth legion. Regarding the legions themselves, one work has proved particularly useful, this is 2012's *The Complete Roman Legions* by Nigel Pollard and Joanne Berry. Meanwhile, with reference to one specific chapter, the work of Dominic Perring has defined Chapter 4, with his breakthrough work referenced there. Richard Hingley's 2018 *Londinium: A Biography* has also proved invaluable in that part of the narrative. Meanwhile, Tim Cornell and John Matthews' *Atlas of the Roman World* has provided much detail regarding the far-flung provinces of the Empire where the IXth legion might have met its fate.

To the above sources of contemporary research used in my attempt to track down what really happened to *legio* IX *Hispana* I can add my own academic research over the last fifteen years through my MA in War Studies with King's College London, MA in Archaeology with University College London, and PhD in Classics and Archaeology from the University of Kent, where I am honoured to be an Honorary Research Fellow. Additionally, my recently published works on Roman themes have proved a fertile source of new information regarding the IXth legion and its times, including *Sea Eagles of Empire: The Classis Britannica and the Battles for Britain*, *Empire State: How the Roman Military Built an Empire*, *Septimius Severus in Scotland: the Northern Campaigns of the First Hammer of the Scots*, *Roman*

Legionaries, and the shortly to be published *Pertinax: the Son of a Slave Who Became Roman Emperor*.

Meanwhile, other specific sources of information on the IXth legion have included the archaeological record, epigraphy, analogy, and where appropriate anecdote. In particular, epigraphy plays a key role in the history of the career and later disappearance of *legio* IX *Hispana*. The word epigraphy, derived from the ancient Greek word for inscription, describes the study of the latter as a form of writing. In that regard we are fortunate that the Romans were prolific inscribers in stone, which was an everyday occurrence across the Empire. Such inscriptions were used in the widest range of circumstances, ranging from details of the deceased on funerary monuments, through to altars referencing the lives of those who set them up, to the detailing on buildings of the individuals who funded them or built them. Roman inscriptions are particularly useful in this work as they not only detail the individual, individuals or units concerned, but almost always name the reigning emperor, including his honorific and other titles at the time. When cross-referenced with other evidence, this provides a fairly precise way of dating when the inscription was made.

Roman academics have long used epigraphy in their studies and in the 1850s Theodor Mommsen, referenced above given his early interest in the IXth legion, developed an international scheme for referencing each individual inscription called the *Corpus Inscriptionum Latinarum* (CIL) project. From that point each inscription recorded was referenced with a CIL number. In the 1920s scholars in Britain then diverged from this system with their own method of recording Roman epigraphy here, this was called the Roman Inscriptions in Britain (RIB) project. They were then followed by their French counterparts who dubbed their inscriptions L'Année Epigraphique (AE). Thus the various inscriptions cited in this work are numbered as either CIL, RIB or AE. Such inscriptions have been specifically used by some scholars in the discipline of prosopography, the study of a group of persons or characters within a particular historical or literary context through their careers, in this case detailed on epigraphy. Their work has shed much light on the careers of various officers of the IXth legion.

In terms of housekeeping regarding my investigation into the fate of the IXth legion, this story takes place in the late Roman Republic and the Principate period of the Roman Empire. The latter name is derived from the term *princeps* (chief or master), referencing the Emperor as the leading citizen of the Empire following the Senate's acclamation of Augustus as the first emperor in 27 BC. While not an official term, later emperors often assumed it on their accession, it clearly being a conceit allowing the Empire to be explained away as a simple continuance of the preceding Republic. The Principate Empire featured a number of distinct dynasties and phases that provide a chronological template when studying the disappearance of *legio* IX *Hispana*. These are (Kean and Frey, 2005, 18):

- The Julio-Claudian Dynasty, from the accession of Augustus in 27 BC to the death of Nero in AD 68.
- The 'Year of the Four Emperors' in AD 69, with Vespasian the ultimate victor.
- The Flavian Dynasty, from Vespasian's accession through to the death of his son Domitian in AD 96.
- The Nervo-Trajanic Dynasty, from the accession of Nerva in AD 96 to the death of Hadrian in AD 138.
- The Antonine Dynasty, from the accession of Antoninus Pius in AD 138 through to the assassination of Commodus in AD 192.
- The 'Year of the Five Emperors' in AD 193, with Pertinax the first incumbent.
- The Severan Dynasty, from the accession of Septimius Severus as the ultimate victor in the 'Year of the Five Emperors' through to the assassination of Severus Alexander in AD 235.
- The 'Crisis of the 3rd Century', from the death of Severus Alexander to the accession of Diocletian in AD 284. This was a period when the Empire was under great stress from a multitude of issues that collectively threatened its very survival. These included civil war and multiple usurpations, the first deep and large scale incursions into imperial territory by Germans and Goths over the Rhine and Danube, the deadly Plague of Cyprian, and the emergence in the east of the Sassanid Persian Empire which presented the Romans with a fully symmetrical threat there for the first time. Collectively they caused a major economic crash. The steps taken by Diocletian to drag the Empire out of this chaos, in what is often styled his reformation, were so drastic that from that point we talk of the very different Dominate phase of the Roman Empire.

Meanwhile, given much of the story of *legio* IX *Hispana* is played out across the distant frontiers of the Empire, military installations play a key role in its activities. In that regard I have used the current size-based hierarchy as a means of describing their size as they occur in the narrative. Starting with the largest, these are 20 ha-plus legionary fortresses for one or more legions. Such fortresses were built around the fringes of the Empire, not only to provide a launch pad for campaigns of Imperial conquest and to defend the Imperial frontier, but also to keep the legions deliberately as far from Rome as possible, the aim here being to diminish the possibility of a successful usurpation. In that regard it was very unusual for any provincial governor or *legate* to command more than four legions at any one time, though note the huge force deployed to defeat the Third 'bar Kokhba' Jewish Revolt detailed in Chapter 6 (Cornell and Matthews, 1982, 81). Meanwhile, next down the scale were the 12 ha-plus vexillation fortresses holding a mixed force of legionary cohorts and auxiliaries, then the one ha-plus forts for outpost garrisons, and finally fortlets for part of an auxiliary unit. Military settlements associated with such fortifications are called a *canaba* when connected with a legionary fortress, and a *vicus* elsewhere.

In terms of the built environment, this again features heavily in the story of IXth legion as it travelled across the territory of the Republic and Empire. Here, larger towns are referenced as one of three types. These are *coloniae* chartered towns for military veterans (in Britain for example Colchester, Gloucester and Lincoln), *municipia* chartered towns of mercantile origin (in Britain for example St Albans) and *civitas capitals*, these last the Roman equivalent of a County town featuring the local government of a region (in Britain for example Caerwent, Silchester and Canterbury). Settlement below this level is referenced as either a small town (defined as a variety of diverse settlements which often had an association with a specific activity such as administration, industry or religion), villa estates or non-villa estates.

Staying with human geography, the IXth legion's chronological journey was played out across the provinces of the later Roman Republic and Principate Empire. The word province itself provides interesting insight into the Roman attitude to its Empire, the Latin *provincia* referencing land '*for conquering*' (Matyszak, 2009, 60). There were actually two kinds of province by the time of the Principate Empire. These were Senatorial provinces left to the Senate to administer, whose governors were officially called proconsuls and remained in post for a year, and Imperial provinces retained under the supervision of the emperor. The emperor personally chose the governors for these, they often being styled *legati Augusti pro praetor* to officially mark them out as deputies of the emperor. Senatorial provinces tended to be those deep within the Empire where less trouble was expected. At the beginning of the first century AD these were:

- Baetica in southern Spain
- Narbonensis in southern France
- Corsica et Sardinia
- Africa Proconsularis in North Africa
- Cyrenaica et Creta
- Epirus
- Macedonia
- Achaia
- Asia in western Anatolia
- Bithynia et Pontus.

In this work I will specifically use proconsul to reference the governor of these Senatorial provinces, and governor to reference this position in an Imperial province.

Staying with classical and modern name use, I have been pragmatic in the narrative to ensure that the work is as accessible as possible for the reader. By way of example, where there is a classical version of a modern name for a given city or town I have used the modern name, referencing the Roman name at the point of its first use. However, with common and well-understood classical names for a given role, for example *legate* (general), I use that throughout the work, providing the modern name in brackets at the first point of use as illustrated here. One final very specific point to make here regarding names relates to how the Roman's themselves styled the IXth legion. In normal circumstances it was called *legio* IX *Hispana*, though in a couple of specific cases *legio* VIIII *Hispana* was used. The former is used throughout this work, while the latter is explained in detail in Chapter 4.

Moving on to the chapter flow of the book, this Introduction is followed by two background chapters to enable the reader to follow the subsequent evidential trail with me as I track the fate of the IXth legion. The first details the Roman military of the Principate phase of Empire, this including a description of the original IXth legion, and then some detail on the early history of its successor, the IXth legion covered by this book. I then look at early Roman Britain given this provided the setting for much of the activities of *legio* IX *Hispana* before it disappeared. I then Sequentially test to breaking point, in four successive chapters, the key hypotheses regarding the fate of the IXth legion. These are that it was lost or disbanded in the north of Britain, that it was lost or disbanded in an insurrection in the south of Britain, that it was lost or disbanded on the Rhine or Danube, or that it was lost or disbanded in the east. At the end of each of these four chapters I have a closing discussion regarding the evidence presented there. I then gather these together in the Conclusion where I set out my own opinion, based on all that has gone before in the book, about what really happened to the IXth legion. The book then ends with a timeline of the late Roman Republic and Empire, and a full bibliography.

Lastly, here I would like to thank the many people who have helped make this detective story regarding the fate of *legio* IX *Hispana* possible. As always this includes Professor Andrew Lambert of the War Studies Department at KCL, Dr Andrew Gardner at UCL's Institute of Archaeology, and Dr Steve Willis at the University of Kent. Next, my publisher and friend Phil Sidnell at Pen & Sword Books. Also, Professor Sir Barry Cunliffe of the School of Archaeology at Oxford University and Professor Martin Millett at the Faculty of Classics, Cambridge University for their encouragement. Next, my patient proofreader and lovely wife Sara, and my dad John Elliott and friend Francis Tusa, both companions in my various escapades to research this book. As with all of my literary work, all have contributed greatly and freely, enabling this work on the fate of the IXth legion to reach fruition. Finally I would like to thank my family, especially my tolerant wife Sara once again and children Alex (also a student of military history) and Lizzie.

Thank you all.

Simon Elliott

January 2020

Chapter 1

Background: The Principate Military

The IXth was a classic legion of the Principate period of the Roman Empire, though had its roots in the earlier Roman Republic. It fought across a wide range of geographies and against many different enemies of Rome before its mysterious disappearance. To enable the reader to fully understand its nature, this first Chapter therefore considers the Roman military of the later Republic and early Empire, beginning with an analysis of that most elite soldier of the ancient world, the Roman legionary. There then follows a specific consideration of the early history of *legio* IX *Hispana*, designed to set the scene for its later exploits. The Chapter then concludes with a discussion of the Principate Empire troop types that supported the legions when on campaign and in battle, namely the auxiliaries and regional fleets.

The Roman Legionary

The Roman legionary of the later Republic and early Empire was a heavy infantryman whose battlefield role was, more often than not, fighting other lines of battle heavy infantry. His appearance by the late first century BC was the result of over 700 years of military evolution in terms of equipment and tactics. This reflected the fact that, even when the Romans lost in war or battle, they were quick adopters of opposing ideas and technology, ensuring they usually won in the long run. This progression featured five distinct phases:

- The Tullian system devised by Servius Tullius, sixth king of Rome and the city's second Etrusco-Roman king who reigned from 575 BC to 535 BC. This was based on his Servian Constitution, with these first Roman armies built around an Etruscan-style hoplite phalanx of armoured spearman, wealthy citizen cavalry, and four classes of supporting troops.

- The Camillan System of Marcus Furius Camillus who became consular tribune for the first time in 401 BC. He completely reformed the Roman military system after its devastating defeat by Brennus' Senones Gauls at the Battle of Allia in 390 BC, and the traumatic sack of Rome that followed. Camillus introduced the manipular legion of 3,000 men (this later growing to 5,000), featuring three classes of legionary, this term being applicable for the first time from this point on. The classes were the *triarii* veterans, *principes* older warriors and *hastati* '*flower of the young men*'. Among his other reforms of the Roman military, Camillus also introduced regular pay for his legionaries after the eight-month siege of the Etruscan city of Veii that finally ended in 396 BC.
- The Polybian System, a revision of the Camillan system introduced after Rome's narrow victory over Pyrrhus of Epirus in the conflict in southern Italy that lasted from 280 BC to 275 BC. The key change here was the introduction of other troop types to support the legionaries, including *velite* skirmishing javelinmen.
- The Marian System created by the seven-times warrior consul Gaius Marius at the height of the Cimbrian Wars in 107 BC. This totally new system was introduced against a backdrop of the manipular legions losing on a regular basis against the Cimbri Germans and their allies invading Gaul (see Chapter 5 for detail). The new legions of Marius featured 6,000 men organized in centuries rather than maniples. Each had 4,800 legionaries armed as front line troops, all now equipped in exactly the same way, while the remaining 1,200 legionaries were specialists and support staff. Their inclusion enabled the Marian legion to operate as a homogenous unit, unencumbered by siege trains and other subsidiary units. As detailed below, *legio* IX *Hispana* was founded in both of its early forms in this period.
- The Augustan System introduced by the first Emperor after his elevation by the Senate in 27 BC. Having inherited 60 legions as Octavian, his main contribution to the evolution of the legion was rationalizing their number down to 28. This fell to 25 after Varus' loss of *legios* XVII, XVIII and XIX fighting Arminius in the Teutoburg Forest in Germany in AD 9. The total number of legions would then hover around 30 for the rest of the Principate. Augustus also rationalized the number of legionaries in a legion

down to 5,500, though still maintaining the balance between front line fighting troops and legionary specialists. This system was to remain in place throughout the Principate period of Empire.

Given the story of *legio* IX *Hispana* falls into the Marian and Augustan phases detailed above, from this point on the narrative concentrates on the legions of those periods.

The numbering and naming of these legions can seem confusing, but simply reflects their being raised at different times, and by different Republican leaders and later Emperors. Many legions shared the same number but had different names, for example there being five third legions. Meanwhile, others shared the same name but had different numbers, for example *legios* I, II, III and IV *Italica*.

From the later first century BC onwards, as the final phase of the Republican civil wars came to an end, the legions were usually deployed around the borders of the later republic and early Empire. There they were best placed to expand the frontiers of Roman controlled territory when ordered to do so, at the same time providing a fearsome deterrent against any neighbours contemplating a confrontation with Rome. These legions were based at regularly spaced legionary fortresses in Spain, on the Rivers Rhine and Danube, along the eastern frontier with Parthia, in North Africa, and later in Britain. The legions were often stationed at these locations for significant periods of time and developed a fierce sense of identity, with Goldsworthy (2003, 50) saying: '...*legionaries were proud of their unit and contemptuous of others.*' This sense of self could often get out of hand, with the legions occasionally being prone to mutiny, as happened with *legio* IX *Hispana* in Pannonia (see below). This phenomenon is further detailed in Chapter 3.

The 6,000 men of the Marian legions and 5,500 men of the Augustan legions were organized into ten cohorts. Using the latter as our example here, the first of these had five centuries of 160 men, with the rest six centuries of 80 men each. The normal century was then broken down into ten eight-man sections called *contubernia*, whose men shared a tent when on campaign and two barrack block rooms when in their legionary fortress. Additionally, the legions also featured 120 auxiliary cavalry, these acting as dispatch riders and scouts. We know specifically of one such individual who actually served in this latter role in *legio* IX *Hispana*. This is Quintus Cornelius whose now-lost tombstone was found around 1800 on the south side of the churchyard of St Peter-at-Gowts in Lincoln. His inscription (RIB 254) reads:

> Quintus Cornelius, son of Quintus, of the Claudian voting-tribe, trooper of legio IX from the century of Cassius Martialis: aged 40 years, of 19 year's service, lies buried here.

Later Marian and all Augustan legions were led by a Senatorial-level *legatus legionis*, with the second-in-command from the time of the Principate being a *tribunus laticlavius*. This was a young Senator gaining personal experience to enable him to command his own legion in the future. Third in command of the legion was the *praefectus castrorum* camp prefect, a seasoned former centurion responsible for logistics and administration. Below him were five younger equestrian-level tribunes, these known as the *tribuni angusticlavia* who were allocated responsibilities in the legion as required. Meanwhile control of each cohort in the legion was the responsibility of centurions, with six to a normal cohort. Each had a specific title that reflected their seniority, the names based on the old manipular legions of Camillus. In ascending order, these were:

- *hastatus posterior*
- *hastatus prior*
- *princeps posterior*
- *princeps prior*
- *pilus posterior*
- *pilus prior*.

Senior officers and centurions controlled their legions with standards and musical instruments. In terms of the former, each legion had a variety of types. By far the most important was the gold *Aquila* eagle standard carried by the *aquilifer*. This only left camp when the entire legion was on campaign, and the Roman authorities heavily frowned upon its loss. As will be seen, the fate of the eagle standard of *legio* IX *Hispana* is a subject much debated throughout this book, and indeed gave Rosemary Sutcliff the title of her fictional account of the legion's fate. By the time of the Principate Empire, the next most important standard was the *imago* featuring an image of the Emperor, this either a bust or a portrait within a *phalera* medallion. This standard was carried by an *imaginifer*. Next came the *signa* standards allocated to each individual century and carried by the *signifer*, these featuring the unit's battle honours on medallions fixed vertically to the wooden shaft. We have specific insight here into an actual *signifer* of *legio* IX *Hispana* in the form of his tombstone found on the site of Holy Trinity Priory in Micklegate, York, in 1688. This area, on the south side of the River Ouse, was well away from legionary fortress on the north bank and at the time would have been a cemetery for the early legionaries based in the fortress. Featuring a fine image of the man himself holding his *signa* in his right hand, the inscription (CIL VII 243/ RIB 673) on the tombstone explains he is 'Luciius Duccius Rufinus, son of lucius, of the Voltinian-voting tribe, from Vienne, a standard bearer of the IXth legion, 28 years old. He is laid here.' This shows just how cosmopolitan the Roman Empire really was, with this legionary with his links to a voting tribe in Rome and originally from the south-west of modern France, finding himself fighting on the northern frontier of Britannia.

Additionally, flag-based standards called *vexilla* were also used. One of these showed the name of the legion, while others were allocated to legionary detachments. This gave these sub-units their name, *vexillation*. Each was carried by a *vexillarius*. Standard bearers were joined in their signalling role by *cornicen* musicians who played the *cornu* horn. These always marched at the head of the centuries, along with their *signifer*.

The standard bearers in the Marian and Augustan legions also had another duty, and one of great importance. In an age before popular banking the legionaries often had nowhere to keep their savings and therefore gave them to their standard bearers for safekeeping. Here Rufinus of the IXth legion again gives us direct contemporary evidence of this practice given his image on his tombstone features him holding a *codex ansantus* case of writing tablets in his left hand, there to record his fellow legionaries' accounts.

Regular pay was clearly a central part of legionary life and again dates to the reforms of Marius. Although as detailed Camillus had much earlier introduced payment for legionaries, this was only when the then part-time citizen soldiers were on campaign. The Marian legions were now regular formations, with another key reform being the removal of the wealth qualification to enlist. This opened up a life in the ranks to the lower levels of Roman society that, for the first time, created a plentiful supply of willing manpower. When this was combined with regular pay, standing units that could remain in existence for years were possible for the first time.

Payment of the legionaries in the initial Marian legions was ad hoc, based on the resources of the various late Republican warlords leading them. Julius Caesar was the first to regularise this when he started paying his troops 225 *denarii* a year, a sure fire means of ensuring their loyalty. It is unclear if his *optimates* opponents immediately copied the move, but over time this amount became the standard level of legionary pay through to the time of the Emperor Domitian (AD 81 – AD 96) in the late first century AD. He then increased basic pay to 300 *denarii*, a level it remained at until the reign of Septimius Severus in the later Principate who increased it to 450 *denarii*. Plutarch (*Lives*, Caesar, 17) adds that Caesar was also adept at spreading the plunder from his campaigns among his troops, another means of ensuring their loyalty, and this tradition of largesse continued into the Principate when legionaries could have their basic pay increased through donatives given by the Emperor. A good example is the 75 *denarii* left by Augustus to all of his legionaries in his will. Further, on retirement the legionaries in both the late Republican and Principate periods were also awarded a *praemia* retirement gratuity. For the Marian retiree this was in the form of land, either a parcel of *centuriated* farmland or a plot in a *colonia* veteran settlement. Caesar provides a good example of the latter, his retirees after the campaign in Greece against Pompey in Macedonia and Greece in 48 BC being settled at the Hellenistic city of Butrint (Roman *Buthrōtum*) in modern Albania. By the time of the Principate, following the reforms of Augustus, a one-off cash payment of up to 5,000 *denarii* was also offered as an alternative to land as the retirement gratuity.

In terms of recruitment, the early Marian legions relied on Roman citizen volunteers, usually aged between 17 and 23, though some were as young as 13 or as old as 36. Additionally, in times of crisis, the number of legionaries was bolstered by conscription under a levy called the *dilectus*, and by recruitment from non-Italian citizens. Yet again Caesar provides a good example of the latter, with the native Gallic *legio* V *Alaudae* legion he recruited towards the end of his conquest of Gaul. Each Marian legionary, whether recruit or conscript, and whether Roman or not, signed up for a minimum term of six years. This length of service lasted until at least the Battle of Actium in 31 BC when it began to steadily increase.

Augustus formalized recruitment into the legions and length of service, setting the age a recruit could join at 18, with enlistment again only open to Roman citizens in normal circumstances. Initially the Principate term of service was twenty years, with the last four as a veteran excused fatigues and guard duty. This was later extended by Augustus to twenty-five years, with five as a veteran, a term which lasted into the later third century AD. The increase was due to a shortage of recruits, he being too successful when trimming down the number of legions, and because of the strain placed on the early Imperial *fiscus* treasury to pay the *praemia* retirement gratuity.

Augustus also set a height requirement for new legionary recruits, this at 1.8m. Like all armies the Marian and Augustan legions marched on their stomachs. In his later military manual from the fourth century AD Vegetius detailed that the legionaries should never be without corn and wheat, wine, salt and vinegar. These ingredients were used to make bread and porridge by Roman troops of all periods, with beans, eggs and vegetables added to bolster the diet. The importance of grain in the diet is well illustrated by a type of punishment given to legionaries for bad behaviour, they having their wheat ration replaced with the barley usually used to feed horses (Polybius, 6.38). Meanwhile, meat would also be eaten on feast days, and the wider diet was always supplemented by local produce and hunting. Meanwhile, when on campaign the daily staples for the legionary were hard tack and whole-wheat biscuits, with bread baked at the end of the day's march after the marching camp had been constructed.

Religion played a key role in the daily lives experienced by the troops of the Marian and Augustan legions. Given the legionary was a citizen of Rome, he was always obliged to honour the gods of the Roman pantheon, in particular the Capitaline Triad of Jupiter, Juno and Minerva. To these, in terms of popularity, one can add Mars given his association with the legions as the god of war. Meanwhile, worship of other gods was often associated with the location of a given legion's place of origin or the location it was based in, these often a local deity assimilated into the Roman pantheon. An example of this can be found in York where a carving of the god *Sol* has been found rendered in the fashion of the local Brythonic sun god. Additionally, certain gods also had a specific association with the legions. These included the eastern deity Mithras who was very popular with the Roman soldiery, and indeed an altar stone to Mithras himself was found in Micklegate area of York in 1776. Worship of all these gods, and also the dates of the traditional festivals of Rome, structured the religious year for the legionary, with the Emperor's birthday and accession date added from the time of the Principate Empire. Elsewhere in their daily lives, legionaries were officially unable to marry until retirement, though they often contracted illegal marriages.

In terms of his equipment, the principal missile weapon of the late Republican and Principate legionary was the famous *pilum* weighted javelin. Originally an Etruscan or Spanish design adopted by the Romans, two were carried, one heavy and one light (Cowan, 2003b, 30). Both types featured barbed heads on long, tapering soft iron tangs. These were attached to a lead-weighted socket which was fixed to a wooden shaft. The weighted socket provided the driving force needed to hammer the javelin through enemy shields and armour. Both weapons were thrown as a massed volley to maximize damage, the lighter one as the legionaries approached the enemy and the heavier one immediately prior to impact. The iron shaft was designed to bend after impact, the aim being to disable an opponent's shield. The heavier *pila*, which could easily go through both shield and the man holding it, also doubled as a makeshift spear when needed to help repel any enemy shock cavalry.

However, the main weapon of the late Republican and Principate legionary was the *gladius hispaniensis* sword. Originally a Spanish design, this was first adopted by the Polybian legions after the Romans fought the Iberian mercenaries of Hannibal in the Second Punic War. Rather than being the short stabbing sword of popular legend, the *gladius* was originally a cut and thrust weapon of medium length, around 69cm long and 5cm in width and featuring a tapering sharp stabbing point. Those originally used by the legionaries inflicted gaping injuries on their Hellenistic pike-wielding opponents in the Second Macedonian War. This was because a key feature of the *gladius* was that it lacked any blood runnels to let in air, which would allow easy withdrawal after a penetrating wound (Matyszak, 2009, 64). Therefore the sword had to be viciously twisted to release it. This original type of *gladius* was still the most common in the Marian legions, though by the time of the Principate had developed into the Mainz type. This *gladius* was broader and shorter in shape, but with a longer stabbing point. By the later first century AD this design had developed further into the Pompeii-type, this slightly shorter than the Mainz type and with a shorter, triangular stabbing point. All types of *gladius* were worn on the legionary's right hip, left if a centurion. Many have questioned how a legionary could draw the weapon smoothly into the en-guard position from the right hand side, especially given the pommel sat just below the armpit. However, in his detailed analysis of the weapon, Bishop explains (2016, 46):

> In fact, the gladius can be easily drawn by inverting the right hand, thumb downwards, then grasping the handgrip and pulling straight upwards. It is a quite natural progression to continue this movement forwards to bring the sword down to the side, point forward, in the characteristic 'at the ready' position depicted on relief sculpture.

To complete their offensive weaponry, legionaries in the Marian and Augustan legions also carried a *pugio* dagger, this on the opposite hip to the *gladius*.

For his defensive panoply, in the first instance the late Republican and Principate legionaries carried the curved, rectangular *scutum*. This large body shield was a development of the more oval earlier Republican examples in use from the time of Camillus. The late Republican and Principate version was around 102cm long and 83cm wide, constructed from planed wooden strips laminated together in three layers. The *scutum* was very heavy, weighing up to 10kg, and was held by a horizontal grip using a straightened arm. The shield was used in close conjunction with the *gladius*, with the legionaries employing a bespoke cut-and-thrust fencing technique. This often meant taking the blow of an enemy weapon while the legionary was in the crouch, the *gladius* then being driven upwards into the opponent's midriff. Given its size and weight, the *scutum* could also be used as an offensive weapon in its own right to smash into an opponent, pushing them off balance and again exposing them to a lethal blow from the *gladius*.

For armour, most legionaries of the Marian and early Principate legions wore a *lorica hamata* long chainmail hauberk, this named after the Latin *hamatus* meaning hooked, referencing the interlinked rings of iron or bronze. This was a Gallic design adopted by the Romans from the early third century BC which weighed between 11kg and 15kg, giving a good level of protection to both the thorax and abdomen. It featured alternating rows of closed washer-like rings that were punched from iron sheets, and rows of riveted rings that were made from drawn wire, both running horizontally, this producing a very flexible but resilient suit of armour. Each of the rings had an outside diameter of about 7mm.

However, as the Principate progressed a new type of armour emerged which came to define the legionary for the next two centuries. This was the *lorica segmentata* suit of banded iron armour that provided the wearer with a better level of protection than anything that was to emerge until the later Medieval period, made from articulated iron plates and hoops. Fine examples can be found as sculpture on Trajan's Column, the Column of Marcus Aurelius and on the reused panels from a lost Arch of Marcus Aurelius found on the Arch of Constantine, all in Rome.

The origins of *lorica segmentata* are unclear though it may have originally been a form of gladiator armour. The first types emerge in the archaeological record at the end of the first century BC, and from that point the armour evolved through three specific versions, these being (all named after the location where examples were found):

- The Dangestetten-Kalkriese-Vindonissa type, those found dating to between 9 BC to AD 43.
- The Corbridge-Carnumtum type,those found dating to between AD 69 to AD 100.
- The Newstead type, those found dating to between AD 164 to AD 180.

Each successive version was less complicated than that which preceded it, for example that found in the *principia* of the vexillation fort at Newstead (Roman *Trimontium*) in the Scottish Borders in 1905 featuring rivets to replace earlier bronze hinges, a single large girdle plate to replace the two previous ones, and hooks to replace earlier and more complicated belt-buckle fastenings.

In a minority of cases late Republican and Principate legionaries also wore one other kind of armour, this being the *lorica squamata* scale mail hauberk. Further, extra armour could also be fitted. This included articulated iron *manicae* arm guards, thigh guards and greaves. These are all visible in use on Trajan's Column in Rome to protect the wearer from the vicious *falx* two-handed slashing weapon used by the Bastarnae allies of the Dacians.

Certain troop types within the legions were also often differentially equipped with armour. By way of example, officers are frequently shown wearing iron and bronze muscled cuirasses, and Principate centurions and *aquilifer* standard bearers *lorica hamata*. Interestingly, as the Principate period of Empire transitioned to the Dominate period, the armour preference for the legionary went full circle, with the chainmail hauberk replacing *lorica segmentata,* given the cost of manufacturing and maintaining the latter became too great after the 'Crisis of the Third Century'.

Finally in terms of the defensive panoply, by the time of the Marian legions the helmet of the legionary had evolved into two principal styles. These were:

- The Coolus type with a round cap of bronze and small neck guard, this disappearing by the middle of the first century AD.
- The iron Port type that featured a deep neck guard, this named after the site-type location of Port bei Nidau in Switzerland.

By the early Principate the latter had developed into the classic 'Imperial' Gallic helmet often associated with the Roman legionary of the first and second centuries AD. This ubiquitous design featured an even larger neck guard. All of these helmets had prominent cheek guards and a reinforcing strip on the front of the cap to deflect downward sword cuts, with ear guards added from the AD 50s.

In terms of their non-military kit, the late Republican and Principate legionaries carried their equipment on a T-shaped pole resting on their shoulders. Such equipment included his engineering gear, comprising a saw, sickle, pickaxe, basket, chain, leather strap and two stakes. These were all used to carry out any engineering activities required, for example building the marching camp at the end of every day's march in enemy territory. The pole also carried the legionary's *patera* bronze mess tin, a cooking pot, a water skin in a net bag and canvas bags for grain rations and spare clothing. The legionary's shield was held in place on his back, while his helmet was usually strung from the neck across the chest.

The legionary's personal marching kit also included a *paenula* hooded woollen bad weather cloak, with officers wearing the shorter rectangular *sagum*. This was worn over a short tunic, and here again we have direct evidence in the form of the tombstone of Rufinus, the *signifier* of *legio* IX *hispana* found in York. His image on the monument shows him in his military dress downs, namely the *paenula* over his tunic. Those legionaries in the north of Britain, including those of the IXth legion, would also no doubt have been pleased to make use of one of Roman Britain's most famous exports. This was the *birrus* waterproofed woollen cloak, ideal for keeping out the cold and wet of a typical British winter.

However, the legionary's most important piece of kit when on the march was his *caligae* hobnailed sandals. These were typically made from a leather upper using single leather pieces sewn at the heel which were then stitched to a multiple-layer hide sole shod with a large number of iron studs. Each sandal weighed up to 1kg, with the average marching load of the late Republican and Principate legionary being an impressive 30kg. This led to a popular contemporary nickname for these elite warriors, namely *muli mariani* Marius' mules.

As Goldsworthy (2003, 90) details, the Romans believed in keeping their legionaries busy even when not on campaign. We are here fortunate to have direct evidence of this in the form of a duty roster that survives from *legio* III *Cyrenaica* in Egypt. Here it was based at the legionary fortress of Nicopolis in the provincial capital of Alexandria. Dating to the late first century AD and covering the month of October, the duty roster lists the tasks performed by thirty-one named legionaries. Such duties included guard duty on the fortress walls and gateways and in the *principia* headquarters building, patrolling in and around the fortress, cleaning the fortresses' bath house and latrines, cleaning their own kit (called 'boots'), and training with the legion's ballista artillery and their own personal weaponry. The latter training particularly focused on martial skills and was based on the same methods used to train gladiators (Elliott, 2018b, 36). For example, for sword drill, a large stake the size of a legionary was set up in the training ground. The trooper then practised his fencing technique with a wooden replica sword and wicker shield, the stake being 'the enemy'. The main focus was to ensure that the legionary thrust his sword rather than slashed, a more difficult blow to see coming and parry. They also practised manoeuvring in complex military formations, for example the *testudo* with locked shields to counter an enemy using large numbers of missile weapons, the *orbis* to provide all round defence and the *cuneus* (swine head) wedge formation used to puncture an opponent's battle line. Meanwhile, fitness training was also essential for the legionary given the amount of kit they carried. In that regard one should imagine the troopers of *legio* IX *Hispana* as 1.8m of solid muscle, built like a modern middleweight Olympic weightlifter.

Finally here, as noted earlier, over and above each late Republican and Principate legionary being a trained engineer, within their ranks were also a wide variety of specialists. Their role was to keep the legion in the field no matter what the circumstances. Paternus (in his now lost *De Re Militari*, detailed in Justinian's *Digest*, 50.6.7) usefully identifies many such specialists in his list of legionary *immunes* (soldiers exempted from general duties because of their specialist skills). These included ditch diggers, farriers, pilots, master builders, shipwrights, ballista makers, glaziers, arrow makers, bow makers, smiths, coppersmiths, helmet makers, wagon makers, roof-tile makers, water engineers, swordcutlers, trumpet makers, horn makers, plumbers, blacksmiths, masons, woodcutters, limeburners, charcoal burners, butchers, huntsmen, sacrificial animal keepers, grooms and tanners. Meanwhile, specifically in terms of construction and engineering, such specialist military personnel in the legions also included *agrimensor* land surveyors, *liberator* land levellers and *mensor* quantity measurers (Garrison, 1998, 75). In the case of the military building aqueducts, one can also add here *aqualegus* aqueduct inspectors.

Table 1: The Roman Legions of the Principate.

Legion	When Founded	Destroyed/ disbanded
legio I Germanica	Later republic	Disbanded AD 70 after Civilis Revolt
legio I Adiutrix pia fidelis	Provisionally recruited by Nero, then made a regular legion by Galba.	
legio I Italica	Under Nero	
legio I Macriana	Under Nero	Civil war legion, disbanded AD 69/70
legio I Flavia Minervia pia fidelis	Under Domitian	
legio I Parthica	Under Septimius Severus	
legio II Augusta	Later Republic/ under Augustus	
legio II Adiutrix pia fidelis	Under Nero	
legio II Italica	Under Marcus Aurelius	
legio II Parthica	Under Septimius Severus	
legio II Traiana fortis	Under Trajan	
legio III Augusta pia fidelis	Later Republic/ under Augustus	
legio III Cyrenaica	Later Republic	
legio III Gallica	Under Caesar	
legio III Italica concors	Under Marcus Aurelius	
legio III Parthica	Under Septimius Severus	
legio IV Flavia felix	Under Vespasian	
legio IV Macedonica	Under Caesar	Disbanded AD 70
legio IV Scythica	Under Mark Antony	
legio IV Italica	Under Severus Alexander	
legio V Alaudae	Under Caesar	Disbanded under Domitian
legio V Macedonica	Later Republic	

(*Continued*)

Table 1:   Continued

Legion	When Founded	Destroyed/disbanded
legio VI Ferrata fidelis constans	Under Caesar	
legio VI Victrix	Later Republic	
legio VII Claudia pia fidelis	Under Caesar	
legio VII Gemina	Under Galba	
legio VIII Augusta	Later Republic	
legio IX Hispana	Later Republic	The subject of this book.
legio X Fretensis	Later Republic	
legio X Gemina	Under Caesar	
legio XI Claudia pia fidelis	Later Republic	
legio XII Fulminata	Under Caesar	
legio XIII Gemina pia fidelis	Later Republic	
legio XIV Gemina Martia Victrix	Later Republic	
legio XV Apollinaris	Under Augustus	
legio XV Primigenia	Under Caligula	Disbanded AD 70
legio XVI Flavia Firma	Under Vespasian	
legio XVI Gallica	Under Augustus	Disbanded AD 70
legio XVII	Under Augustus	Destroyed in AD 9 in Germany
legio XVIII	Under Augustus	Destroyed in AD 9 in Germany
legio XIX	Under Augustus	Destroyed in AD 9 in Germany
legio XX Valeria Victrix	Under Augustus	
legio XXI Rapax	Under Augustus	Disbanded under Domitian
legio XXII Deiotariana	Under Augustus	Disbanded under Hadrian
legio XXII Primigenia pia fidelis	Under Caligula	
legio XXX Ulpia Victrix	Under Trajan	

After Goldsworthy, 2003, 51.

The late Republican and Principate legions also included a range of specialist clerical staff drawn from the ranks, responsible for roles such as recording the movements of various *vexillations* of legionaries within their region of responsibility, and the keeping of grain store records. Details of such *immunes librarii* can be found from across the Empire, for example Septimius Licinius of the *legio* II *Parthica* who set up a commemoration to a daughter in Albano, Italy, and Marcus Uplius Firminus who similarly set up an inscription in Potaissa (modern day Torda), Dacia.

The Early History of Legio IX Hispana

The actual origins of *legio* IX *Hispana* are unknown. A IXth legion did participate in the year-long 90/89 BC Siege of Asculum in the Social War when Gnaeus Pompeius Strabo led his Roman army to victory over their former Italian allies. The next we hear of a IXth legion, presumably the same one, is that which Caesar inherited along with *legios* VII, VIII and X when appointed proconsul in the provinces Cisalpine Gaul, Provincia (Transalpine Gaul) and Illyricum in 58 BC. That legion played a major role in his conquest of Gaul from 58 BC through to 52 BC. This included helping defeat the Helvetti at the Battle of Bibracte in 58 BC, the Suebi at the Battle of Vosges the same year, the Belgae Nervii at the Battle of Sabis in 57 BC, participating in the two incursions to Britain in 55 and 54 BC, and playing a key role at the Siege of Alesia in 52 BC. At some stage during its tenure in Gaul this IXth legion may have also been posted to Aquileia in north-eastern Italy to protect the region against Illyrian raiders (Keppie, 1984, 208). The legion then played a full role in Caesar's extensive campaigns against his *optimates* civil war opponents in Greece, North Africa and Spain. This included being key participants in the battles of Dyrrhachium and Pharsalus in 48 BC against Gnaeus Pompey. This legion was then disbanded between 46 BC and 45 BC, though it is unclear why.

The actual IXth legion, and the subject of this book, is the one raised by Octavian shortly afterwards from Caesarian veterans settled in Italy to counter the rebellion of Sextus Pompeius in Sicily in the later 40s BC. This then campaigned against the armies led by the Caesarian assassins Gaius Cassius Longinus and Marcus Junius Brutus in the Balkans, and was almost certainly among those led to victory by Octavian and Marc Antony at Philippi in 42 BC given it shortly afterwards was awarded a cognomen styling it *legio* IX *Macedonia*. This indicates the legion performed particularly well in battle.

The IXth legion is next recorded fighting in the Cantabrian Wars that lasted from 27 BC to 19 BC. This conflict was the final stage of the Roman conquest of the Iberian Peninsula, when Augustus (as Octavian was by now styled after the Senate proclaimed him Emperor in 27 BC) moved to pacify the warlike Cantabri and Astures tribes in northern Spain. This conflict was particularly brutal, ultimately requiring eight full legions plus auxiliaries (in total over 50,000 men) to secure victory. The IXth legion again fought with great bravery in this war, then staying in Spain long enough for its cognomen to change from *Macedonia* to *Hispaniensis* (meaning 'stationed in Spain'). This was later shortened to *Hispana* (meaning 'Spanish').

After the conclusion of the Cantabrian Wars Augustus gradually drew down the number of legions in Spain to three, with his successor Tiberius (AD 14 to AD 37) reducing these to one. By this time the battle-hardened *legio* IX *Hispana* had been long redeployed, in the first instance back to Aquileia as evidenced by a number of contemporary legionary tombstones found there.

By the time of Augustus' death in AD 14 we can specifically locate *legio* IX *Hispana*, this time to the province of Pannonia on the River Danube. Here Tacitus, in his Annals (1.16-30), details it as one of three legions stationed together in the same fortress that mutinied over poor living conditions. Nero Claudius Drusus, Tiberius' son and commander in the region, responded with typical Roman vigour and promptly executed the ringleaders. The three legions were then deployed to separate winter camps under new leadership.

The IXth legion is next recorded being sent to North Africa in AD 20 to support *legio* III *Augusta* in its campaigns against the Numidian rebel leader Tacfarinas. After participating in a major victory in AD 22 it then returned to Pannonia where it moved to the legionary fortress at Sisak (Roman Siscia) in modern Croatia. It is next recorded accompanying the Pannonian governor Aulus Plautius when appointed by the emperor Claudius (AD 41 to AD 54) to command the invasion of Britain in AD 43. Given that assault and the subsequent lengthy campaigns of conquest in Britain form a major part of Chapter 2, the subsequent activities of *legio* IX *Hispana* are considered there. Later chapters then consider its possible later geographical deployments.

The Auxilia

Pre-Imperial Roman armies relied on mercenary and allied troops to add diversity to the heavy infantry-focused Camillan, Polybian and Marian legions. These were recruited to fulfil a wide variety of supporting roles on the battlefield, fighting under their own officers and in their own native formations.

Early on, as Rome began to expand territorially, such troops were recruited from Italy. Examples included warriors from their Latin neighbours, and the hill tribesmen of the Hernici, Aequi, Umbri, Sabini and Volsci. These were later joined by mercenaries and allies from Samnium and Magna Graecia. However, from this point, as Rome began its irresistible advance across first the western and then eastern Mediterranean, the mercenaries and allies began to be recruited from much further afield. These included, in the west, Numidian light cavalry, Spanish cavalry and foot troops, Balearic slingers, and Gallic and German cavalry, the latter especially favoured by Julius Caesar. Meanwhile, in the east, the Romans recruited many other different types of warrior including Cretan archers, Rhodian slingers, Macedonian and Greek cavalry, Thracian peltasts and eastern specialist horse archers.

However, this all changed as part of the Augustan reforms of the military. In addition to his rationalization of the legions, the first Emperor also formalized the supporting troops in the Roman military establishment, and from this time they were called auxiliaries (or auxilia in shortened form, as used in this book). These were now regular troops and featured both cavalry and infantry, recruited from *peregrine* non-Italian freemen, often from recently conquered new Provinces as the new Empire expanded. The number of auxilia quickly grew, with Tacitus (Annals, 4.5) saying that by AD 25 there were as many in the Roman army as legionaries, the latter number at that time around 175,000.

Though auxilia were full line of battle troops, they were the junior partners to their legionary counterparts. Foot troops were paid 100 *denarii* per annum from the later first century AD, with cavalry paid 200 *denarii* (those based on the wing of a battle formation being paid 333 *denarii*). Terms of service were similar to those of the legionaries, with auxiliaries normally serving twenty-five years. Upon retirement the trooper was given a citizenship diploma that granted Roman citizenship to himself and his heirs, the right of legal marriage to a non-citizen woman, and citizenship for existing children.

Auxiliary cavalry were organized into *quingenary alae* of 512 men or *milliary alae* of 768. Each was commanded by a *Praefectus Alae*. The basic cavalrymen were called *equites*, equipped with a *hasta* spear that could be thrown or used as a short lance, and a *spatha* long sword.

Their defensive panoply included flat oval or hexagonal shields, short *lorica hamata* chainmail hauberks and a variety of types of bronze and iron helmets, often with cheek and neck guards. In the early Principate the *equites* were supported by a variety of different types of light cavalry fighting in the style of their native region. Examples included eastern horse archers from Armenia and Syria, and Moorish *symmachiarii* javelin-armed skirmishers.

Auxilia infantry formations in the Principate were based on a single *quingenary* cohort of 480 troops, or a double-sized *milliary* cohort of 800 troops. These cohorts (both the small and large) were divided into centuries of between 80 and 100 men, each commanded by a centurion. Above this level the cohort was commanded by an equestrian, a *praefectus* for a *quingenary* unit and a tribune for a *milliary* unit.

Auxilia foot fought in both close and loose formation, the latter making them especially useful in difficult terrain. The majority were line of battle troops who fought in a similar manner to the legionaries. They were armed with a short, throwable spear called a *lancea* and a sword similar to the legionary *gladius*, this was later replaced by the longer cavalry-style *spatha*. The auxiliary foot shield was usually an elongated oval plank design covering the torso, featuring a central iron or bronze boss. Auxilia are most frequently shown wearing *lorica hamata* chainmail or *lorica squamata* scalemail hauberks, these being shorter and less sophisticated than those worn by the legionaries. Auxilia helmets were also less sophisticated, often cheaper bronze versions of those worn by the legionaries. The auxilia also provided the majority of the specialist warriors in Roman military formations, for example archers, staff slingers, slingers, crossbowmen and javelinmen.

Auxilia units could also be fielded in combined formations that featured both infantry and mounted troops, their organization being less well understood. Such infantry cohorts, cavalry *alae* and combined units were very flexible and could easily be moved around the Empire as needed in the same manner as *vexillations* of legionaries.

The Roman Navy

Republican Roman fleets of the early-to-mid first century BC, at the time of *legio* IX *Hispana*'s foundation, were considerably smaller than at their height during the Second Punic War (218 BC to 201 BC). Given by this time Rome controlled both the western and eastern Mediterranean, their key role was to counter piracy, and also participate in the frequent civil wars as various late Republican warlords strove for power. Their only major activity outside the Mediterranean was to support Caesar's conquest of Gaul, including his two incursions to Britain in 55 and 54 BC.

However, as with all other aspects of the Roman military establishment, Roman naval power was totally transformed as part of the Augustan reforms. He rationalized the ad hoc maritime system he inherited, replacing it with a series of regional fleets which reflected the Empire's expanding geographical reach. By the time *legio* IX *Hispana* had founded York around AD 70 there were ten such navies, each with a specific area of territorial responsibility. These are detailed in the table below, this also shows the annual stipend of each fleet's *praefectus classis* admiral, and so showing their status.

The *Classis Britannica* in Britain, which provides a good example of one of the larger Principate regional fleets, would certainly have served alongside *legio* IX *Hispana* during the various campaigns of conquest in Britain. This fleet featured 900 ships and 7,000 crew, including sailors, marines and support personnel (Elliott, 2016, 63). Each regional fleet had an origin specific to its region of operations, with the *Classis Britannica* coming into being with the original 900 vessels built by Caligula for his abortive AD 40 invasion of Britain. These remained on the north-western coast of Gaul and were still there to later be used by Claudius for his AD 43 invasion, the fleet remaining in existence from

Table 2: Regional Fleets of the Roman Principate.

Fleet	Annual Stipend
Classis Ravennas	300,000 sesterces
Classis Misenensis	200,000 sesterces
Classis Britannica	100,000 sesterces
Classis Germanica	100,000 sesterces
Classis Flavia Pannonica	60,000 sesterces
Classis Flavia Moesica	60,000 sesterces
Classis Pontica	60,000 sesterces
Classis Syriaca	60,000 sesterces
Classis Nova Libica	60,000 sesterces
Classis Alexandrina	60,000 sesterces

Ellis Jones, 2012, 61.

that point until the middle of the third century when it disappears from the historical record.

All regional fleets performed both military and civilian roles. In the former context the *Classis Britannica* had responsibility for the North Sea, English Channel, Atlantic approaches, Bristol Channel and Irish Sea, the east and west coasts of the main island of Britain, the river systems of Britain and the continental coast up to the Rhine Delta. The latter reflected the way the Romans viewed *Oceanus* separating Britain from the continent, not as a barrier as we do today in the context of recent military history, but as a point of connectivity linking Britannia physically with the rest of the Empire. This is reflected in the fact that the *Classis Britannica*'s headquarters were in Boulogne (Roman *Gesoriacum*), in north-western Gaul, with additional bases in Britain including Dover (Roman *Dubris*), Richborough (Roman *Rutupiae*), Lympne (Roman *Portus Lemanis*) and Pevensey (Roman *Anderida*). This fleet would have played a very active role supporting *legio* IX *Hispana* as it fought its various campaigns of conquest in Britannia.

Meanwhile, in its civilian activities the *Classis Britannica* was used in a variety of roles. This included administration, engineering and construction, and running industry and agriculture.

As with all of the Empire's regional fleets, the principal warship of the *Classis Britannica* was the small, mobile ram and ballista-equipped *liburnian* bireme galley. Ships of this type had replaced the large polyreme galleys of the Republican civil wars by the end of the first century BC. The fleet also used a variety of *myoparo* cutters and *scapha* skiffs, and transport vessels of all kinds.

An equestrian-level *praefectus classis* appointed directly by the Emperor commanded each regional fleet, he reporting to the provincial procurator rather than the governor given each fleet's civilian activities, though clearly he fell under the latter's command when on military duty. As part of his headquarters operation the *praefectus classis* had a specialist staff. This included a *subpraefectus* executive officer and aide-de-camp, *cornicularius* chief of staff, *actuarii* clerks, *scribae* scribes and seconded *dupliarii* ratings attached from the fleet.

Meanwhile, the commander of a squadron of ships was called a *navarchus* (the most senior the *navarchus principes*), and the captain of an individual vessel a *trierarchus*. Aboard ship the *trierarchus*' executive team included a *gubernator* senior officer responsible for the steering oars, a *proretus* second lieutenant and the *pausarius* rowing master.

Below this level the ship's company was based on the military organization of their land-based counterparts, with the basic unit called a
century. This reflected the preference for close action when engaged in
naval combat. The century was commanded by a centurion, assisted by an
optio second-in-command, a *suboptio* junior assistant, a *bucinator* bugler
or *cornicen* horn player, and finally an *armorum custos* armourer. The rest
of the ship's complement comprised marines, *velarius* sailors, and plenty
of *remiges* oarsmen. The latter were always professional rather than the
slaves often depicted in popular culture, the whole company being styled
milites (soldiers, the singular being *miles*) as opposed to *nautae* sailors.

In the Principate, service as a naval *milite* was regarded in the same way
as being an auxilia. Terms of service for all ranks was twenty-six years, a year
longer than their auxiliary counterparts, the reward on completion being
Roman citizenship. We have unique insight into this in the form of a recent
archaeological discovery. This was the finding of the copper alloy military
diploma of one Tigernos, a sailor of the *Classis Germanica*, granting his
citizenship after completing his service. Interestingly, he may prove to be
Britain's first named sailor as, despite his service on the Rhine, the diploma
was found broken into eight pieces at the Roman fort in Lanchester
(Roman *Longovicium*), County Durham.

Each naval *miles* received three gold pieces or 75 *denarii* upon enlistment.
Their basic annual pay at the beginning of the Principate for the lower ranks
was 100 *denarii*, with crewmembers with greater responsibilities being paid
an additional amount on top.

For weaponry, the marines of the regional fleets were armed in a similar
manner to the land-based auxilia. Principal missile weapons, in addition to
artillery, included bows, slings, javelins and darts. For hand-to-hand work
the marines also carried boarding pikes, the *hasta navalis* naval spear, various
types of sword and the *dolabra* boarding axe.

Clothing for the naval *milites* differed between the regional fleets,
reflecting differing climatic and operational conditions. Again using the
Classis Britannica as an example, an essential item of clothing in northern
waters was the *birrus*. Other key items of clothing for the *milites* of this
regional fleet would have included the *pilos* conical felt hat, a belted tunic
with trousers, and sandals or felt stockings with low-cut leather boots
rather than *caligae*. The short *sagum* cloak was worn when on formal duty.

Chapter 2

Background: Early Roman Britain

T he young province of Britannia played a key role in the later history of *legio* IX *Hispana*, with many speculating it is the location of the legion's mysterious disappearance. Given in this work two of the four main hypotheses regarding its fate are based here, it is useful to set out in this chapter a brief history of the early province and the key role played by the IXth legion in the campaigns of conquest here. Firstly, Late Iron Age (LIA) Britain is considered to set the scene for the arrival of Caesar. His two incursions of 55 BC and 54 BC are then detailed, putting the main island of Britain firmly on the Roman map for the first time. Next, the Claudian invasion of AD 43 (with *legio* IX *Hispana* a full participant) is set out, followed by a detailed narrative covering the lengthy forty years of conquest that followed.

Britain Before Rome

Britain was culturally an integral part of north-western Europe well before the arrival of Rome, and this was particularly evident in the Iron Age. This began here around 800 BC and featured five phases:

- The Earliest Iron Age from 800 BC to 600 BC, when Britain was part of the Hallstatt culture that predominated in western and central Europe.
- The Early Iron Age from 600 BC to 400 BC, when Britain continued to be part of the Hallstatt culture, and was later part of its La Tène evolution.
- The Middle Iron Age from 400 BC to 100 BC, where La Tène culture continued to predominate.
- The Late Iron Age (LIA) from 100 BC to 50 BC, once more La Tène in nature, which included Caesar's two incursions.
- The Latest Iron Age from 50 BC to the creation of the Roman province of Britannia in AD 43. Though again La Tène in nature,

with Britain its last redoubt after Caesar's conquest of Gaul in the 50s BC, Rome's influence here grew throughout this period.

Enter Caesar

Gaius Julius Caesar's two incursions into Britain in 55 BC and 54 BC were set firmly within his campaigns of conquest in Gaul. He had a number of reasons for invading:

- Britain remained a source of trouble on the north-western flank of his conquests in Gaul.
- Caesar was always on the lookout for an opportunity to make money. He knew there were exploitable natural resources in Britain, himself noting (Caesar V.2): '...tin is found inland, and small quantities of iron near the coast.' The Romans were also aware there was gold, silver, tin, lead and copper, much of it in the South West and Wales.
- Caesar was never one to pass the chance for new glory, relying on conquest after conquest to cement his reputation amongst his *populares* supporters back in Rome.

This latter point is particularly important. It is hard to explain to a modern audience what a truly fantastical adventure Caesar planned here. In the first instance his force would have to cross *Oceanus*. Such a voyage was a frightful proposition to sailors and legionaries used to the comparatively benign *mare nostrum*, as the Mediterranean was then styled in Rome. Next, once in mysterious Britain, he would be campaigning in a land of which the Romans knew little, other than the few pieces of intelligence provided by Mediterranean merchants and geographers from the previous few centuries (for example the metal resources). Invading Britain was truly a leap in the dark for the Romans. Interestingly in that regard, when Caesar sought intelligence from the Veneti tribe on the Gallic coast who knew the islands here well through trade, they tried to protect their friends across the water by playing dumb.

Unusually for Caesar, his first incursion to Britain in 55 BC was ill planned. Not only did he fail to gain intelligence from the Veneti, but his own pre-invasion reconnaissance for a landing place was also a failure. This consisted of a single trireme galley commanded by a tribune called Gaius Volusenus. After spending four days sailing up and down the eastern coast of Kent, the latter made the unlikely recommendation of the beaches beneath the White Cliffs of Dover. Caesar took the advice and set off with *legio* VII and *legio* X (around 12,000 men) in eighty transports, escorted by war galleys from the Mediterranean. An additional eighteen vessels modified to carry his cavalry set off separately, but crucially never arrived after missing the tide.

Unsurprisingly, when his fleet arrived off Dover the cliff tops were swarming with native British warriors, forewarned of the Roman invasion by their Gallic friends. Caesar quickly realized his mistake and headed north, the fleet eventually dropping anchor between Walmer and Pegwell Bay below Ramsgate. However, the Britons had tracked his fleet and were again arrayed along the shore. Caesar now had to carry out that most dangerous of military operations, an amphibious assault on a well-defended coastline. First he drove his war galleys hard ashore to the north of the landing area, aiming to turn the Britons' right flank. From here they could enfilade the landing zone with ballista. The legionaries were reluctant to land, however, and now a famous incident occurred. This was the *aquilifer* of *legio* X leaping into the shallows and declaring (Caesar, V.1): 'Leap, fellow soldiers, unless you wish to betray your eagle to the enemy. I, for my part, will perform my duty to the Republic and to my general.'

This worked, with the shamed legionaries swarming ashore and eventually winning a hard fought victory after which they built a large marching camp. However, bad weather later damaged many of Caesar's ships, this needing half of his force to carry out repairs. Then, after some desultory local campaigning but unable to scout or pursue because of his lack of cavalry, the Romans returned to the continent.

Caesar now showed typical Roman grit. He determined to return, and this time with a much greater force. This comprised five legions (up to 30,000 men, and almost certainly including the IXth legion) and 2,000 allied cavalry. For the new campaign he also built a fleet of 600 specially designed ships, these featuring much lower freeboards than his Mediterranean designs to enable easier disembarkation, and wider beams to carry bulkier loads. To these he added 200 locally chartered transports, a further 80 ships used in the previous year's incursion, and 28 war galleys.

The enormity of Caesar's force this time intimidated the Britons who avoided opposing his landing, this again on the east coast of Kent. However, as in 55 BC, bad weather intervened. While Caesar was campaigning inland against a large British force a storm badly damaged many of his transports anchored off the coast of Kent. He quickly returned to the landing area, initiating an urgent repair operation again. His legions then renewed their campaign, with the legionary spearheads forcing a crossing of the Thames and capturing the main base of the British leader Cassivellaunus. The latter then sued for peace. Terms were quickly agreed, including the Britons supplying hostages and agreeing to pay an annual tribute to Rome. Honour satisfied, Caesar then withdrew back to Gaul.

Elephants and Camels

Plans to revisit Britain started early. Augustus himself, founder of the Empire, planned at least three invasions in 34 BC, 27 BC and 25 BC. The first and last were abandoned because of issues elsewhere in the Empire, the second cancelled after successful diplomacy. Such false starts were certainly viewed negatively at the time, with first century BC poet Horace reflecting that (*Odes*, III.5): 'Augustus will be deemed a God on Earth when the Britons and the deadly Parthians (also targets for early Imperial Roman expansion) have been added to our Empire.'

Next, in AD 40 Caligula also abandoned a planned invasion of Britain while actually on the beaches of northern Gaul, having built 900 ships and stocked warehouses there to do so, as detailed in Chapter 1.

It was therefore left to the ill-favoured Claudius to actually invade Britain with a true intention to stay. Having become the most unlikely of emperors at the hands of the Praetorian Guard in Rome, he determined to make his name and secure his legacy through conquest. Opportunity was provided by the death of Cunobelinus, king of the Catuvellauni tribe based in the region of modern Hertfordshire and Buckinghamshire. His sons Caratacus and Togodumnus succeeded him, immediately launching an offensive against their Atrebates neighbours in the Thames Valley. Roman allies, the latter were defeated, with their king Verica fleeing to Rome and the protection of Claudius. Caratacus and Togodumnus then overplayed their hand by demanding Verica's extradition. Claudius refused, with disturbances then following in Britain against Roman merchants already embedded there following Caesar's incursions. With the means already available thanks to Caligula and his ready-built fleet and stocked warehouses, Claudius now had the opportunity and decided to invade.

Claudius took no chances given the enormity of the task. He appointed the highly experienced Pannonian Governor Aulus Plautius to command his army of conquest. This comprised four legions (*legio* II *Augusta*, Plautius' own *legio* IX *Hispana* from Pannonia, *legio* XIV *Gemina* and *legio* XX *Valeria*

Victrix) that together with their associated auxiliaries created an army of 40,000 men. Claudius also loaded the invasion fleet with 3,000 tonnes of grain to feed the invasion force for at least three months after arrival.

However, once again an event now occurred which showed how fearsome the task ahead was, with the legionaries refusing to board their ships. At the last minute the day was saved by one of Claudius' own freedmen called Tiberius Claudius Narcissus, a senior figure in the emperor's *Consilium Principis* advisory council.

He boarded a vessel and shamed the soldiery into following him, they shouting '*Io Saturnaila*', referencing the end of year role-reversing winter festival. The huge force then set sail in three divisions, arriving in late summer to land unopposed given the British warriors had dispersed to gather their harvest. The landing place was again the east Kent coast. Once ashore Plautius secured the beachhead by building a huge 57ha marching camp, the remains of which can still be seen today within the wall circuit of the later Saxon shore fort at Richborough.

The Romans soon began their breakout, the 40,000 men snaking along the Pilgrim's Way, the well-known prehistoric ridgeway running for much of its length in Kent along the south side of the North Downs. Given the south-facing slopes, this would have had the added advantage of ensuring that Plautius' force was exposed to the maximum amount of sunlit daylight as the legionary spearheads progressed, helping them stay on the march for longer each day.

Plautius quickly defeated Caratacus and Togodumnus in two small engagements in eastern Kent as the Britons tried to interdict his line of march, after which the Dobunni (a tribe based in the Welsh Marches who supplied troops to support the Catuvellauni) became the first of the British kingdoms to sue for peace. Plautius then continued his advance, arriving on the eastern bank of a large river where Dio (60.19) describes his famous river crossing battle taking place. Many believe this was at Aylesford on the River Medway, a location naturally arrived at when travelling along the Pilgrim's Way given it is only a short distance down today's Bluebell Hill to reach the site (Elliott, 2016, 116). This two-day affair was a close-run thing, with the Romans unable to deploy their fleet in support as the site was above the river's tidal reach, then downriver at modern Snodland. The Romans finally won after Plautius sent a detachment of Batavian auxiliaries (natives of the Rhine Delta region) to swim the river and outflank the Britons who then routed. They fled downriver to the Thames which they crossed, regrouping on the northern shore. Plautius pursued, hot on their heels. He then fought another contested river crossing battle, winning this one with ease given he could use his fleet.

Once in the region of modern Essex Plautius paused and consolidated his position, learning that Togodumnus was dead and Caratacus had fled west to find sanctuary with the Silures and Ordovices tribes in southern and central Wales. He regrouped for a final push, sending for Claudius to join him to share the final victory. The Emperor quickly crossed the Channel, arriving at Plautius' camp with war elephants and camels to intimidate the native Britons. The force then broke camp and headed north at speed for the Catuvellaunian capital of Camulodunum (later Roman *Colonia Victricensis*, now modern Colchester), arriving in late October. This lightning strike eviscerated all before it and the Catuvellauni quickly sued for peace, with eleven other British tribes following. All submitted to Roman rule. Claudius then declared the province of Britannia founded, establishing Camulodunum as its capital and appointing Plautius its first governor. He then left, never to return, having stayed for only sixteen days.

Up to this point the conquest of Britain had followed a similar pattern to that of Gaul. That now changed. It took Caesar only eight years to pacify Gaul. It took the Romans another forty years to finally establish a northern border in Britain, along the Solway Firth–Tyne line later fortified as Hadrian's Wall, in a brutal series of campaigns of conquest.

Conquest and Rebellion

Claudius' new province was only the area covered by the modern south-east of England, and moves to conquer more territory to the north and west began almost immediately. Firstly, *legio* XX *Valeria Victrix* built a fortress at Camulodunum (renamed *Colonia Claudia* in AD 49), establishing it as a *colonia* for retiring veterans.

The three remaining legions then headed out in different directions. Plautius' *legio* IX *Hispana* headed north, skirting the territory of the Iceni tribe in modern Norfolk, by this time a Roman client kingdom, and reaching the River Nene where it established a vexillation fort at Longthorpe (Roman name unknown). This built, the IXth legion continued north to found another vexillation fort at Leicester (later, Roman *Ratae*) on the River Soar, and then a full legionary fort at Lincoln (later, Roman *Lindum Colonia*) on the River Witham. The legion certainly left its mark there during its stay, with many inscriptions to soldiers of *legio* IX *Hispana* found there in addition to that of the legionary dispatch rider Quintus Cornelius. A fine example is the tombstone of legionary Gaius Saufeius, found at the corner of Salthouse Lane on the High Street in the modern city. The inscription (RIB 255) on his fine two-metre tall limestone monument reads: 'To Gaius Saufeius, son of Gaius, of the Fabian voting-tribe, from Heraclea, soldier of legio IX, aged 40, of 22 year's service: he lies here.'

If Saufeius' tombstone is contemporary with the IXth legion's stay in Lincoln then here is a warrior that, given his twenty-two years service at death, could easily have taken part in the Claudian invasion itself.

Meanwhile *legio* XIV *Gemina* headed north-westwards deep into the Midlands, establishing vexillation forts at Great Chesterford (Roman name unknown), Mancetter (later, Roman *Manduessedum*) and Alchester (Roman name unknown). Finally, and most famously, *legio* II *Augusta* under the future emperor Vespasian (AD 69 to AD 79) struck out for the South West where the tribes were notably hostile, particularly the Durotriges in the region of modern Dorset, southern Wiltshire, southern Somerset and eastern Devon. Suetonius (*Vespasian* 4) goes into great detail here, telling us he:

> fought 30 battles, subjugated two warlike tribes (the Durotriges and Dumnonii), captured more than 20 oppida (fortified native urban centres), and took the Isle of Wight.

Vespasian's speedy westward advance was greatly aided by his use of the British fleet to provide close support in the littoral zone along the coast and down river systems. This included exercising military control there, scouting and raiding ahead of the land forces, carrying out all of the logistical heavy lifting, and building fortified harbours to supply the troops as they advanced (Elliott, 2016, 120). Archaeological data supporting the latter comes in the form of large-scale Claudian-period storage buildings and Claudian pottery on the site of the later Roman settlement of *Clausentum* (today a suburb of Southampton) at the tip of the Bitterne Peninsula. From here supplies arriving via the regional fleet would have been ideally placed for forward deployment up the River Itchen to the advancing legions and auxilia. Vespasian's progress can be tracked today by these coastal supply bases, the next at Wimborne in Dorset, then Weymouth Bay in Dorset, and finally at Topsham in Devon. The latter later became the port for the later legionary fortress built by *legio* II *Augusta* around AD 55 on the site later to become Exeter (Roman *Isca Dumnoniorum*). After four seasons of intense campaigning, with Vespasian using this combination of land-based shock troops supplied by his new series of fortified harbours, the South West was conquered and incorporated into Britannia.

At the point of Plautius' departure, Britannia comprised the region below a line from the River Severn to the Wash, excepting the client tribes of the Atrebates in the Thames Valley and the Iceni in northern East Anglia. This new frontier broadly tracked the river valleys of the River Avon in the South West and River Nene in the East. By this time manifestations of *Romanitas* were emerging across the conquered territory, with the former native British nobility encouraged to learn formal Latin, wear togas on official business and invest in grand stone-built public building enterpises (conveniently for the Romans, funded with loans from the leading Senatorial families in Rome). More practically, given the always-urgent need to make a new province pay its own way, Roman patterns of local government were also imposed. As Oosthuizen (2019, 27) details:

> The (new) administration of Roman Britain was based on a set of nested hierarchies: broadly speaking from vicus, a small local centre (as opposed to the vici civilian settlements associated with Roman forts), to pagus, the locality, to civitates, a region often reproducing a prehistoric territory (as for example with the Cantiacii in modern Kent).

The next governor in Britain was called Publius Ostorius Scapula. He put down an early rebellion by the Iceni, campaigned in Wales against raiders led by Caratacus (the fugitive leader harboured by the Silures and Ordovices), put down a rising among the Brigantes in the north and finally campaigned against the Deceangli tribe in northern Wales.

Ostorius was replaced by Didius Gallus in AD 51 who continued campaigning in Wales, being replaced by Quintus Veranius Nepos in AD 57 who died within a year of taking office. However, the next leader here was one of the truly great British governors, Gaius Suetonius Paulinus. Soon after arriving he targeted Anglesey at the north-western tip of Wales, deep in the heart of Deceangli territory. This mysterious island was home to the Druids, the leaders of pre-Roman religion in Britain. Paulinus staged a major amphibious assault here in AD 60, a Claudian invasion in miniature. The native Britons deployed in a dense mass on the shore and, driven by religious fervor, fought desperately. After a vicious battle, Paulinus was successful and the island captured.

Next, however, he faced an existential threat to the survival of the province from a totally unexpected direction. This was the AD 60/61 revolt of Boudicca, queen of the Iceni. The context was the earlier death of Boudicca's husband, the Iceni king Prasutagus. An ally of Rome, in his will he left his kingdom to his daughters and also the emperor Nero (AD 54 to AD 68). However, when he died the Romans predictably ignored his wishes and annexed the kingdom. Boudicca protested but was flogged, with her daughters allegedly raped, though another factor was Roman financiers calling in their loans to the British elites there.

Soon Boudicca's incendiary rebellion had ignited most of the South East above the Thames against the Romans. Marching south at the head of an army close to 100,000 strong, she first targeted the then provincial capital at Colchester. Here *legio* IX *Hispana* takes centre stage once more, though in this case in the context of ignominious failure. The nearest military formation to the insurrection, its *legate* Quintus Petillius Cerialis (a future governor of the Province) led a large force comprising legionary *vexillations* and auxiliaries to intercept Boudicca. This arrived too late to save Colchester, which by that point had already been torched with great loss of life. It was then decisively defeated by the main British army, with Cerialis fleeing for his life alongside his cavalry, leaving his legionaries to their fate. They then remained incongruously holed in up in a nearby fort until after the insurrection had been defeated. Interestingly, some have speculated that Quintus Cornelius and Gaius Saufeius, referenced earlier in the context of their tombstones found in Lincoln, may have fallen in this engagement.

In Wales, Paulinus had abandoned his assault on the druids as soon as he heard of the revolt. The governor immediately headed south-east along the route of Watling Street, accompanied by most of *legio* XIV *Gemina*, some *vexillations* from *legio* XX *Valeria Victrix* and a few auxiliary units including two *ala* of cavalry. Reaching High Cross in modern Leicestershire where Watling Street crossed the Fosse Way (the military trunk road linking Lincoln with Exeter) Paulinus then sent for the Exeter-based *legio* II *Augusta* to join him. However, the unit's *legate* and second-in-command were away, with its *praefectus castrorum* in charge.

Called Poenius Postumus, he ignored the call, bringing shame on the legion. Clearly he thought the province about to fall and wanted to stay on the River Ex from where he could evacuate his troops if necessary. Meanwhile, some stragglers from *legio* IX *Hispana* also found their way to

Paulinus, giving him a total force of around 6,000 legionaries from the three legions, 4,000 foot auxiliaries and around 1,000 mounted auxiliaries.

At this point Tacitus has Paulinus marching in person to London (Roman *Londinium*), the recently founded major trading port on the River Thames, from where the provincial procurator Catus Decianus had fled to Gaul as Boudicca and her growing force marched on the town. It is useful to quote the historian in full at this point given the real sense of jeopardy he presents as the new province fell into chaos (*Annals*, 14.33):

> Paulinus…with wonderful resolution, marched amidst a hostile population to Londinium, which, though undistinguished by the name of a colony (it was styled by the Romans a *municipium* mercantile town), was much frequented by a number of merchants and trading vessels. Uncertain whether he should choose it as a seat of war, as he looked round on his scanty force of soldiers…he resolved to save the province at the cost of a single town. Nor did the tears and weeping of the people, as they implored his aid, deter him from giving the signal of departure and receiving into his army all who would go with him. Those who were chained to the spot by the weakness of their sex, or the infirmity of age, or the attractions of the place, were cut off by the enemy

The key reference here is that which describes the local population as hostile when Paulinus was marching down Watling Street through Leicestershire and Hertfordshire, indicating that the Catuvellauni certainly, and perhaps even the Trinovantes to their east, had joined the Iceni in the great revolt. In these circumstances Paulinus' force would have been constructing defended marching camps at the end of each day's match as they travelled south-east. It is therefore unlikely that if Paulinus did indeed travel in person to London, he took his whole army. More likely he would have travelled with a bodyguard of auxiliary cavalrymen, or even more likely have sent an advance guard to assess the situation with authority to order an evacuation if needed.

In the event, when Boudicca did arrive in London, any remaining Romans or Romano-British were butchered and the town burned to the ground. Boudicca then targeted the new *municipium* of St Albans (Roman *Verulamium*), razing this also. The primary sources say that 80,000 were killed in the three sacking events by this point, indicating the scale of the insurrection and its rank savagery. However, the stage was now set for Roman retribution, and on a devastating scale.

By this point the primary sources say Boudicca's force had grown to 230,000, though only 100,000 were still likely warriors. This was an enormous force to keep in the field and she knew that a meeting engagement with Paulinus would be needed quickly to keep her army and its swelling number of dependent camp followers together. She also knew that if the governor was defeated, the Romans might abandon the province for good. Boudicca therefore advanced north-west along Watling Street to seek out the Roman army. As she progressed she would also have received intelligence about the size of Paulinus' force, and no doubt felt the outcome of the forthcoming battle was a foregone conclusion.

In that she was wrong, as the wily Paulinus was ready for her and chose the place to make his stand very carefully. This was in a steep defile with woods on either side and behind. These protected his flanks and limited the frontage of the line of battle, negating the British superiority in numbers and playing to the martial superiority of his own legionaries. The location of the battle is unknown, with most historians and archaeologists favouring a site along Watling Street. Leading candidate sites include High Cross where Paulinus had awaited the arrival of *legio* II *Augusta* in vain, Church Stowe in Northamptonshire and Markyate in Hertfordshire. Interestingly, the latter is between Dunstable, a Roman site not destroyed by Boudicca (indicating she didn't arrive there), and St Albans to its immediate south-east which she did destroy. All three sites also have a significant water source, essential with so many engaged in the battle.

Paulinus deployed his legionaries and auxilia uphill of the Britons. He divided his foot troops into four main bodies with a centre, left and right flanks, and with a reserve to the rear of the centre. He then positioned an *ala* of auxiliary cavalry on either extreme flank hard against the woods there, where he finally deployed field defences for additional protection. Boudicca deployed her enormous force opposite, though in much denser formation, with the chariots in front manned by her own elite warriors. So confident were the Britons of victory that the families of the warriors joined the baggage train at the rear of her battle line to watch events unfold.

Boudicca now exhorted her army to more slaughter, then opened the battle with a wild uphill charge with both the chariots and foot warriors. The former rode across the front of the Romans, hurling insults and javelins, before turning square on to close for hand-to-hand combat. The foot troops followed close behind. The discipline of the legionaries now shone through. En masse they released their lighter *pila*, 6,000 iron-barbed javelins arcing high in the air in a steep parabola and then dropping on the heads of the Britons, many without helmets. The auxiliary infantry joined in with their own *lancea*, and with ballista, bows and slings used by specialist missile troops. Then, at point-blank range, the legionaries unleashed their second, heavier *pila*. These flew in a flat arc, hammering into the front ranks of Britons who came to a shuddering halt in a tangle of dead horses, overturned chariots, bodies and wounded.

Paulinus saw that the British advance had faltered and seized his chance to take the initiative. He now ordered the legionaries to move forward in a series of *cuneus* wedge formations, with centurions and standard bearers to the fore. The auxiliaries followed suit on the flanks. Swords were drawn and shields set hard forward. The wedges then charged downhill into the dense mass of Britons, causing slaughter everywhere and forcing the natives into a huge, desperate crush where the warriors couldn't use their weapons. A massacre ensued as the Britons broke and tried to run away. However, they were trapped on the field by the surrounding families and baggage train. All were hacked down where they stood, the legionaries giving no quarter.

The result was a mighty victory for Paulinus, with Tacitus saying (*Annals*, 14.35):

> The troops gave no quarter even to the women: the baggage animals themselves had been speared and added to the pile of bodies. The glory won in the course of the day was remarkable, and equal to that of our older victories: for, by some accounts, little less than eighty thousand Britons fell, at a cost of some four hundred Romans killed and a not much greater number of wounded. Boudica ended her days by poison; while...Postumus, camp-prefect of the second legion, informed of the exploits of the men of the fourteenth and twentieth, and conscious that he had cheated his own corps of a share in the honours and had violated the rules of the service by ignoring the orders of his commander, ran his sword through his body.

The Romans then quickly drafted in 2,000 more legionaries from Germany together with 1,000 auxiliary cavalry and eight units of auxiliary foot to help stamp out the last flames of resistance. This was carried out with such vigour in the Iceni homelands of north Norfolk that the region remained for many years under-developed compared to the rest of the province.

Thus ended the Boudiccan revolt, the province secured for another 340 years. However, Paulinus didn't receive the plaudits he might have expected. This was because the absent procurator Decianus hiding in Gaul was quickly replaced by the emperor Nero with a new man named Gaius Julius Alpinus Classicianus. The latter was critical of Paulinus' post-revolt punitive actions against the Britons, fearing it might spark another revolt. He reported this to the emperor who sent his own freedman Polyclitus to conduct an investigation. Though we don't have the full details of its findings, the investigator did report that Paulinus had lost some ships from the regional fleet. This excuse was used to relieve him, he being replaced by the more conciliatory Publius Petronius Turpilianus as governor. However, Paulinus does not seem to have returned to Rome in disgrace, as a lead tessera found there features both his and Nero's names alongside symbols of victory, and a man with his name was nominated as consul for AD 66. Nevertheless, the Romans had been badly rattled by the rebellion, and in my view if Paulinus had lost his battle Britannia would have fallen, with the Romans perhaps unlikely ever to return.

Calm restored, rebuilding in Britain began, with the provincial capital moving to London. Things had settled down to such an extent that by the mid AD 60s Nero pulled the *legio* XIV *Gemina* out of the province. Consolidation was now the watchword, and the slow process of northward conquest didn't begin again until AD 69 when the new governor Marcus Vettius Bolanus campaigned against the Brigantes. These were Rome's erstwhile allies in the north. This huge confederation of tribes was resident in what is now Yorkshire, Lancashire, Cumbria, Northumberland and south-western Scotland. Cause was provided by the usurpation of Rome's ally there, Queen Cartimandua, by her estranged husband Venutius. Though the governor achieved some success in his campaigns he was soon replaced from AD 71 by the first of three great warrior governors. The first was Quintus Petillius Cerialis, with orders from Vespasian (Emperor since AD 69) to achieve military glory for the new Flavian dynasty. By this time he had rebuilt his reputation as a military leader following his failure against Boudicca a decade earlier, in particular leading the campaign to defeat the Batavian Revolt of Gaius Julius Civilis in the Rhine Delta.

Now in Britain, Cerialis immediately targeted the Brigantes in the north again, being given another legion in *legio* II *Adiutrix* to help achieve the task. First he ordered *legio* IX *Hispana* from Lincoln into Yorkshire where they constructed a new fortress at York (later, Roman *Eboracum*) on an easily defendable plateau at the confluence of the Rivers Ouse and Foss, deep in Brigantian territory. Located on the northern bank of the former, this original fortress was classically playing card shaped, enclosing a large area of over 20 ha and easily able to host the 5,500 men of the IXth legion. Its initial defences were a 2.5m deep V-shaped ditch and a 3m high turf/ clay rampart topped with a palisade, featuring wooden towers and gates. This was to be the home for *legio* IX *Hispana* for the rest of its time in Britain.

At the same time *legio* II *Adiutrix* was sent to the River Dee where a new naval facility and fort was constructed on the west coast at Chester. When all was ready, Cerialis then launched a savage offensive, with legionary spearheads from *legio* XX *Valeria Victrix* and *legio* IX *Hispana* driving up the north-western and north-eastern coasts, supported by the *Classis Britannica*. *Legio* II *Adiutrix* formed the strategic reserve.

The progress of the campaign is evidenced by the multitude of vexillation-size forts built as the operation unfolded. The end was never in doubt, with the Romans crushing the final stand at the Brigantian capital of Stanwick St John in North Yorkshire. Venutius was killed, and by the time Cerialis returned to Rome in AD 74 the north of England had been incorporated into the province of Britannia, including parts of the modern Scottish Borders. The fate of Cartimandua is unknown.

The next warrior governor was Sextus Julius Frontinus, another Flavian favourite. Arriving in Britain with the north now pacified, Frontinus turned his attention to the unfinished business in Wales. Here, in spite of the campaigns of Gallus, Nepos and Paulinus, the native tribes were still troublesome. Deploying *legio* II *Augusta* from its base in Gloucester (later, Roman *Glevum*), Frontinus launched a campaign that took three years to defeat the tribes of southern and central Wales. To secure the region he then redeployed the legion from Gloucester to Caerleon (later, Roman *Isca Augusta*) where they built a large legionary fortress and harbour to oversee southern Wales and the Bristol Channel. To complete the subjugation of the region he then had *legio* II *Adiutrix* rebuild the fort at Chester into a full legionary fortress, this was even bigger than those at York and Caerleon, to maintain Roman authority in northern Wales. As a final act while governor he also campaigned against the Brigantes, who were still clearly not happy with their recent subjugation by Rome. As will be seen in Chapter 3, this was not the last time there was trouble in the north.

One can sense here of how slow, painful and bloody the Roman occupation of the increasingly large province of Britannia was. Because of the need to physically lock down newly occupied areas with fortifications large and small, the legacy of Roman conquest here is physically written across the landscape. Many of today's leading cities and towns in England and Wales were originally Roman legionary fortresses and their *canabae* civilian settlements. Think Exeter, Gloucester, Chester, York and Lincoln. Other key cities and towns were originally smaller Roman vexillation forts and their *vicus* civilian settlements. Examples include Leicester, Manchester (Roman *Mamucium*), Carlisle (Roman *Luguvalium*) and Corbridge (Roman *Coria*). This system of fortresses and forts, designed to put the stamp of Rome across the province, was matched by a series of military trunk roads that to this day form the backbone of the pre-motorway A-road network in Britain. As Bishop details (2014, 41):

> Since most of the major roads in (Roman) Britain…had their origins in the military campaigns of the conquest period, it is not unreasonable to suggest that the various components of the network can be dated to the aftermath of the earliest military activity in each area.

Examples proliferate. Think the A2 following the line of Watling Street from the Imperial Gateway at Richborough on the east coast of Kent through to London. The A5 then follows the same road through to the Welsh Marches where it branches north to the legionary fort at Chester and south to the legionary fort at Caerleon. Similarly the Fosse Way, for much of its length the modern A46, links the legionary fortress at Lincoln through the fort at Leicester and on to the legionary fortress at Exeter. Meanwhile, Ermine Street links the provincial capital London with the legionary fort at Lincoln, and then on to that at York. To this day, for much of its length the modern A1 follows its line.

The Far North

To this point the province of Britannia, carved out of the pre-Roman landscape of Britain at great cost to both native Britons and Romans, still had no settled northern border. This task was left to the last and greatest warrior governor, Gnaeus Julius Agricola. Having been commander of *legio* XX *Valeria Victrix* under Cerialis he was already familiar with the troublesome province. Returning as governor in the late summer of AD 77, he immediately launched a savage offensive against the

Ordovinces in Wales in response to the near annihilation of a Roman cavalry detachment. Within a month he'd hacked his way through to Anglesey, again the centre of resistance, annihilating any further opposition.

Encouraged by Vespasian to greater glory, Agricola now turned his gaze to the far north. In AD 78 he redeployed his legions to the former territory of the Brigantes. There he spent a year pacifying any remaining rebels and building a string of vexillation forts to secure his rear. In AD 79 he then launched his assault into the Scottish Borders. This followed the same pattern Cerialis had used in his campaign against the Brigantes, with legionary spearheads forging up the west and east coasts supported by the *Classis Britannica*. The IXth legion again took the lead on the eastern route. Success is indicated by the building of a substantial fort at Newstead (Roman *Trimontium*) on the River Tweed, site of the Selgovae tribe's major population centre. Tacitus adds that the eastern spearhead may actually have reached as far north as the River Tay (Agricola, 20). Certainly Agricola's accomplishments were well regarded back in Rome, with Dio (66.20) saying the new Emperor Titus (AD 79 to AD 81) was given his fifteenth salutation by way of celebration.

Agricola spent AD 80 consolidating his position in the Scottish Borders and Fife, constructing new military harbours to forward deploy the *Classis Britannica*. Examples include Kirkbride, Newton Stewart, Glenluce, Stranraer, Gurvan, Ayr and Dumbarton on the west coast, and Camelon on the east. A major naval base may also have been established at Carpow on the Tay.

In his third year of campaigning in AD 81 Agricola targeted the south-west of the Scottish Borders where the Novantae tribe had proved particularly difficult to pacify. For this he launched an amphibious assault, with himself in the lead vessel. This was either northwards across the Solway Firth, or westwards across the River Annan in Galloway. Again he achieved total success.

Next Tacitus (*Agricola*, 24) says Agricola considered invading Ireland late in the campaigning year with one legion. He certainly had the means given much of the *Classis Britannica* was already deployed in the north-west for his campaign against the Novantae (Elliott, 2016, 78). Gathering in Loch Ryan or Luce Bay in Galloway, this fleet would only have 32km to travel to reach Belfast Lough. The invasion never took place, however, with the new Emperor Domitian (AD 81 to AD 96) refusing permission (Mason, 2003, 100).

With new imperial orders, in AD 82 Agricola headed back north once more. This time the legionary spearheads forged above the Clyde and Forth line, focusing on the east coast given the inhospitable terrain in the west in the Scottish Highlands. The native Britons here, collectively called the Caledonians, now began to fight for their very survival. Tacitus (*Agricola*, 27) has them desperately attacking military installations, including Rome's most northerly legionary fortress at Inchtuthil on the Tay. Agricola once more prevailed, the campaigning season ending with the Romans poised for one final assault on the farthest north.

Agricola took no chances in AD 83 for his fifth and final campaign, fielding an army of 30,000 men. First he sealed off the east coast with the *Classis Britannica*, then launched his huge force north towards the Grampians and Moray Firth. His aim was to force the Caledonians into a decisive meeting engagement. In this he succeeded, the gathered tribes offering battle at a place called Mons Graupius. While the exact location isn't known, the outcome is. Total Roman victory, the Caledonians massacred. Interestingly, although *legio* IX *Hispana* and its sister legions were in attendance here, all of the fighting was carried out by the Roman auxiliaries. Agricola now considered the farthest north, and so the whole main island of Britain, conquered. To mark this he ordered the *Classis Britannica* to circumnavigate the northernmost tip of the island (*Agricola*, 10), then reported total success to Domitian who, to monumentalize the success, ordered a grand triumphal arch to be built at the Imperial Gateway of Richborough where Claudius had landed back in AD 43.

This satisfactory situation wasn't to last, however. Domitian quickly lost interest in Britain, and sometime between AD 83 and AD 85 he recalled Agricola to Rome. Despite his immense success he was only awarded a statue and triumphal decorations. He never again held high military or civil office and died in AD 93.

Without the political imperative from the emperor to stay in the far north, within four years of Agricola's departure the forts cutting off the Highland Line in the upper Midland Valley had been evacuated. Next the legionary fortress at Inchtuthil on the Tay was abandoned, even before it was fully completed by *legio* XX *Valeria Victrix*. By the end of the century Rome's most northerly border had settled on the Solway Firth–Tyne line, where we can once more pick up the story of *legio* IX *Hispana* as the second century AD began.

Chapter 3

Trouble in the North

As detailed in the Introduction, the most popular theory regarding the loss of *legio* IX *Hispana* is that it was destroyed while campaigning in the north of Britain in the early second century AD. This is certainly the view held by many in the wider public after the story's popularization in historical fiction and by Hollywood. But what are the facts behind this dramatic theory? In truth, they are very few in number in terms of any specific disaster. Therefore, to test this hypothesis, in this Chapter I first provide context by detailing Roman York where the IXth legion was based for much of its later existence. I then consider its theatre of operations in the north of the province and across the frontier in the region of modern Scotland. Next I detail how it actually carried out its duties there. Finally, I then set about examining every aspect of its later life in Britain to see if any evidence at all points to a dramatic end in the far north. Only once I have followed this evidential trail do I take a view about its potential fate there.

Roman York, Home of the IXth Legion

As set out in Chapter 2, *legio* IX *Hispana* founded York when it built a legionary fortress there at the confluence of the Rivers Ouse and Foss as part of the governor Cerialis' campaigns against the Brigantes in the early AD 70s. By the early second century AD this turf wall and palisade structure, with its wooden towers and gates, and its associated *canaba legionis* civilian settlement, were well established as the most significant Roman town in the north of the province. The IXth legion chose the location of its fortress well, constructing it on the northern bank of the Ouse which provided ready access to the eastern coast of Britain and the North Sea through the Humber Estuary. This position was also particularly defensible, with the Foss tributary of the Ouse providing riverine protection on its south-eastern flank.

As detailed in Chapter 2, the original fortress was classically playing-card in shape and very large. Its defences featured a deep ditch with ankle breakers in the bottom designed to snap the ankles of those trying to scale the far side, and a 3m high turf rampart topped by a wooden palisade. The corners of the fortress were positioned at the four points of the compass, facing north, south, east and west, with its principal streets the *via principalis* ('main street') and the *via praetorian*. The latter tracked the line of today's Stonegate, crossing the Roman bridge across the Ouse to link the fortress with its *canabae*. This bridge was the third longest in Roman Britain, after those in London crossing the River Thames and the River Medway crossing at Rochester in Kent.

The fortress featured four heavily fortified *portae* gates that were set in the centre of each of the four walls, these still correlating with the modern entrances to the portion of the city on the north bank of the river today. Of these, the river-facing *Porta Praetoria* gave access to Ermine Street, the great northern road linking York with Lincoln and then on to London, while at the opposite end of the fortress the *Porta Decumana* opened onto the twin north-westerly roads to Malton (Roman *Derventio*) and Stamford Bridge (Roman name unknown), also giving access to the east coast. Meanwhile the north-western *Porta Principalis Dextra* opened onto Dere Street giving access to the far north, while on the south-eastern side the *Porta Principalis Sinistra* gave access to the road leading to the port of Brough-on-Humber.

This latter gate is particularly important in the story of *legio* IX *Hispana* as it is near this location that an inscription was found in 1854 that is the latest dated anywhere in the Empire which mentions the legion. This key and iconic piece of evidence was discovered by workmen digging a deep drain seven metres beneath King's Square in the city. The inscribed limestone slab, now in the Yorkshire Museum, is over one metre square in size. It formed the centre section of a monumental inscription that, once reconstructed by the best scholars of the day, read (RIB 665): 'The Emperor Caesar Nerva Trajan Augustus, son of the deified Nerva, Conqueror of Germany, Conqueror of Dacia, Chief Priest, in his twelfth year of tribunician power, acclaimed imperator six times, five times consul, father of his country, built this gate through the agency of the ninth Hispana legion

The reference to tribunician power allowed the inscription to be dated to AD 108, there being no later epigraphic inscription mentioning the IXth legion anywhere. The context for the find was the rebuilding programme that began in the early first century AD which saw the original turf and palisade fortress replaced with a new stone built structure on the same grid plan as the original fortification. Campbell (2011, 48) speculates that the inscribed slab was installed to celebrate the new stonebuilt south-eastern gateway's construction.

As with other Roman legionary fortresses, that at York existed to provide accommodation for the men and equipment of its legion, in this case initially *legio* IX *Hispana*. It had three principal specific functions:

- In the first instance to protect the legion if their base was attacked. It should be remembered here that at this time Hadrian's Wall had yet to be built, with the northern frontier set along the Solway Firth–Tyne line marked by the east-west Stanegate road (see below for detail).
- To act as a base for the legion to maintain control of Brigantian territory in the north of the province.
- To provide troops to patrol the northern border and project power northwards into the modern Scottish Borders and beyond.

The fortress, in both its original turf and later stone built phases, featured a grid pattern of streets and buildings seen in most similar structures across the Empire. At the centre, dividing the *via praetorian* and with the *via principalis* passing across its front, was the parade ground featuring the 'headquarters' *principia* building which housed the senior base commander and his staff. The parade ground at York was 78m wide and square in form, on one side featuring a *basilica* great aisled hall running perpendicular to the *principia*. The scale of this hall was immense given the size of the single column recovered in 1969 during excavations of the structure. At 68m long, 32m wide and 23m in height, the *basilica* would have stood just short of the modern height of today's Minster. At one end stood the *tribunal* (podium) from where the commanding officer addressed his gathered troops and received visiting dignitaries. From the *principia* building the legion at York was administered, with rows of rooms set out across its rear serving as offices. The central one was the most important, this called the *aedes* and serving as the legionary shrine. It was here that *legio* IX *Hispana*'s standards were kept. This room also had a more practical function in that beneath its floor sat a vault in which the legionary pay chest was kept.

Other buildings in close proximity to the *principia* included the *praetorium*, the commanding officer's house where the *legate legionis* of the

IXth legion lived. This was built in the same manner as a fine town house and was used for business as well as domestic purposes. The south-west corner of that at York is thought to be part of the Roman structural remains exposed beneath the Minster today, resplendent with its fine painted wall plaster.

Meanwhile, also around the central parade ground and again next to the *principia* to provide ease of access, was the building that housed the *praefectus castrorum* legionary supply officer. Opposite this across the parade ground was a *forum* market, used by the troops and their suppliers.

The rest of the fortress interior was packed out with a wide variety of buildings and structures, some stone built and some wooden, set out in a regularized pattern such that any incumbent in the fortress would know as a matter of fact where every amenity was. Such buildings included a large number of barrack blocks to house the IXth legion's troops, granaries to feed them, workshops to manufacture and maintain all of their equipment, a hospital and a bath house. The latter was a very important feature of the Roman cultural experience and served to remind many of the troops of their Spanish and Pannonian roots. One can imagine how popular this bath house would have been in the heart of a northern British winter, with its piping hot steam rooms. The actual legionary bath house building in York was located in 1972 in the southern corner of the fortress, this was a large structure occupying an area of 9,100m².

The legionary fortress, with its fine *principia* and associated *basilica*, was not the only manifestation of the built environment in Roman York. Just across the River Ouse was the *canabae* where resided all of those who, in a huge variety of ways, supported the military presence in the fortress. These early civilian residents of Roman York ranged from the families of the troops across the river (official and otherwise), merchants of all types, those operating the sophisticated transport infrastructure (using not only the road network but more importantly the region's river systems), those participating in the wide variety of industrial activities not already located within the fortress, and finally any manifestations the reader can think of for the purveying of entertainment of all types for the troops. The cosmopolitan nature of the *canabae* in York is well illustrated by the wide variety of deities worshipped there, based on various forms of archaeological evidence (Parker, 2019, 45). Even from its earliest times, these include Classical gods such as Hercules and the Imperial Cult, Eastern gods including Osiris and Serapis, personification gods such as Fortune and Victory, and local gods including Dioscuri and Toutatis. After the time of *legio* IX *Hispana*'s stay in York, this substantial *canabae* was to grow even more in stature and eventually became a full-scale *colonia* veteran's settlement. With the Severan division of the province into two it then became the capital of the province of Britannia Inferior, and later when Diocletian created his new administrative system of diocese containing smaller provinces, it finally became the capital of Britannia Secunda (Cornell and Matthews, 1982, 172).

Finally here, mention should also be made of Brough-on-Humber to the south-east of York. This town on the northern bank of the Humber was the port through which those travelling to York from the Continent arrived in Britain. Called *Petuaria* during the occupation, the site was originally a fort founded around AD 70 whose *vicus* later developed into the *civitas* capital of the native Parisi tribe. The town also featured the ferry-crossing point carrying the original route of Ermine Street across the Humber, thus facilitating the vital road link from London and Lincoln to York, before the more westerly spur of this major trunk road was later built to bypass the Humber (given the ferry crossing would have been impassable in bad weather).

The Route North

York's *Porta Principalis Dextra* opened onto Dere Street (sometimes called Deere Street), the modern name for the major Roman trunk road that ran to the far north of the province and onwards from the town. Its route was one well trodden by the legionaries of *legio* IX *Hispana* as they switched backwards and forwards to man the northern frontier and campaign in modern Scotland.

The road owes its name to the Anglo-Saxon kingdom of Deira that existed from AD 559 to AD 664, its territory covering an area ranging in the east from the Humber to the River Tees, and westwards to the Vale of York. This kingdom possibly derived its name from the River Derwent. The road corresponds roughly with the first British route identified in the Antonine Itinerary.

Having left York, the first place of note along its length is Aldborough (Roman *Isurium Brigantum*) in North Yorkshire, the *civitas* capital of the former territory of the Brigantes. This site also featured a fort, one of many scattered across the region that date to the time of Cerialis' campaigns against the Brigantes. It guarded the point where Dere Street crossed the River Ure.

Heading further north along Dere Street one next reaches Catterick (Roman *Cataractonium*). Again in North Yorkshire, this was the site of a Roman fort guarding the road's crossing of the River Swale built on a bluff on the south bank in the early AD 70s. Soon a *vicus* emerged which spread to the north bank of the Swale, this later being fortified, again reflecting the troubled nature of the north of the province (Ross and Ross, 2020, 19). Mattingly (2006, 147) says that this base became the long-term transit camp for those heading to the northern frontier and beyond and as such would have featured a significant presence from *legio* IX *Hispana* during its time in the north. In that regard recent archaeological research by Northern Archaeological Associates has located two timber granaries to the immediate south, together with a stock enclosure and well.

Continuing north, the next site reached is Piercebridge where a Roman presence existed at this Dere Street crossing of the River Tees from around AD 70. Continuing onwards, Binchester (Roman *Vinovia*) in County Durham is the next site, to the immediate north of Bishop Auckland where another fort was built guarding the Dere Street crossing of the River Wear. This again featured an extensive *vicus*.

Moving on, one next reaches Ebchester (Roman *Vindomora*) in County Durham, this an auxiliary fort protecting the Dere Street crossing of the River Derwent. Finally in terms of Roman settlement, just short of the northern frontier along the Solway Firth–Tyne line is Corbridge in Northumberland where Dere Street met the eastern terminus of the Stanegate road. The most northerly town in the Empire, initial Roman settlement here was a fort built around AD 85. This was replaced by a town featuring two walled military compounds from the early second century AD.

The 61km long Stanegate road itself (named after 'stone road' in Northumbrian dialect) was built by Agricola as part of his northern campaigns. After the withdrawal of Roman forces from the far north it marked the northern frontier of the province of Britannia. It ran from Roman Carlisle in the west to Corbridge in the east through the natural gap formed by the valleys of the Rivers Irthing and Tyne. The Stanegate was a substantial military trunk road almost 7m wide and was built to facilitate rapid west to east passage for military forces defending the northern border. Troops along its length, both legionaries from *legio* IX *Hispana* and auxiliaries, were housed in a series of vexillation forts, for example that at Vindolanda. The line of the road was then later used to mark the route of Hadrian's Wall when the northern frontier was fortified, this built to the Stanegate's immediate north.

This region in the north of the province, ranging from York all the way to the Stanegate road, had a very different feel to the increasingly wealthy south and east of Britannia at the time *legio* IX *Hispana* was based at York. Here in the north, settlement and the local economy was totally bent towards maintaining the huge military presence, particularly during times of campaigning north of the border. Mattingly (2006, 149) is very specific in this regard, saying:

> A considerable portion of northern England remained under direct military supervision long after the *civitas* centre of the Brigantes was established at Aldborough (see above). The scale of the garrison was also remarkably static between the first and third centuries: a legionary fortress (at York) and over fifty smaller forts spread across the region. The impact of such a large and prolonged garrison on the (native) Brigantes must have been colossal.

The longevity of this military presence within the former territory of the Brigantes as the region was bent to the will of Rome is shown by recent excavations at the fort at Brough near Castleton in the Derbyshire Peak Distict. Here, recent excavations have shown that a fort built around AD 80 as part of Agricola's early campaigns was occupied by a military garrison all the way through to AD 125 (interestingly it was still being used in some capacity as late as AD 350).

Another factor in this differential experience of living in the north of Britain compared to the south and east was the fact that the region had been brutalized by the campaigns of the governors Bolanus, Cerialis and Agricola against the Brigantes. It was therefore almost certainly suffering from economic hardship and depopulation at the time *legio* IX *Hispana* was resident in York as it gradually recovered from the hugely disruptive Roman campaigns of conquest. Additionally, another equally disruptive factor impacting settlement and the economy in the north of the province was the frequent raiding from the far north as the unconquered tribes there sought to test this new frontier to their south.

Despite these depredations, those remaining continued the rural lifestyle of their forebears as they rebuilt the regional economy. The agricultural landscape here was defined by ditch enclosures, with the roundhouse continuing to be the main type of dwelling throughout the occupation. Although villa estates did exist, they were much fewer in number when compared to the south, with Mattingly (2006, 419) saying those evident were located either in the Vale of York or north of the Humber, with a few also found in the broad valleys on the Wolds or on moorland areas. Meanwhile, in terms of commerce, the regional markets at the *canabae* in York, and in the emerging towns at Brough-on-Humber and Aldborough, were the principal vectors for the flow of capital to the provincial economy.

In terms of the regional economy as it recovered, agriculture was the dominant factor as elsewhere in the Roman Empire. Arable production improved as the occupation progressed into the second century AD, through the introduction of new technology including the grain-drying kiln. A fine example of this was found at Crambe near Malton featuring a limestone flue lining. A new type of plough was also introduced which featured a coulter for the first time. This was a vertically mounted component that cut an edge ahead of the ploughshare itself. Meanwhile, in terms of fauna, cattle remained the predominant meat type eaten in the north, ahead of sheep and pigs.

Industry also had an important role in the regional economy, though less so than agriculture. For example, advanced pottery manufacturing is evident at the beginning of the second century AD, with mass-produced wheel-made vessels of a Roman type evident rather than the earlier handmade pottery of the LIA (Ottaway, 2013, 200). It is no surprise that the military was the major source of demand for these products, with many found in the archaeological record in York and along the northern border. Meanwhile, metalworking was also an important factor in the economy in the north, again especially in the context of supplying and maintaining the military presence. Some of this metalworking was actually carried out in a bespoke military context, for example in the form of the small *fabricae* (industrial workshop) at the fort at Corbridge. Here, archaeological evidence includes arrowheads, iron scales from *lorica squamata* scalemail hauberks and iron slag found alongside hearths and tempering tanks. Outside of such direct military control, though still driven by military demand, one also sees in the region civilian industrial metalworking in York in the *cabana*, at Brough-on-Humber and in Catterick. Other goods manufactured in the region at the beginning of the second century AD included glass, again in York, ceramic building materials, leatherwork and local jewelry, and a millstone grit quern manufacturing industry. Further, significant extractive *metalla* industries included lead mining, iron manufacturing in East Yorkshire and a quarrying industry that supplied the building stone to urbanise and later fortify the region.

Into the Far North

When the legionaries of the IXth legion crossed the Stanegate road they exited the Empire, entering a border territory where the Romans kept a close eye on the native population using a series of vexillation size forts. A fine example was located at High Rochester in Northumberland, with another at Newstead near Melrose in the Scottish Borders, both along Dere Street. Birley (2007, 355) argues that there wasn't actually a clear distinction between the Empire to the south and *barbaricum* (as the Romans would have thought it) to the north of the Stanegate, especially as the natives on both sides were almost certainly Brigantes. In that context, it seems certain that in addition to their full-time presence at the various forts north of the border, the Romans were always politically active amongst both the northern Brigantes and, above them, the tribes of lowland Scotland. Further, when necessary additional military units were also deployed to deal with specific issues as they arose.

Going further north Roman influence waned, particularly above the Highland Boundary Fault where lay the Scottish Highlands. Here was a true Conradian heart of darkness as the geographical territory there would have seemed to the Romans at the time, even after the campaigns of Agricola.

At the time of the IXth legion's deployment in York the various tribes in modern Scotland had yet to coalesce into the huge Maeatae and Caledonian confederations later encountered by the likes of Septimius Severus in the early third century AD. Instead, they were still a complex patchwork of tribes, with Jones and Mattingly (1990, 21 and 45) using the second century AD geographer Ptolemy and others to detail them as follows (set out south to north):

- The Votadini in the eastern Borders.
- The Selgovae in the central Borders.
- The Novantae in the western Borders.
- The Dumnonii around the Clyde.
- The Epidii in the Mull of Kintyre.
- Above the Clyde on the west coast, going south to north, the Creones, the Carnonacae and (at the far north-western tip of Scotland) the Caereni.

- On the east coast around the River Tay, the Venicones.
- In Aberdeenshire, going south to north, the Vacomagi and Taexali.
- Broadly, throughout the Grampians, the Caledonii (in a specific context).
- Above the Moray Firth, again going south to north, the Decantae, Lugi, Smertae and Cornacii.

There were no towns as such north of Hadrian's Wall excepting the *vicus* settlements associated with the Roman fortifications at sites such as High Rochester and Newstead. In terms of native settlement north of the border, Mattingly (2006, 422) says that: 'In most areas, social organisation was characterized by dispersed small settlements, suggesting a high degree of social fragmentation into family groups or clan.'

In part many of these settlements did have distinct similarities (particularly those in the modern Scottish Borders) to those in the northern part of the province in the south, although with a particularly regional feel. For example the roundhouses of south-east Scotland (the most common type of dwelling there as in the Brigantian south) often used dry stone walls in their construction, with an internal ring of posts utilized to support an 'attic' to give extra living space (Kamm, 2011, 15).

Meanwhile, highlighting the ephemeral nature of security in the far north, hill forts featuring many such roundhouses were common in the LIA and Roman period. Mattingly (2006, 423) highlights examples at Traprain Law, Dryburn Bridge and Broxmouth. Defences here included 6m high dry stone walls and wooden palisades. A number of these regional forts feature the stone walling being vitrified through the use of fire, it previously being thought that this was a deliberate measure to strengthen them. Recent research, however, shows it actually weakened the defensive structures, and so a modern interpretation sees the vitrification process as a deliberate attempt at slighting the defenses, perhaps in the context of Roman offensive operations.

Some other types of settlement and dwelling were unique to Scotland. One example was the wheelhouse found in the exposed coastal areas of the Western Isles. This featured spokes of stone walling radiating out from the centre to support a solid outer wall, with the lower section of the structure sunk down into a pit and with an entrance in the form of a tunnel covered in stone and peat slabs. Another example was the crannog, a fortified timber and thatch roundhouse built on piles or on an artificial island in a lake (again emphasising the perceived need for security). A further building type was the broch dry-stone walled tower, common in the north-east of Scotland and, with up to four storeys, by far the most imposing structures north of the frontier. Over 500 of these have been found, each built around a central court yard with a very narrow and easily defendable entrance, and with the inhabitants living in galleries constructed within. All were built between 200 BC and AD 150 and their standard design seems to indicate they were built by travelling specialist broch builders. Once more, their substantial nature emphasises the need for security at the time.

The economy north of the border was also different to that in the south, although noting there would have been some commonality among the Brigantes living either side of the Stanegate road frontier amid one of the densest of military concentrations anywhere in the Empire. Indeed, the economic differences became most pronounced as one headed into the far north. In his appreciation of the Roman invasions of Scotland, Kamm (2011, 15) says that many of the advances in economic and manufacturing sophistication that were visible across the Roman world by the second century AD were lacking in Scotland. He adds:

> As crafts became more sophisticated and mass production was introduced, particularly of iron objects and pottery, so trade increased and urban development occurred around centres of industry and commerce. This happened from Spain right across central Europe, and in Britain on the east and south-east coasts. Scotland remained largely untouched by such advances until the thirteenth century AD...

There is some evidence that the coalescence of power through proximity to the Roman world did have an economic impact in at least the Scottish Borders as early as the time of the IXth legion's stay in the north. Mattingly (2006, 423) describes the creation of boundary features and progressive deforestation taking place here as more land was cleared for agricultural use. The latter in particular would have required substantial societal organization to be carried out in such an organized manner, and highlights an expanding population. Mattingly (2006, 426) also highlights another manifestation of the impact of Rome from south to north, namely the finding at over 200 native sites of Roman artifacts. Such data may indicate commercial contact, or may be in the context of conflict, although interestingly there is a blank area in the western borders that probably illustrates the eastern coast focus of the majority of the Roman campaigns in the north.

Finally, here it is worth considering why the Romans never actually succeeded in incorporating the far north of the main island of Britain into the province of Britannia. James (2011, 144) makes the case that it was because of the failure of the 'open hand alongside sword' strategy that he believes underwrote much of Rome's early Imperial growth. This required an elite sophisticated enough in the newly conquered territories to buy into Rome's Imperial project once any conquest had taken place. He believes that, despite the two determined attempts to conquer the north of the islands of Britain under Agricola and Septimius Severus, such an elite appears to have been singularly lacking in the territories of modern Scotland (this view backed up by the above analysis of the economy north of the Stanegate road border). This was certainly the case early in the Roman occupation of Britain at the time of *legio* IX *Hispana*'s deployment in York, and even when the larger Maeatae and Caledonian confederations began to appear later on it may still have been a factor given the challenging climate and geography. Therefore, the political will to conquer the far north of Britain for glory was exponentially more important given the perceived limited economic potential there. Even then, this desire for Imperial triumph in the far north only manifested itself in full twice, initially when the first Flavian emperor Vespasian needed a major victory to herald the onset of his new dynasty, and then when the great warrior emperor Septimius Severus decided to crown his reign with one last mighty achievement. Both ultimately failed given the Romans never stayed in the far north in force after each attempt, in the first instance because the last Flavian emperor Domitian lost interest in Britain, and secondly because Severus died in York in AD 213.

Campaigning in the North

Having established the nature of the campaigning theatre experienced by *legio* IX *Hispana*, we can now consider its military activities in the far north. Here, rather than detail the low level policing activity more than likely still needed among the recently conquered Brigantes in the north of the province, I concentrate on campaigning further north in the region of modern Scotland.

In the first instance, their opponents there when on campaign and battle proved exceptionally hardy who, even when well beaten, frequently returned to continue their predation of the new Roman province to the south. Dio is useful here in giving a near contemporary view of these most northerly warriors in the British Isles. Describing the opponents in the region faced by the Romans in the AD 180s, he says (77.12.1-4):

> ...(the) tribes inhabit wild and waterless mountains and desolate and swampy plains, and possess neither walls, cities, nor tilled fields, but live on their flocks, wild game, and certain fruits... their form of rule is democratic for the most part, and they choose their boldest men as rulers. They go into battle in chariots, and have small, swift horses; there are also foot soldiers, very swift in running and very firm in standing ground. For arms they have a shield and a short spear, with bronze apple attached to the end of the spear shaft, so that when the enemy is shaken it may clash and terrify the enemy; and they also have a dagger. They can endure hunger and cold and any kind of hardship; for they plunge into swamps and exist there for many days with only their heads above water, and in forests they support themselves upon bark and roots, and for all emergencies they prepare a certain kind of food, the eating of a small portion of which, the size of a bean, prevents them from feeling either hunger or thirst.

The hunger-preventing food described here has been identified as the heath pea (*lathyrus linofolius*) by Dr Brian Moffat (2000, 13) of the Soutra Aisle research centre.

Goldsworthy (2003, 164) usefully identifies four types of conflict engaged in by the Romans, these being wars of conquest, the suppression of rebellion, punitive expeditions and a response to raiding and invasion. The Romans only really attempted the first on two occasions, with Agricola's Flavian campaigns in the later first century AD and Septimius Severus in the early third century AD, both ultimately failing for the reasons set out above. The IXth legion played a full role in the former, leading one of the east coast legionary spearheads. However, though present it didn't participate in fighting in the conflict's only meeting engagement at Mons Graupius in AD 83 given only the Roman auxiliaries were utilized to defeat the Britons there, as detailed in Chapters 1 and 2.

With regard to Goldsworthy's three other types of Roman conflict, all were to a greater extent features of Roman campaigning in the far north of Briton. In that regard *vexillations* of *legio* IX *Hispana*, when deployed north of the Stanegate road, would most commonly form the core of a combined arms force including *alae* of auxiliary cavalry and cohorts of auxiliary foot. This would range far and wide, often using the forts north of the border as supply bases, to target a given threat. When they did so with menacing intent the *alae* of cavalry would range far and wide, providing a scouting function, pursuing defeated enemies, protecting the flanks and rear of the infantry force and brutalizing the local economy. The scouting function of the mounted troops was assisted by specialists deployed even further proud of the main legionary spearheads when on campaign in enemy territory. These included the *speculator* scouts from within the ranks of each legion. Further, we know from epigraphy and literary sources that the Romans deployed elite scouting units called *exploratores* in Britain, these analogously similar to today's Special Forces, from forts in the north of the province including High Rochester, Risingham and Netherby (Bishop, 2014, 51).

A key feature of this deep penetration type of Roman campaigning in enemy territory was the marching camp. These were large-scale temporary fortifications built by the legionaries and auxila at the end of every day's march. They were constructed in a few hours and came in a variety of sizes dependent on the scale of the force that needed protection. Almost always playing card in shape, they generally featured a deep ditch two metres wide with the usual ankle-breaker step in the bottom, with the spoil then being used to create an internal rampart. Atop this ran a palisade created by the stakes the troops carried as part of their specialist engineering equipment, either a continuous wooden barrier or one created by the stakes being lashed together to form large caltrops. Within this barrier the camp would then be set out for the night, effectively recreating the interior layout of a permanent Roman fortification. The next day (or longer if the camp was occupied for more than a night), the camp was struck in swift order. This was in a very specific way, with the first trumpet call from the *cornicen* signalling the legionaries to strike their tents, the second telling them to ready the pack animals and destroy the camp, and the third to fall into marching ranks.

As seen in the Agricolan campaigns, the native Britons in the far north avoided set piece battles with the Romans if at all possible, and indeed in the Severan campaigns in the early third century AD when he deployed a huge force of 50,000 men there wasn't a single 'battle' as such in either of his two campaigns. Therefore, the two most common types of conflict were either guerilla warfare as the Britons sought to impede and interdict Roman military activity, or punitive siege warfare against native settlements, particularly hill forts.

In terms of the former, the natives were clearly far more experienced to a life living rough in their indigenous terrain, with Herodian (3.14) saying they often dispensed with breast plates and helmets 'which would impede their movement through the marshes'. However, the legionaries of the IXth legion and their auxiliaries were also highly experienced in countering this type of conflict. Roman military textbooks detail how to conduct such a specialist style of warfare, for example former British first century AD warrior governor Frontinus (1.6.3) explaining in his *Strategemata* (Stratagems) how to deal with ambushes using classical world examples:

> When Iphicrates was leading his army in Thrace in a long file on account of the nature of the terrain, and the report was brought to him that the enemy planned to attack his rear-guard, he ordered some cohorts to withdraw to both flanks and halt, while the rest were to quicken their pace and flee. But from the complete line as it passed by, he kept back all the choicest soldiers. Thus, when the enemy were busy with promiscuous pillaging, and in fact were already exhausted, while his own men were refreshed and drawn up in order, he attacked and routed the foe and stripped them of their booty.

What seems clear from these primary sources is that, despite the difficulties pinning down their opponents (who were often fighting for survival), the Romans always adapted to the tactics being used against them, even if often at great cost as in the Severan campaigns. Such adaptation to the circumstances was one of the great characteristics of the Roman military, they relying on their sophisticated organization, training, élan and well organized supply system to eventually give them an advantage in all kinds of warfare, including against an opponent who avoided confrontation. In particular, the legionaries would destroy the local economy employing slash-and-burn tactics to deprive the natives of their homes and food. In the AD 210 campaign in Scotland this reached its peak with Severus' ordering his troops to kill all of the natives the legionaries came across. Thus, while things were often grim for the Romans when campaigning in the north against an opponent most often fighting desperate guerilla campaigns, they usually overcame the adversity and ensured that the discomfort felt by all levels of native northern British society was far more brutal.

Faced with such frightful odds in terms of capability and manpower, the native Britons of the far north more often than not sought sanctuary in their hill fort protected settlements, though usually this did little to help them. We actually have a specific example here which shows the brutality they faced through the sophisticated techniques used by the Romans in overcoming their defences. This is in the context of recently published research regarding the 7ha hillfort site at Burnswark in Dumfriesshire in the Scottish Borders. Here, a debate has taken place as to whether data previously considered (from antiquarian and 1960s archaeological excavations) showed an actual Roman siege at the site (either Hadrianic or early Antonine in date) or that the site was actually an example of a Roman siege training exercise. The key items of interest in that regard were the north and south Roman siege camps there, and also a plethora of ballista bolts/balls and lead slingshots found at the site. To reach a conclusion either way the Melrose-based Trimontium Trust recently carried out a new review of the existing research and also secured fresh data, the latter based on a systematic metal-detecting survey to identify more lead sling shots (with a view to plotting their scatter) and also experimental archaeology regarding the use of slings in siege warfare (Reid, 2016, 22). The results of this research suggest yet another grim interpretation for the activities of the Romans north of the frontier, with the two camps now being seen as a real-world tactical response to the topography in the context of a full siege, and the widespread scatter of sling shots and other missiles (and their quality) suggesting deadly intent. As Reid (2016, 26) says, the evidence shows that:

> ...there was a massive missile barrage at Burnswark. This was not just restricted to the gateways, but extended along a full half kilometer of native rampart. The simplest explanation for this distribution is that the defenders on the hilltop were suppressed by a hail of sling bullets with an accurate range of 120m and the stopping power of a modern handgun, as well as ballista bolts, and arrows. This presumably covered an attacking force sweeping out the three huge gateways and storming the hilltop. Such a combination of missile troops and conventional infantry is likely to have been brutally effective.

Further, one other factor adds even more insight into the awful experience of the native Britons on the receiving end of this devastation. This is because some of slingshots were hollowed out with a 4mm hole through their centre, this designed to make a screeching noise when slung. This is an early example of psychological warfare on the battlefield, bringing to mind the screaming sirens of diving Junkers Ju-87 Stukas during the Blitzkrieg early in the Second World War, adding to the misery of those on the receiving end.

Lost in the North?

Having considered the home of *legio* IX *Hispana* in York at the time of its disappearance in Britain, the theatre of operations in the far north where it campaigned, and how it carried out its duties there, we can now turn to the first hypothesis concerning its fate. This is the suggestion that it was lost fighting in the far north of the province of Britannia, being so comprehensively defeated that it completely disappears from history. As can be seen above, given the usual Roman dominance in the region when it engaged in force, such an event would have been truly shocking. By way of background, there were of course other legions that ceased to exist, either due to destruction at the hands of an enemy or because they were simply disbanded. A number of these are considered below. However, it is highly unusual for a legion to simply disappear completely with no reference to its fate. One suggestion here is that *legio* IX *Hispana*'s performance in defeat was so shaming that it had a *damnatio memoriae* (translating as 'condemnation of memory') declared against it by the Senate on behalf of the emperor. The latter was a very deliberate, discrediting act that removed it from ever having existed. This is also considered below.

As set out in the Introduction, this theory regarding the fate of the 'lost' legion has existed since at least the eighteenth century when John Horsley published his *Britannia Romana or the Roman Antiquities of Britain*. It was then picked up by the renowned German scholar Theodor Mommsen in the 1850s and was soon projected into the public imagination by various historical fiction works, particularly Rosemary Sutcliff's *The Eagle of the Ninth* first published in 1954. This story's popularity was such that by the early twenty-first century it was receiving the Hollywood treatment in the form of major feature films.

In many ways these later works of fiction are distractions from the very real fact that, at least in Britain, *legio* IX *Hispana* really does disappear. To consider the validity of this Chapter's hypothesis that it was destroyed in the far north I therefore consider the undisputed facts regarding the end of the IXth legion's time in Britain. First, its last mention in contemporary writing. Then, its last mention in epigraphy in the province. Next, the fact that at some stage in the late AD 110s an emergency force of legionaries from the continent was deployed to stabilise the northern frontier in Britannia. Then, the fact that when Hadrian's Wall was built in the AD 120s all of the units which contributed manpower left inscriptions to mark their work. None is to be found mentioning *legio* IX *Hispana*. Moving on, the fact that from AD 122 *legio* VI *Victrix* replaced the IXth legion in York, it arriving in the province with the emperor Hadrian. Then, the first time a contemporary list of Roman legions is published which doesn't mention the IXth legion. I next move on to consider why some legions were physically disbanded, and whether through analogy this could apply to *legio* IX *Hispana*. It is in this context that I also discuss whether the legion was subject to an act of *damnatio memoriae*. Finally, I consider the mysterious finding of what might be a legionary *Aquila* standard buried beneath the *forum* of Silchester (Roman *Calleva Atrebatum*) in modern Berkshire.

The IXth legion is last mentioned in AD 82, by Tacitus in the context of Agricola's campaigns to conquer the far north of Britain. This references a specific incident in the governor's sixth year in office and fourth year campaigning in the north, when his legionary spearheads were driving through Fife up to the River Tay and beyond. Given its importance the reference is recorded here in full, with the historian saying (Agricola, 25-27):

> The natives of Caledonia turned to armed resistance on a grand scale…They went so far as to attack our forts, and inspired alarm by taking the offensive…But just then Agricola learned the enemy were about to attack in several columns. To avoid encirclement by superior forces familiar with the territory, he likewise divided his own army into three parts and so advanced. As soon as the enemy got to know of this they changed their plans and massed for a night attack on the IXth legion, which seemed to them the weakest [this in itself an interesting observation]. Striking panic into the sleeping marching camp, they struck down the sentries and broke in. The fight was already raging inside the camp when Agricola was warned by his scouts of the enemy's march. Following closely on their tracks, he ordered the speediest of his cavalry and infantry to harass the assailants' rear and then had his whole army join in the battle cry; the standards gleamed in the light of dawn. The Britanni

were dismayed at being caught between two fires, while the men of the IXth took heart again: with their lives now safe they could fight for honour. They even effected a sally, and a grim struggle ensued in the narrow passage of the gates. At last the enemy broke under the rival efforts of the two armies – the one striving to make it plain that they had brought relief, the other that they could have done without it.

This last contemporary written reference to the *legio* IX *Hispana* seems a rather ignominious way for the famous IXth legion to disappear from history, with its marching camp almost overrun in the far north of Britain, a highly unusual development, perhaps a precursor to its later fate.

Next we can turn to the last recorded inscription referencing the IXth legion in Britain. This is that set out above earlier in the chapter, on the inscribed limestone slab that formed the centre section of a monumental inscription referencing the rebuilding of the south-eastern gate at the legionary fortress in York. This has been accurately dated to AD 108 based on the nature of the reference to the Emperor Trajan.

Moving on, I now consider an event which could point to the disappearance of *legio* IX *Hispana*, at least in a British context. This is tantalisingly trailed in the *Historia Augusta* (Hadrian, 5.1-2), it saying that on the new emperor's accession in AD 117 there was widespread trouble across the Empire. Specifically, it says that 'the Britons couldn't be kept under control.' Further, the noted Roman rhetorician Marcus Cornelius Fronto, writing in the AD 160s to his former pupil Marcus Aurelius, says that the heavy casualties suffered by the Romans in the Roman-Parthian War at that time (this covered in detail in Chapter 6) were comparable to those suffered at the beginning of Hadrian's reign in Britain (Birley, 2005, 118). Epigraphy also references a dramatic event in the north of Britain at this time, in the form of the funerary monument to Titus Anneus, a centurion of the I *Tungrorum* auxiliary cohort. His tombstone at the vexillation fort at Vindolanda, dating to this period, references him being killed 'in the war' (Southern, 2013, 175). Other contemporary evidence at Vindolanda from this time is also instructive, in the form of the famous writing tablets excavated there. Specifically, tablet number 164 references 'nasty little Britons…(Brittunculi).' This certainly shows there was no love lost between Rome and the natives of northern Britain, whether in the province itself or north of the frontier. Further, a coin dating to AD 119 features Britannia for the first time ever, this on the rear.

On the coin the iconic figure is depicted in a typically martial manner, with spear and shield and seated on rocks. Moorhead and Stuttard (2012, 124) describe it as conjuring up an image of a rugged, warlike province, this certainly an impression given by contemporary writers. The coin has been interpreted by some as representing an issue minted to celebrate a Roman military triumph in the far north. This was a frequent later occurrence when a major victory was won in the province, for example in the context of the Severan campaigns in the early third century AD.

This troubling level of insurgency, which Moorhead and Stuttard (2012, 124) say threatened the very survival of the province, required the creation of a special task force. This is referenced on the career inscription on the tombstone of Titus Pontius Sabinus found in Farrentino (Roman *Farrentinum*) in Italy (CIL X.5829). Though it mostly details the high offices he later achieved, the most interesting reference is that which states that while he was serving as the *primus pilus* senior centurion of *legio* III *Augusta* in the province of Germania Inferior (note this legion was normally stationed in North Africa so he may have been commanding a vexillation deployed out-of-theatre) he was seconded by the emperor Hadrian to command an emergency task force which the inscription calls the *expeditio Britannica*. This featured vexillations from three legions, these being *legio* VIII *Augusta* and *legio* XXII *Primigenia*, also from Germania Inferior, and *legio* VII *Gemina* from Hispania Tarraconensis. This gives a likely force size of around 3,000 men, it being unclear from the inscription if more troops were also drawn from the vexillation he himself originally commanded. That would increase the legionary force to nearer 4,000 men, almost the size of a full legion, giving real context to events in Britain when the expedition took place. The legionaries may also have been joined by auxiliaries given another inscription from an alter found at Maryport in modern Cumbria, which references one Marcus Maenius Agrippa who, when commander of the *cohors* I *Hispanorum* auxiliary cavalry regiment, was tasked by Hadrian to lead them on a *expeditionem britannicam*. Southern (2016, 175) says that these deployments indicate '...a disaster of some considerable proportions'. To provide context, the last occasion when such reinforcements had been required in Britain was in the wake of the Boudiccan Revolt in AD 60/61, when the then new province nearly fell.

Above I have detailed two events, a serious conflict of some kind in Britannia dated to the accession of Hadrian in AD 117 referenced by both primary sources and epigraphy, and the expeditions to Britain of Sabinus and Agrippa. The timing of that by Sabinus in particular is significant as it seems unlikely such a large-scale intervention in Britain would have been made if the northern border was secure. The implication is therefore that when this expedition took place the IXth legion was for some reason unable to perform its principal task, namely maintaining Rome's most northerly frontier. To provide balance here, Frere (2000, 25) and Campbell (2011, 50) have both argued that based on the career paths of Sabinus and Agrippa the expedition to Britain may have occurred about a decade later. However, there is no reference anywhere to any conflict in Britain at this later time. I therefore believe that common sense dictates this significant emergency redeployment of legionaries and perhaps auxilia was most likely the response to the crisis in Britain at the beginning of Hadrian's reign, perhaps necessitated because *legio* IX *Hispana* had for some reason become incapacitated. In the same context Southern (2013, 175) says '…there is nothing to disprove the suggestion that the legionaries arrived in Britain c. AD 119' as replacements for heavy casualties, with Birley (2005, 118) also earlier arguing this case. Whatever the exact date of the expeditions of Sabinus and Agrippa, the former certainly seems to have been highly successful in restoring security along the northern frontier given there is no mention of trouble in the region again until the later reign of Antoninus Pius (AD 138 to AD 161).

If we follow the above narrative that trouble broke out in the north of Britain at the beginning of Hadrian's reign, that the IXth legion suffered extensive casualties, and that Sabinus' *expeditio Britannica* was the Imperial response to save the province from further predation, then the next question is, who was the actual enemy the Romans were fighting? When Mommsen published his theories in the 1850s he speculated that *legio* IX *Hispana* had been the subject of an uprising by the Brigantes tribe, subjugated by the Romans in the late AD 60s and AD 70s. He went further, arguing that the legion was wiped out in its legionary fortress in York. It was this event, he suggested, that prompted the building of Hadrian's Wall. Others then followed his lead, from noted historian Wilhelm Weber in the early twentieth century (1907, 136) to Sir Charles Oman (1938, 109) in the 1930s. More recently, in discussing possible causes of the trouble in the north of the province, Southern (2013, 175) says one of the reasons may have been forced conscription into the Roman military. This would have been into auxiliary units, with the conscripted troopers then having to serve abroad, well away from their homes. She describes this process as 'neither gentle or welcome'. Such a move, when added to the heavy economic dislocation in the north following the earlier conquest campaigns there, may have been the tipping point leading to widespread insurrection and, in the hypothesis being tested in this chapter, the destruction of the IXth legion. Certainly, as detailed above, the *Historia Augusta* suggests this, saying the Britons couldn't be kept under control (Hadrian, 5.1-2).

However, a key issue with Mommsen's original theory is that we now know there is no archaeological evidence to suggest that the early fortress in York was destroyed at all. An alternative theory therefore is to consider whether the IXth legion was lost not fighting for survival in its own back yard, but much further north, campaigning in the region of modern Scotland. This was certainly the theory popularised by Rosemary Sutcliff and others, with the legion marching north of the Stanegate road and never being heard of again. Once more though, we are hampered here by the fact that there is no evidence in the archaeological record of the IXth legion ever heading north into modern Scotland, even if anecdotally (given it was the northernmost legion) we can argue it must have done. It is therefore equally difficult to identify the tribes with whom it may have fought and lost there, under this hypothesis. The most likely candidates would have been the Votadini, Selgovae and Novantae in the Scottish Borders, and the Dumnonii around the Clyde. However, given the size of force needed to defeat a battle-hardened Roman legion, even if it was ambushed or similar, a more likely scenario here would feature a general uprising of the tribes north of the frontier, perhaps even including those in the Scottish Highlands. Southern (2013, 175) again considers that one of the triggers may have been forcible conscription of native warriors into the Roman military.

Next I turn to three events tied to Hadrian's AD 122 visit to problematic Britannia. First, the building of the 117 km long wall named after him that fortified the northern frontier. Here, the accepted version of events has him ordering its construction to physically secure the northern border on his arrival that year, after the earlier insurrection had been put down. However, new evidence is beginning to emerge to show that its initial construction might actually have begun well before he came to Britain, with sections prepared for him to view as part of an inspection of the wider Roman northern frontier, including the *limes Germanicus* (Graafstall, 80). If this new theory is correct, it seems he was unimpressed with what he found in Britain as at least some parts of the new frontier fortification were radically altered after his visit, a key change being the building of major forts along its length including those at Birdoswald, Housesteads and Chesters. Whenever it was actually built, what is clear about Hadrian's Wall is the vast cost in terms of material and manpower needed to complete it. This forensically highlights the seriousness of the earlier conflagration in the north of the province, perhaps backing the view that *legio* IX *Hispana* may have met a grim fate.

Hadrian's Wall was anchored in the west at Bowness-on-Solway (site of the Roman fort of *Maia*) on the Irish Sea, and in the east at Wallsend (Roman *Segedunum*) on the Tyne. Some have argued that this substantial fortification was built for purposes other than being a hard military frontier, for example saying it was some kind of customs or frontier control barrier between the Empire to the south and native tribes and later confederations to the north. For example, Breeze and Dobson (2000, 40) say:

> The purpose of the barrier was to control movement, not to prevent it, as the liberal provision of gateways demonstrates. Civilians, whether merchants or local farmers moving their cattle and sheep, or simply local people visiting relatives on the other side of the wall, would be allowed through the gateways...

However, as Bishop rhetorically counters (2014, 50): 'If Hadrian's Wall was not a defence against invading enemies, what was it?' He goes on to make the case it was purely a military fortification with both strategic and tactical functions, and I agree. Certainly, to my mind those in favour of a less militaristic purpose for the wall seriously underestimate the marked sense of otherness when comparing the Roman military to their civilian counterparts. This was certainly not a relationship of equals.

As finally completed after Hadrian's visit, the wall was threaded with watchtowers and milecastle fortlets (in addition to the larger forts detailed above, hence the number of gateways alluded to by Breeze above), commonly two of the former between each of the latter. The western part was initially constructed from compacted turf blocks, these later being replaced with stone. This was the section built first, and quickly, giving insight perhaps into the direction of the principal threat during the earlier insurrection, surprising given most Roman campaigning was usually in the east when north of the frontier. Meanwhile, the eastern section was constructed as new from stone, with 3.7 million tonnes of sandstone and limestone eventually used for the facing alone.

The wall featured a north-facing fore-ditch, where this was possible, and additionally a large *vallum* constructed to its immediate south. The latter included a broad flat-bottomed ditch up to 3m deep, up to

6m wide at the top and 2m wide at the bottom, with a mound up to 6m wide on either side. This provided rearward defence for the wall and suggests that the Romans continued to be wary of any further agitation among the Brigantes.

Construction of the wall and its associated infrastructure, which took at least six years to complete, was carried out by *vexillations* from nearly every known military unit in Britain at the time. We know this as they have all left inscriptions marking out the sections they built. For example, an inscription to *legio* II *Augusta* (RIB 1637) can be found at the Hotbank milecastle, while one made by a *vexillation* from the *Classis Britannica* regional fleet (RIB 1340) can be found on the granary wall of the fort at Benwell (Roman *Condercum*). Notably, no inscriptions exist from the IXth legion, perhaps hard evidence that the legion by AD 122 was no longer in the province, if it still existed at all.

This conclusion is further backed up by the fact that when Hadrian arrived he came with a new legion, *legio* VI *Victrix*, which immediately took the place of *legio* IX *Hispana* in York. The newly arrived legion had been founded by Octavian in 41 BC at the height of the final round of Republican civil wars. It first fought at the siege of Perusia in northern Italy in that year, where lead slingshots have been found featuring the legion's stamp, before engaging Pompeian forces in Sicily and then taking a leading role in the naval Battle of Actium in 31 BC when Octavian finally defeated Mark Antony and Cleopatra. The legion then served extensively in Spain in the final stages of the Roman conquest of the Iberian Peninsula, where it founded the legionary fortress of León. For this it was awarded its first cognomen, *hispaniensis* (confusingly given the legion it replaced in York). There it was to remain for a century, before deployment to the Rhine frontier at the end of the 'Year of the Four Emperors' in AD 69 when it then participated in the campaign to defeat the Batavian Revolt of Gaius Julius Civilis. Afterwards the legion was granted its second cognomen *Victrix* by the new Emperor Vespasian. The legion then remained in Germania Inferior, redeploying to Neuss where the troops then rebuilt the legionary fortress there destroyed by Civilis. It next helped defeat the rebellion of Lucius Antonius Saturninus, governor of Germania Superior, against the emperor Domitian in AD 89, before relocating to Xanten at the end of the first century BC, where it also rebuilt the fort there. *Vexillations* were then sent to accompany Trajan in his Dacian campaigns, before *legio* VI *Victrix* finally travelled to Britain and York in AD 122 with Hadrian.

Some have speculated that the arrival of *legio* VI *Victrix* in Britain was actually to bolster the IXth legion in the north rather than to replace it, specifically in the context of helping build Hadrian's Wall. This was first postulated by then leading archaeologist Eric Birley of Durham University who, writing in the Durham University Journal in 1948 in a paper entitled 'The End of the Ninth Legion', argued the case. This view has since given impetus to the opinion that the legion was not lost in Britain, but simply deployed elsewhere, perhaps after the northern frontier was fortified. However, the fact that not a single inscription from *legio* IX *Hispana* has ever been found in the context of Hadrian's Wall mitigates against this view that the two legions served together for a time, as does the fact that the legionary fortress in York was immediately occupied by *legio* VI *Victrix* on its arrival, indicating it was already empty. The new legion's appearance in Britannia was certainly noted at the time, with for example two altars dedicated to Neptune and Oceanus found in the River Tyne at Newcastle marking its safe arrival (Birley, 2005, 121).

The final event marked by the arrival of Hadrian in the UK was the advent of a new governor. This was Aulus Platorius Nepos who replaced the previous incumbent Quintus Pompeius Falco. The latter had been one of the early provincial appointments of Hadrian, almost certainly as part of the response to the insurrection in Britain at the beginning of his reign. For some reason, by AD 122 the emperor had decided on a change and when he travelled to Britain Nepos, previously governor of Germania Inferior, came with him along with *legio* VI *Victrix* which had also been based in the province. This can be dated to before 17 July that year based on two military diplomas that mention Nepos' arrival. The new governor was an interesting choice given he was a close friend and ally of Hadrian, they both belonging to the same Sergia *gentes* tribe. He was also an experienced military leader. His deployment to Britain was therefore a purposeful move by the emperor who wished to place a loyal strongman in charge of the province.

When Hadrian arrived in Britain things were clearly still far from well following the earlier trouble in the north, with the *Historia Augusta* (Hadrian, 11.2) saying he 'corrected many things' and then quoting the poet Florus as saying 'I do not want to be Caesar, to walk among the Britons' (Hadrian, 16.3). The emperor may also have had issues with the legions and auxilia in the province, perhaps in the context of whatever had happened to *legio* IX *Hispana*, as another altar found in the Tyne references the discipline he imposed on the military. Coins minted to commemorate his visit also show him addressing the *Exercitus Britannicus*, this broadly translating as the military in Britain.

Next, having established the IXth legion is last mentioned in contemporary history in AD 82, and last referenced in epigraphy in AD 108, we can now put a definitive end date by which time we can say with confidence it had ceased to exist. This is in the context of a column (originally two, nearly identical) known as the Collonetta Maffei pillar, erected in Rome around AD 168 during the diarchy of Marcus Aurelius and Lucius Verus. This features a *nomina legionum* list (CIL VI.3492) of all of the legions then active within the Roman military, and specifically includes *legio* II *Italica* and *legio* III *Italica*, legions that had only just been founded by the joint emperors. A number of legions (in addition to the three lost by Varus in AD 9) are notable for their absence, but whose fates are known. These include:

- *legio* I *Germanica*, disbanded by Vespasian after siding with Vitellius during the 'Year of Four Emperors' in AD 69, and then later rebelling during the Batavian Revolt.
- *legio* IV *Macedonica*, disbanded by Vespasian after siding with Vitellius during the 'Year of Four Emperors'.
- *legio* V *Alaudae*, which suffered heavy casualties in the Batavian Revolt and was then later disbanded by Domitian after suffering further defeat fighting the Sarmatians north of the Danube around AD 92.
- *legio* XV *Primigenia*, disbanded in AD 70 after being wiped out during the Batavian Revolt.
- *legio* XVI *Gallica*, disbanded by Vespasian after rebelling during the Batavian Revolt.
- *legio* XXI *Rapax*, disbanded by Domitian after being destroyed fighting the Sarmatians north of the Danube around AD 92.
- *legio* XXII *Deiotariana*, likely disbanded by Hadrian after suffering heavy casualties during the Third (bar Kokhba) Jewish Revolt from AD 132 to AD 135.

There is of course one other legion we know disappeared before AD 165 given it is also not listed on the pillar, this being *legio* IX *Hispana*. However, there is a difference in that it is the only one whose ultimate fate we simply do not know. It just completely disappears. The detail on the Collonetta Maffei pillar is later confirmed by Dio (55.23.4) who, when writing in the early third century AD, also provides a list of legions extant in his day, which is also devoid of the above legions including the IXth. It does differ in one way in that it includes the three Parthian legions raised by Septimius Severus in AD 197 for his eastern campaigns. This brought the number of legions then in service to thirty-three, the largest number ever fielded by Rome.

One further suggestion here is that, if the IXth legion was defeated or even wiped out campaigning in the far north, the event was so ignominious that it had a *damnatio memoriae* declared against it. Such a move would go far beyond the usual disbandment for serious defeat, as happened with *legio* XVII, *legio* XVIII and *legio* XIX after Varus's AD 9 defeat, and some of the others listed above too. The name *damnatio memoriae* is actually comparatively modern, being first used in 1689 to describe the very public act of memory condemnation by the Senate in ancient Rome. More often than not this was used against an individual, for example when Caracalla directed this as a posthumous punishment against his brother Geta after ordering his murder at the end of AD 211 (Elliott, 2018a, 171). Thus, many of the images of Geta which survive today have been deliberately defaced, with his name often removed from public monuments. However, a key issue regarding this theory and the fate of the IXth legion is that there are no other examples of a legion suffering *damnatio memoriae*. Therefore, it is difficult to say whether it was deliberately removed from the historical record or not. As already mentioned, by AD 165 it had simply disappeared.

The last piece of evidence considered here regarding the fate of the IXth legion in the context of it being lost in the north of Britain is actually found far to the south of the province, at Silchester in Berkshire. Here, in the *civitates* capital of the Atrebates tribe, a bronze casting of an eagle was found in 1866 by the Rev. J.G. Joyce in what had been the Roman town's *basilica*. Some 15cm high, about the correct size for the *Aquila* eagle atop a legionary standard, its finding prompted some to argue that this was the eagle of the lost IXth legion, tucked away after its demise in the rafters of what might have been the *aerarium* treasury room in the *basilica*. This certainly featured in Rosemary Sutcliff's *The Eagle of the Ninth*, she saying at the time of writing that the eagle was one of the factors which motivated her to write the book. However, sadly for this theory, more recent investigations have dated the eagle to the later Antonine period, it is therefore most likely an adornment to a statue of Jupiter or an emperor.

Finally here, for balance, I set out one of the key arguments used to argue the case that *legio* IX *Hispana* survived intact after its time in

Britain. This is based on the discipline of prosopography, detailed in the Introduction, used in this case to consider the career paths of various Roman officers based on epigraphic recordings of their lives (Campbell, 2011, 50). Antiquarians and later historians have identified a number of senior officers and officials who served in the IXth legion around the time it 'disappeared' in Britain but who later went on to have highly successful careers. Some have argued this would have been extremely unlikely if the legion had been shamed in some way. Specific examples include Lucius Aemilius Karus, a tribune in *legio* IX *Hispana* who in the early AD 140s was the governor of the province of Arabia Petraea and may later have been consul in Rome in AD 144, another IXth legion tribune called Lucius Novius Crispinus Martialis Saturninus who was consul in AD 150, and the one time *legate* of the legion Lucius Aninius Sextius Florentinus who died when the governor of Arabia Petraea in the later AD 120s/early AD 130s.

While the above points are valid, some have suggested there may be confusion here based on individuals of the same name, with the epigraphic listings linked to later governors and consuls perhaps referencing offspring instead. Another point to consider is that, even if these individuals had served with *legio* IX *Hispana* at the time it disappeared in Britain, they may have been absent for some reason. For example, it was not uncommon for officers to be seconded away to serve on the staffs of governors and procurators as *beneficiarii*, or to command *vexillations* redeployed on short term Imperial duty elsewhere (with Sabinus and his *expeditio Britannica* being a prime example, and with others directly referencing the IXth legion detailed in Chapter 5).

Closing Discussion

To conclude this chapter, I holistically consider the above evidence regarding the lost IXth legion and its time in the north of Britain. Firstly, this was a highly experienced military unit tasked with securely holding the most northerly of Roman frontiers, against a challenging foe intent not only on preventing further Roman conquest in their own territory, but also on predating the new province to the south at every opportunity. Further, based in its legionary fortress in York, *legio* IX *Hispana* was firmly embedded in the territory of the only recently conquered and clearly recalcitrant Brigantes tribe. Yet it was clearly up to its challenging task, trusted by successive governors in Britannia to protect the new province.

However, unlike *legio* II *Augusta* and *legio* XX *Valeria Victrix*, the IXth legion was not to remain in Britain for the rest of the existence of the province. Below I have set out five key known facts about its fate:

- The last time it is mentioned historically dates to AD 82, by Tacitus in the context of the campaigns of Agricola in the far north of Britain.
- The last inscription mentioning it is dated to AD 108, from the rebuilt south-eastern gate at the legionary fortress in York.
- It was replaced in York by *legio* VI *Victrix* in AD 122 when the latter travelled to the province with the emperor Hadrian.
- There are no inscriptions referencing the legion when Hadrian's Wall was built around the same time, unlike the other military units engaged there.
- It is missing from the AD 165 Collonetta Maffei list of extant legions.

This is a powerful evidential trail, though it is not definitive. Therefore, from this point we have to rely on informed speculation. It does seem probable, based on the contemporary commentaries detailed above, that there was some kind of military crisis in the north of Britain around the time of Hadrian's accession in AD 117. This was almost certainly the event that required the *expeditio Britannica* of Sabinus to stabilize the situation. The longer-term solution was then the arrival of the new legion in York, and the building of Hadrian's Wall. So, could *legio* IX *Hispana* have been destroyed around the time of this military crisis, fighting against the Brigantes in a northern revolt, fighting the tribes further north in the region of modern Scotland, or fighting against both in a 'Boudiccan'-style conflagration, this time in the north? Based on analogy and anecdote, the answer is of course yes, but to date there is no hard evidence to support the argument that this is what happened. However, it does remain a leading candidate hypothesis regarding the fate of the IXth legion. There are others to consider though, and in the first instance I stay in Britain, looking further south to the provincial capital of London.

Chapter 4

The Hadrianic War in London

In 2017 Dr Dominic Perring of UCL's Institute of Archaeology published a groundbreaking new theory. In an article in the leading classical journal *Britannia*, this leading expert on Roman London looked at three different events that occurred there during the reign of Hadrian. His aim was to see if together they could be interpreted as evidence for what he termed a 'Hadrianic War' in the provincial capital, this on the scale of the previous century's Boudiccan Revolt. The events he considered were:

- The finding of large numbers of human crania within the town boundaries in the upper courses and tributaries of the Walbrook valley.
- The well-known though disputed Hadrianic fire in London.
- The building of the *vexillation*-sized fort at Cripplegate in the north-west of the town.

Above in Chapter 3 I have considered whether *legio* IX *Hispana* was led to its destruction in the north of the province. Yet here we have a theory that the provincial capital itself was the subject of a 'war' early in Hadrian's reign. Therefore, the hypothesis tested in this chapter is to see whether the legion was actually lost in this dramatic incident rather than in the north, either rebelling itself or being defeated when trying to prevent the 'Hadrianic War'. To do that I first provide a description of the Roman town in the early second century AD. I then go into detail regarding Dr Perring's theory based on the three events, each considered in turn. Finally, having detailed his broad hypothesis, I set this against the fate of the IXth legion to see if all can be linked together to tell one of the great untold stories of Roman Britain.

Roman London

London was a Roman colonial settlement founded around AD 50. It became the provincial capital in the early AD 60s, taking over from Colchester after the Boudiccan revolt of AD 60/61. By the beginning of the second century AD it was the leading urban settlement in Roman Britain, a thriving town with a diverse population of 45,000 from all corners of the Roman Empire. Later enclosed by the 3.2km land wall circuit built by Septimius Severus in the late second century AD, it wasn't the biggest of provincial capitals, but was certainly wealthy.

Londonium was founded on the northern bank of the River Thames. This major waterway in the Roman period was very different to that today given its modern canalization that restricts its width to around 200m in the region of the Roman town. Myers (2016, 197) says that at the time of London's founding the river's formal channel was at least three times its modern width, with much of the area between Southwark and Lambeth on the south bank low-lying mudflats. At high tides many of these would have been submerged, increasing the river's width to more than 1km (Milne, 1985, 84).

The Roman town was founded on the then steep-sided and defendable Cornhill, this most likely site of a pre-existing Roman trading post given it bordered Catuvellauni territory to the north-west, Trinovantes territory to the north-east and Cantiaci territory to the south across the river. Others have argued that it was also the first point upstream where the Thames could be bridged (Merrifield, 1965, 33), and where shipping could still make use of tides to facilitate their passage to and from the sea (Rowsome, 2008, 25).

Cornhill was one of the three hills that went on to define the Roman town, the others being Ludgate Hill to the west and Tower Hill to the east. The former was separated from Cornhill by the steep-sided valley of the Walbrook stream, then a far more significant feature than today, and the latter by the smaller but still steep-sided and now lost Lorteburn stream.

The Walbrook is a key feature of this chapter and deserves close attention here to provide context to what follows, particularly regarding the Walbrook skulls. Though it had a comparatively small topographical catchment area of 4.7km in the Roman period (Myers, 2016, 327), its dense network of tributaries, particularly upriver, meant that the northern region of Roman London was marshy and often prone to flooding and wider damage from storm surges. Indeed, there was no gate in the Severan land wall section there until Moorgate was built in the fifteenth century AD. Further, when the bastions were added to the land wall in the later third century AD, none were thought needed along this section such was the marshy nature of the land outside the walls there, the building of which actually exacerbated the problem.

The main sources of water for the Walbrook were the ponds and springs originating in the gravels and clays across its catchment area, but principally those along the Islington Ridge well to the north of the Roman town. It had two main source streams, the first to the west that, at 3.4km long, originated amid the springs at Barnsbury above the Angel, Islington and at St Mary le Clere at the Old Street intersection with City Road. Meanwhile, the eastern source stream was fed by the diffuse springs on the slopes below Highbury, Canonbury, and at Hoxton and Holywell. The point of confluence of the two source streams was at Blomfield Street, immediately east of Finsbury Circus (Myers, 2016, 327). Now conjoined, the Walbrook then passed through the Roman town boundary along the line of today's London Wall to the south-east of Finsbury Circus. Its main tributary (one of many) rose in springs near the modern Barbican, passing through the Roman town boundary near today's Moorgate and then joining the Walbrook itself above Lothbury. Once within the Roman town boundary the main stream ran for 0.9km before reaching the Thames. In the early second century AD it was only tidal a short distance, up to Cannon Street.

The original Roman town grew on Cornhill throughout the Julio-Claudian and Flavian periods, despite being burnt to the ground during the Boudiccan Revolt. It was soon a thriving emporium where many of the goods imported from the continent to the east coast of Britannia arrived. These were then broken down in the Roman Port of London into smaller loads for onward shipment around the east and south coast and along the regional river systems. The town's commercial nature from the beginning is marvellously brought to life in it earliest known financial transaction. This is in the form of a stylus-writing tablet, one of 405 found between 2010 and 2014 during the Museum of London Archaeology's (MOLA) excavations at the Bloomberg site on Walbrook. These tablets originally featured wax in their wooden frames, this decaying after they were discarded in the Walbrook valley. However, many still have discernible messages scratched into their wooden backs by heavy-handed authors. One such is that of Tibullus, freedman of Venustus, his message a formal acknowledgment that he owed a trader called Gratus, freedman of Spurius, a debt of 105 *denarii* for goods sold and delivered. Incredibly, it is dated to 8 January AD 57 (Tomlin, 2016, xiii), less than a decade after the town was founded.

Londinium's official status is unclear, but given its mercantile and cosmopolitan nature it was almost certainly a *municipium* rather than a *colonia* veteran's settlement or *civitates* capital county town. As it continued to grow its rivers continued to play a key role in its development. Given the original town was on Cornhill, this was where all of the grand public buildings associated with a provincial capital could be found. This included a *basilica* and *forum*, London's second, which was the largest stone built structure in the Empire north of the Alps (today lying beneath the modern city's Leadenhall Market). At 166m by 167m square, the *forum* was five times larger than the original it replaced, and specifically built with monumentalism in mind, a powerful statement of Rome's intention to stay in Britain after the defeat of Boudicca. The construction of this *forum* was particularly remarkable, involving the dumping of huge quantities of gravel, brickearth and re-cycled building material to raise its flagstone-covered surface over one metre above the natural ground level. Meanwhile, the four-storey *basilica* was even more striking, with white limewashed walls and its roof clad in thousands of soft orange *tegula* and *imbrex* roof tiles. This massive structure was visible well beyond the town boundaries, and designed to impress those arriving by road or river for miles around. Such was their scale that the *forum* and *basilica* complex took thirty years to complete, this at some stage in the early second century AD (Hingley, 2018, 123). Meanwhile the Governor's Palace, beneath modern Cannon Street railway station, was equally grand. This featured finely decorated 25m by 20m state reception rooms with high-quality mosaics, ornate pools, and a spacious bathing complex with fine views across the riverfront. The eastern part of the town also featured the major official places of worship, including temples to the Capitoline Triad of Jupiter, Juno and Minerva, and also to the Imperial Cult.

By the early second century AD continued growth then saw the town jump the Walbrook stream, spreading to the west where the Fleet River (another Thames tributary) marked a new natural western boundary on the far side of Ludgate Hill. This created a town of two halves, the original eastern half where the fine public buildings remained on Cornhill and a less salubrious western half on Ludgate Hill on the far side of the Walbrook. Here were found the more mundane buildings associated with the day-to-day lives of *Londinium*'s inhabitants, including the large public bath house at modern Huggin Hill near modern St Paul's Cathedral dating to the AD 80s, a smaller one on Cheapside dating to the AD 70s, and Roman London's first amphitheatre. The latter was constructed from timber and also dated to around AD 70.

Additionally, in this less salubrious part of the town, a number of eastern cult religions were worshipped including those associated with Mithras (the famous Mithraeum was later built here on the western bank of the Walbrook), Cybele and Isis. Also later built here was the 4.7 ha *vexillation* fort in the north-west corner of the town, together with its associated stone-built amphitheatre (which replaced the earlier wood built structure), these both detailed below in the context of the 'Hadrianic War in London' hypothesis.

The last stage of town growth took place in the late second century AD when it spread north-west of the *basilica* and *forum* into the upper reaches of the Walbrook valley, and further to the east where it crossed the Lorteburn stream onto Tower Hill (Bentley, 1984, 13). The whole was then enclosed by the Severan land walls, built around AD 199/200 following the failed usurpation of the governor Clodius Albinus. This circuit delineated the city from Ludgate Hill in the west to Tower Hill in the east and still defines the 'square mile' of the City of London to this day. Roman London's gateways were also built at this time (they may have been monumentalised earlier as smaller stone built entrances to the town) at Ludgate, Newgate, Aldersgate, Bishopsgate (where Ermine Street originated and the likely entrance to the town for any legionaries travelling south from the IXth legion's base at York, see below), Aldgate, and the Watling Street London Bridge crossing from Southwark (these running west to east).

All of the grand structures of Roman London, together with many of the town's houses, shops and warehouses, were constructed of Kentish ragstone, excavated in five state-run *metalla* quarries in the upper Medway Valley. This fine limestone was transported the 127km down the Medway and up the Thames in a two day journey, using the tides where possible, on vessels manned and operated by the *Classis Britannica* regional fleet (Elliott, 2017, 108).

Meanwhile, Roman London featured two principal industrial zones. That within the town boundary was the lesser of the two, based in the northern reaches of the Walbrook valley. This featured small-scale industries including tanning, butchery, bone rendering, glass recycling and small-scale metal working, their waste products discarded in the Walbrook stream. These industrial enterprises were sited here on low-value land, well away from administrative, commercial and high-value residential areas to the south (Myers, 2016, 328). Meanwhile, outside the town boundaries across the Thames the principal industrial zone of Roman London was located in Southwark on a series of islets sitting proud of the mudflats there. This featured large-scale major metal working enterprises whose noxious fumes and noise were even further away from the town centre than those of the Walbrook industrial zone. A number of key roads met here in Southwark, including those transporting iron from major iron working *metalla* sites in the Weald (Elliott, 2017, 101).

Finally, *Londinium* also featured a number of official cemeteries, their founding actually setting the formal town boundaries early on given the Romans always buried their dead away from the living in the pre-Christian era. Such town boundaries had religious significance in the Roman world and were called the *pomerium*. In London, prior to the construction of the Severan land walls, this featured a substantial ditch and bank.

By the beginning of the second century AD the burial grounds of the provincial capital included the western cemetery between the roads to Silchester (Roman *Calleva Atrebatum*) and St Albans, the northern cemetery either side of Ermine Street as it set out north for Lincoln and York from Bishopsgate, and the eastern cemetery to the south of the road to Colchester. There were also a number of burial grounds in Southwark, and on the western bank of the Fleet.

A Hadrianic War in the Provincial Capital?

Having provided detail of Roman London at the beginning of the second century AD we can now consider Dr Perring's theory regarding a dramatic event there during the reign of Hadrian, with the Walbrook skulls, the Hadrianic fire and the Cripplegate fort detailed in turn. Note should be taken that London features in no written contemporary histories between those covering the Boudiccan revolt and the late second century AD. Therefore the below narrative relies heavily on the archaeological record.

The initial skulls found in the Walbrook and its tributaries were first commented on by early antiquarians, and were possibly the inspiration for Geoffrey of Monmouth's story of a massacre of Roman soldiers beside a brook or stream in his twelfth century AD *Historia regum Britanniae* (2007, 5.4). Then, as the city expanded in the nineteenth century and early twentieth century, hundreds more were discovered by workmen digging new sewers and erecting new buildings in the north of the original Roman town, for example at Blomfield Street, London Wall and Copthall Avenue.

Many of these skulls were darkly stained given the wet conditions of the Walbrook catchment area, and nearly all were found in identifiable Roman contexts.

In the 1920s Mortimer Wheeler presented two theories to explain the finding of so many bodiless skulls in the Walbrook system. His observations coalesced over time into the three broad interpretations that have come to dominate debate over their origins. First, he noted that the presence of crania alone might show they had been deposited along the banks of the stream and its tributaries by storm-surges given their rounded shape that would provide greater buoyancy than other skeletal remains (Wheeler, 1928, 15). In this theory the crania originated in the burial grounds to the north of the town boundary, particularly the principal 'northern' cemetery. Others have since made the same observation, for example Knüsel and Carr (1995, 162) who drew on taphonomic studies (this the research of the biogeochemical, ecological and sedimentary processes that occur in the environment before and after organisms are buried) to show that the clustering of skulls could be caused by fluvial sorting of the bodies. The impact of fluvial activity on the distribution of skulls was also illustrated by the excavations around Eldon Street from 1987 to 2007 that examined a small roadside cemetery where 135 burials, mostly inhumations dated to shortly after AD 120, were catalogued. Most of these were set along a major water channel that fed into the Walbrook stream. Some of these burials had been eroded by watercourse flooding given the human remains were present in the stream channel itself. These disturbed remains included both isolated skulls and groups of skulls, a discovery suggesting that the crania had indeed been washed out from burials in this cemetery and other burial grounds further upstream. Most recently, Myers (2016, 76) in his study of the Roman Walbrook also highlights the frequency of skulls being washed down the stream and its tributaries from the northern cemetery and other burial grounds, with the land there being disturbed by such storm surges.

Wheeler also cautiously suggested that some skulls were those of victims of Boudicca's sacking of London in AD 60/61. The debate following this led to the final two theories regarding the skulls origins, both associated with violence. The first was that they were trophy heads after some kind of conflict, the second that they had been ritually placed and were probably the heads of execution victims. With regard to his initial Boudiccan idea, more recent research by Marsh and West (1981, 86) highlighted that most of the skulls were actually from young males, indicating they are unlikely to have been the old and infirm members of the population left in London, unable to escape Boudicca, as detailed by Tacitus (*The Annals*, 14). They suggested instead that the Walbrook skulls were deposited in religious practice involving watery burial, this argument then developing into suggestions that the skulls illustrated the Celtic veneration of the human head. Cotton (1996, 85) developed this hypothesis further by finding parallels with the evidence of headless sacrificial or war victims from LIA Gaul, suggesting an association with headhunting cults and decapitation rites (see below).

Some of the skulls certainly show signs of trauma. A study of thirty-nine skulls found on the west bank of the Walbrook at 52–63 London Wall, where the stream exited the Roman town boundary, showed they had been left to decompose in waterlogged pits. Dog gnawing and puncture marks indicated these decapitated heads had soft-tissue on when deposited, exposing them to scavenging. Further, the lack of weathering on them indicates this process was unlikely to have taken place over an extended period. Pottery amid the human remains suggests the skulls were deposited between AD 40 and AD 200, with stratigraphic evidence narrowing this date range to between AD 120 and AD 160. Nearly all of the skulls came from young males aged between 28 and 35 years old. Additionally, most carried injuries inflicted around the time of death, with one a clear case of decapitation with a sword. The violence evident on some of the skulls was grossly excessive, with some featuring massive cheekbone damage (Perring, 2017, 37). Given this, the overall assemblage is most likely a collection of either trophy heads or those carefully deposited after a mass execution event.

The most recent Walbrook skull discoveries were made during the construction of Crossrail, near where Liverpool Street and an earlier Roman road crossed the Walbrook. These finds continue to be studied by MOLA and were recovered from two main areas. Firstly, in 2013 during tunnelling operations thirty-five skulls were found within gravels dumped against the east bank of the Walbrook in late second century AD engineering works. The date range of these is between AD 80 and the late second century AD. Preliminary analysis shows nearly all were male, with some of them polished by water action. Meanwhile, in 2015 twenty more skulls were found in a Hadrianic roadside ditch on the eastern approach to the Walbrook crossing. Most were placed at intervals along the southern side of the road, indicating deliberate placement. Again the most likely interpretation is that they were a collection of trophy heads or decapitated crania carefully deposited after a mass execution.

These latest finds bring the total number of Walbrook skulls detailed in published accounts to over 300. Further, it should be noted that these are only the ones known about, given many earlier skulls found in the stream and its tributaries are recorded and now lost. Perring (2017, 40) says these total 'an immense number', especially skulls found in sewer digging. Even the known number of more than 300 is an astounding figure given only 29 other human skulls have been found within the Roman town boundary, and these all singly. By way of contrast, some 2,180 Roman burials have been recorded from London's main cemeteries, with at least 320 of these consisting of cremations. Therefore, this large number of bodiless skulls from one location is surprising. Further, to illustrate the number that have yet to be discovered, records of sewer excavations and archaeological investigations encompass only about 5 per cent of the projected line of the Walbrook and its tributaries. Additionally, in those parts of the valley where detailed surveys have been undertaken they illustrate only limited sampling. For example, the detailed descriptions of investigations at 15–35 Copthall Avenue and 43–44 London Wall show that less than 4 per cent of the fills of the roadside ditches were archaeologically sampled, with the river channels barely explored at all.

To summarise the evidence here, we have a huge number of crania found in one area of Roman London, this the poorly settled upper reaches of the Walbrook valley and its tributaries in the north of the Roman town. Perring (2017, 40) contextualizes here, saying:

'The exceptional nature of the second-century concentration of skulls in the upper Walbrook deserves emphasis. The record of over 300 crania represents a significant part of the total of human remains recovered from Roman London.'

Of these most were young males, and most date to between AD 120 and AD 160, a time when extensive engineering was being used to introduce a planned grid of streets to an area previously undeveloped on the northern marshy extremity of the Roman town. This process canalized many of the tributaries of the Walbrook, buried many of the earlier roadside ditches and reclaimed much marshland, this all capping the earlier channels and wetlands and thus sealing the skulls in place.

What might account for this phenomenon? As detailed earlier, the options considered above are that they are either:

- The result of fluvial erosion by storm surges carrying the skulls downstream from burials in formal cemeteries, particularly the large northern one.

- The result of violence, in this case trophy heads from mass beheadings (anti- and post-mortem) after some kind of conflict, noting the unusually high numbers involved.
- The result of ritual placement in wet places in a type of votive practice, particularly of the heads of public execution victims, again potentially on a mass scale.

Clearly, these are not mutually exclusive possibilities and the different assemblages may have been formed in different ways. Nevertheless, considering each is instructive.

In terms of the first, Perring (2017, 42) is dismissive of this as an option to explain all of the crania. He says:

> It is evidently the case…that skulls found in stagnant wet places and roadside ditches could not have been carried directly to these locations by fluvial action. It is also impossible to identify an upstream source of burials to account for large numbers of skulls within the river. Extensive investigation between Moorgate and Bishopsgate shows that the area north of the Roman settlement remained under-utilised pasture and marsh. Numerous excavations have confirmed the absence of cemeteries throughout almost all of this area, while disturbed human remains were not present in 'natural' or residual contexts.

He concludes that the evidence shows while some burials were washed into tributaries of the Walbrook, they are too few in number to account for the bulk of the evidence.

In terms of the skulls being the result of deliberate placement, either as the result of headhunting or public execution, Perring (2017, 43) clearly feels it more likely that most of the skulls entered the water through direct human agency, arguing that this was demonstrably the case for the non-fluvial finds. He says:

> It is…reasonable to identify a deliberate pattern of disposing of human remains, disproportionately the heads of young men, in the river and associated wet places. The deposition of skulls and bodies in wet places is widely attested in northern Europe in both the Iron Age and Roman period. Lakes, springs and bogs are liminal places on the threshold between the living and other worlds. The deposition of skulls in boundary ditches is also likely

to have been influenced by a widespread association of heads with gateways and thresholds that constituted sacred borders separating the worlds of the living and the dead. The places in London where skulls were found are also areas where horse remains were unusually frequent and, while this was probably the product of a common approach to the disposal of human and horse remains within the urban pomerium, it might additionally reflect on the fact that the horse could serve as a psychopomp (a guide to lead the souls of humans to the place of the dead).

Looking first at the trophy head theory, evidence gathered by Redfern and Bonney (2014, 214) suggests at least some were definitely of this nature, most likely obtained in warfare. In that regard, while the violence witnessed in the London Wall assemblage shows them to be victims of extraordinary punishment, they are not the only Walbrook skulls to show evidence of weapon injury, as many others also show evidence of such trauma. Headhunting was well-known in the British and Gallic LIA prior to the arrival of the Romans, who viewed it on the scale carried out as a fascinating though disturbing practice (Perring, 2017, 45). As an example, the first-century BC commentator Diodorus (5.29. 4-5) says:

> The Gauls cut off the heads of their enemies slain in battle and fasten them about the necks of their horses. They hand over the blood-stained spoils to their attendants to carry off as booty, while striking up a paean over them and singing a hymn of victory. They nail up the heads on their houses, just as hunters do when they have killed certain wild beasts. They embalm in cedar oil the heads of their most distinguished enemies and keep them carefully in a chest. These they display, with pride, to strangers, declaring that one of their ancestors, or his father, or the man himself, refused the offer of a large sum of money for this head. They say that some of them boast that they refused the weight of the head in gold.

Writing shortly afterwards, the Greek geographer, philosopher and historian Strabo (4.4.5) echoes these views, adding that Roman travellers in Gaul had seen many such heads, so many in fact that eventually they got used to the sight. Today, most of the evidence of this practice comes from hillfort sites, particularly in boundary ditches and next to gateways where many of the crania found display weapon injuries. It is unclear if these were placed there deliberately, or were the casually discarded heads of decapitated lower-class warriors.

It is clear from primary sources and particularly sculpture and epigraphy that the practice of headhunting, probably by a limited number of troops, gradually found its way into Roman military practice. The vector appears to have been the employment of Gallic and German allied and mercenary troops in the late Republic, the tradition then continuing into the Imperial period when Augustus formalized such troops into regular auxilia units. By way of example, when Caesar won the final victory over his Pompeian rivals at Munda in Spain in 45 BC some of his troops erected a palisade on which they displayed the severed heads of slain opponents to intimidate any surviving Pompeains who had fled within the town walls of Munda. Interestingly, it seems these were legionaries from *legio* V *Alaudae*, a unique legion that was recruited from native Gauls (as opposed to Roman citizens, see Chapter 1) in *Gallia Transalpina* during Caesar's later AD 50s Gallic campaigns (Elliott, 2019, 123). This is the only reference we have to legionaries being involved in headhunting, an important distinction as we will see.

By the time of the Empire only auxilia are depicted in sculpture brandishing severed heads. Four prime examples include those on the Great Trajanic Frieze. This comprises slabs from a monument to Trajan's two Dacian campaigns of AD 101–AD 102 and AD 105–AD 106, later reused and visible today on the early fourth century AD Arch of Constantine. On one panel spanning two of the slabs, three auxiliaries stand with right arms raised presenting the heads of Dacians to Trajan. The style of their armour and shields indicates they are cavalry. Meanwhile another auxiliary, this time mounted, reaches down with his left hand to grasp the hair of a Dacian, his right hand holding a *spatha* ready to decapitate his opponent. Next, on Trajan's Column in Rome one of the helical friezes shows the severed heads of two Dacians impaled on poles next to two auxiliary cavalrymen as nearby legionaries build a fort. Moving on, a gruesome scene is depicted on the Bridgeness Slab, the easternmost distance slab along the Antonine Wall which records the building of '4652' paces of the then northern frontier by legionaries of the Caerleon-based *legio* II *Augusta*, the original now in the National Museum of Scotland in Edinburgh. The inscription on the slab is flanked by scenes of victory, with that on the left showing an auxiliary cavalryman riding down four natives. One has been decapitated, with his headless body slumped forward in a seated position while his head falls to the ground. Finally, on the Column of Marcus

Aurelius in Rome which commemorates his victories in the Marcomannic Wars, one of the helical friezes (scene LXVI) shows the seated emperor listening to an advisor while two auxiliaries to his left distract him by holding up severed German heads.

Meanwhile, Roman military tombstones also show headhunting practices openly professed by members of auxiliary cavalry units while based in Britain. A good example is provided by the late first century AD memorial to Aurelius Lucius in Chester. This shows his groom holding up a severed head. Meanwhile, a tombstone dated to between AD 75 and AD 120 from Lancaster shows Insus, a citizen of the Treviri and trooper with the *Ala Augusta*, grasping the head of a decapitated enemy.

Isolated skulls found on Romano-British sites have also been identified as possible trophies. Skull fragments in Flavian pits at the fort at Newstead are thought to be discarded military trophies, while the skull of a young male found in the fort ditch at Vindolanda has sword wounds to the head and has also been interpreted as a trophy. Meanwhile, at Colchester six skulls, mostly young males and with some showing trauma associated with decapitation, were found in the town ditch and have also been identified as trophies.

For balance, it should be noted that in terms of the sculptures and tombstones, none of the scenes and images indicate the auxiliaries involved were of Gallic or German origin, though Fields (2006, 11) believes they most likely were. He says:

> It should come as no surprise…that since the days of Caesar large numbers of Celts, principally Gallic horsemen, had been enlisted to serve in Rome. It is a fair presumption that these auxiliary troops, displaying severed heads in time-honoured Celtic fashion, were Gauls.

Perring agrees, saying (2017, 46):

> Rome's recruitment of auxiliary cavalry from Gallic and Germanic provinces may have contributed to an evolution of battlefield practice (that had) become acceptable in an army that, with Hadrian's encouragement, was increasingly willing to learn from customs previously considered barbarian.

On the subject he concludes that auxiliary cavalry in particular are likely to have been at the centre of any policing exercise in the provincial capital,

Above: Auxiliary cavalryman tombstone from Kirkby Thore, Cumbria, showing him riding down a native British warrior.

Right: Tombstone from the AD 60s of Gaius Saufeius, soldier of the IXth legion who died at the age of 40 after twenty-two years' service. Found in Lincoln.

Roman auxiliary cavalrymen and foot beheading German prisoners during the Marcomannic Wars, Column of Marcus Aurelius, Rome.

Roman legionaries in testudo formation assaulting a German camp during the Marcomannic Wars, Column of Marcus Aurelius, Rome.

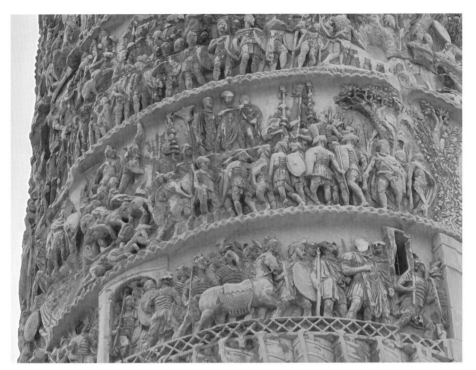

Marcus Aurelius addresses Roman legionaries during the Marcomannic Wars, Column of Marcus Aurelius, Rome.

Roman auxilia in scale mail and chainmail during the Marcomannic Wars, Column of Marcus Aurelius, Rome.

Roman auxiliary cavalrymen during the Marcomannic Wars, Column of Marcus Aurelius, Rome.

Box-flue tile from the legionary fortress at York, made by specialist troops in *legio* IX *Hispana*.

Above: North-western wall of the legionary fortress at York. The IXth legion began the process of replacing the original earth bank and palisade wall with one built from stone.

Right: Tombstone of Lucius Ducchius Rufinus, signifier of *legio* IX *Hispana*, found at Holy Trinity Church, Micklegate, York.

'The Emperor Caesar Nerva Trajan Augustus, son of the deified Nerva, Conqueror of Germany, Conqueror of Dacia, Chief Priest, in his twelfth year of tribunician power, acclaimed imperator six times…(built) through the agency of the ninth Hispana legion.' The last stone inscription to ever mention the IXth legion, dated to AD 108 and installed to celebrate the construction of the new stone-built south-eastern gateway in the legionary fortress at York.

Multangular Tower, legionary fortress, York. Built by *legio* VI *Victrix* which replaced *legio* IX *Hispana* there from AD 122.

Right: Bronze head from a
statue of the Emperor Hadrian,
found discarded in the River Thames.
Possibly the result of the Hadrianic
War in London.

Below: Detail of Sarmatian cavalry
scale-mail armour, either bronze
or horn, base of Trajan's Column in
Rome. Note the dragon standard.

Above: Sarmatian banded leather armour, detail of the base of Trajan's Column in Rome.

Left: Commodus, sole Roman Emperor from AD 180 to AD 192.

Replica Roman Principate Empire legionary helmets, Trimontium Museum of Roman Scotland.

Arch of Titus, *Forum Romanum*, Rome. This shows his triumph after sacking Jerusalem in AD 70 during the First 'Great' Jewish Revolt.

Right: Painted wall-plaster from the *praetorium* commanding officer's house in the legionary fortress in York, found today beneath York Minster.

Below: Wall of the *praetorium* commanding officer's house in the legionary fortress in York, found today beneath York Minster.

Sequence of defensive ditches at the Roman fort site at Ardoch, Perthshire, Scotland.

The Medway Gap as seen from Bluebell Hill on the North Downs. Aylesford, centre, is thought to be the location of the river-crossing battle described by primary sources during the Claudian invasion in AD 43 in which *legio* IX *Hispana* participated.

Right: Tombstone of Insus, son of Vodullus, a Roman auxiliary cavalryman. Found in Lancaster. Note the severed head of a native Briton.

Below: Interior of the motte of Castle Dykes Norman castle in Northamptonshire, originally a Roman marching camp. Associated with the possible site of the defeat of Boudicca by Gaius Suetonius Paulinus.

Left: Bust of the emperor Hadrian who visited Britain in AD 122, bringing *legio* VI *Victrix* with him which was installed in York.

Below: Amphitheatre at the Roman legionary fortress of Caerleon, Wales, home of *legio* II *Augusta*. That at the legionary fortress in York, yet to be found, would have been similar.

Interior of the Roman legionary fortress at Caerleon, Wales, showing the typical layout of the barrack blocks, with ovens in the foreground.

Roman legionaries in *lorica segmentata* on a panel from a lost Arch of Marcus Aurelius in Rome, reused on the Arch of Constantine.

Left: Column from the basilica in the Roman legionary fortress, York. Home of *legio* IX *Hispana*.

Below: Roman fort site at Newstead (Roman *Trimontium*), Melrose, Scottish Borders. A typical Roman fortification north of the border.

and the evidence from London supports the suggestion that headhunting practices inspired by Gallic tradition had become normalised within the early second century AD Roman army. While the Walbrook skulls may have been trophies obtained in reprisals that continued over several decades and certainly drew on practices that continued for the better part of two centuries, the exceptional scale of the second century evidence he argues is more consistent with a major massacre concentrated within a shorter war. An event of this nature could have contributed to exaggerated ritual practices within the upper Walbrook *vicus* (see below), which drew on the warrior culture associated with auxiliary troops, whose identities were in part formed in Gaul and Germany.

Of relevance to this work and for discussion later, at the time of *legio* IX *Hispana* in the early second century AD we know of at least seven Gallic auxiliary units based in Britain (four cavalry and one with a mounted component), these being the *ala (Gallorum) Agrippiana miniata*, *ala Gallorum Pianacentia*, *ala Gallorum Sebosiana*, *ala I Tungrorum*, *cohors II Gallorum Equitata* (a mixed infantry and cavalry unit), *cohors III Nerviorum CR* and *cohors V Gallorum*. Later in the reign of Hadrian, Hodder (2003, 145) suggests there were 10,688 auxiliary cavalry (between 11 and 14 *alae*) and 25,520 auxiliary infantry in the province, in addition to the (by then) 16,500 legionaries of *legio* II *Augusta* at Caerleon, *legio* XX *Valeria Victrix* at Chester and *legio* IV *Victrix* at York.

Turning to the final explanation regarding the Walbrook skulls, this is the argument that the heads belonged to the victims of public executions, deliberately deposited in this way as some kind of votive practice. Ritual activity involving excarnation (the practice of removing the organs and flesh of the dead before burial, in this case leading to bodiless skulls) took place in both the LIA and Roman Britain. It therefore makes sense to look for wider evidence of this practice in the Roman world to understand how and why the crania entered the Walbrook under this theory.

Normal Roman burial practice involved acts of expiation (making amends for wrong doing) and purification and took place in graveyards beyond the town boundary. In the Roman world the corpse demanded respect as it was believed the departed souls would suffer if the body was not properly buried. Therefore, funerary rites were important sacred duties involving calming the spirits of the dead, whose trespass in the land of the living while unburied threatened misfortune. A proper Roman burial demanded the body be covered, even if by only by a few handfuls of dust, and it was an offence to damage bodies during or after the interment process. Relevant to this work, such rights extended to enemies killed on the battleground and even executed criminals, where the reunion of decapitated heads with the body was an important concession to the bereaved. Perring (2017, 43) says denial of burial was in this context an exceptional punishment, reserved only for those who challenged public and social order, and specifically those considered guilty of treason and betrayal. In these cases corpse abuse might include decapitation, then a denial of burial rites and exposure to scavenging by wild dogs and birds, these combining to achieve the public obliteration of victims in a *damnatio memoriae* context. The distancing of the head from the body meant that funerary rituals could not be properly carried out, nor the remains properly interred, in this case leading to bodiless skulls.

Given these unburied dead risked contaminating sacred areas, including those defined by the town boundary, their remains therefore required some form of ritual cleansing to prevent their spirits from troubling those still living. In such cases the Roman world therefore developed various mechanisms to remove unburied human remains. For example, in Rome itself the Tiber was used as part of the purging process and consequently river disposal came to be associated with corpse abuse and the denial of burial. Several histories make a point of describing how the bodies of those who betrayed Rome were casually thrown into the Tiber. An extreme example is that of the bodies of executed Samnite prisoners who were thrown in the river in their thousands by the supporters of Lucius Cornelius Sulla after the Battle of the Colline Gate in 82 BC. Using the Tiber as his comparator, Perring says: 'The evidence from the Walbrook, although open to other interpretations, is consistent with the picture obtained from Rome. Like the…Tiber, the Walbrook and Thames formed sacred boundaries to the settlement they circumscribed.'

Other towns and rivers also offer analogy here. For example Eusebius (*Ecclesiastical History*, 5.1.63) describes the AD 177 execution of Christian martyrs from Lyon and Vienne, some of who were beheaded in the amphitheatres there. Their bodies were deliberately mutilated by wild animals, exposed for six days under guard to prevent their burial, then burnt and swept into the Rhône.

Following on from this analogy, the upper Walbrook valley of the Roman town was a highly suitable environment for the disposal of the deliberately unburied dead, or at least their skulls. It formed part of the city *pomerium*, an area favoured in the Roman world for the execution and burial of criminals. It also lay to the north-west of the town, this a direction naturally associated with mortality beyond the setting sun. The area also formed part of the hinterland of London's amphitheatre, this itself occupying a liminal space. Built at the latest in the early AD 120s in its stone-built form (which replaced the wooden original), this had a seating capacity of between 7,000 and 10,500 spectators. The amphitheatre was certainly a place where public executions took place, and also gladiatorial combat, and could certainly be the place of origin for some of the skulls, with many of these victims denied a formal burial. As Perring (2917, 45) says:

> London is bound to have witnessed frequent executions, as the city held a pivotal role in Rome's administration of Britain, remaining under the direct command of the provincial governor until at least the early Flavian period. The governor's judicial duties included imposing the death sentence and ordering public execution.

We have direct evidence of this in the form of the second century AD tombstone of Celsus, a *speculator* (scout) of *legio* II *Augusta* whose memorial was found near Blackfriars, and who was an officer on the staff of the governor responsible for judicial killing.

Above I have set out the history of the Walbrook skulls, and the three principal theories used to explain their provenance. Though some may well have been the result of fluvial action, to my mind most weren't given their deliberate placement. We are therefore left with the trophy head and public execution theories, noting in the case of the latter the exceptional nature of such methods of body disposal, even of executed crinimals. Given the fact that most of the skulls are of young men, and date from between AD 120 and AD 160, their relevance to the disappearance of *legio* IX *Hispana* is discussed later in this chapter.

Finally here, I turn to one final beheading event associated with a possible Hadrianic War in London. This is in the form of a bronze head of the emperor Hadrian recovered from the Thames just below London Bridge. Recent studies show that this casting was probably commissioned from a London workshop, and it was possibly made to commemorate his accession to the Imperial throne in AD 117. The statue from which the head had been roughly hacked was intended to be viewed from the front, and most likely would have stood prominently within a niche in the new *forum* still being finalised at the time. Many scholars have assumed that the head was removed from the statue in later antiquity, possibly by iconoclasts.

However, there is no evidence for this. Since both the *forum* and *basilica* were extensively damaged by fire in the Hadrianic period (detailed below), it is difficult to see how the statue would have escaped destruction at this time unless it had been moved. In that regard, Perring (2017, 51) says:

> This suggests an alternative context for the events that resulted in its decapitation and the disposal of Hadrian's head in the waters of the Thames. There are other instances of heads being removed from imperial statues and thrown into rivers in ritual acts of desecration analogous to the abuse vested in trophy heads. Here the decapitation of the Imperial image mirrored corpse abuse and could have symbolised the rejection of Hadrian's imperial authority, while also drawing on wider practice in the ritual disposal of body-parts from bronze statues in water to expel spirits from the image. This event could have happened soon after the statue was first erected rather than centuries later, hence unintentionally saving the head from fire damage.

The decapitation of this important new statue of Hadrian in this context would therefore be directly related to the insurrection event being discussed in this chapter.

I now turn to the next key piece of evidence considered by Dr Perring in his hypothesis regarding a Hadrianic War in London, namely a town-wide conflagration in the second century AD. Roman London has long been associated with a major burning event, namely that of the Boudiccan Revolt in AD 60/61. Here the primary sources say the town was destroyed with great loss of life. Direct evidence of this exists in the archaeological record, in the form of a well-recognized bright red destruction horizon (mostly the remains of timber-and-clay buildings) followed by a subsequent phase consistent with military reoccupation and rebuilding as the town was restored, this time as the provincial capital.

Then, in the 1940s, evidence of another razing of Roman London came to light. This was the result of work by archaeologist Gerald Dunning, then the Inspector of Ancient Monuments in Britain. As Hingley (2018, 116) explains:

> Excavations…found widespread evidence for second destruction of Londinium during the AD 120s or AD 130s. It has long been argued that there was one substantial phase of burning in which

large parts of Roman London were destroyed, perhaps around AD 125 during the reign of the emperor Hadrian. The burnt layer resulting from this conflagration has long been interpreted as the second destruction of Londoninium after the fire of the Boudiccan uprising.

Perring (2017, 47) argues that since this burning event shows such a remarkable similarity to the Boudiccan fire, it opens up the possibility that it was also the result of conflict. He says that numerous excavations subsequent to that of Dunning have found prime examples of this Hadrianic destruction horizon, arguing there are near-contiguous sightings of fire debris that indicate a single conflagration destroyed most of *Londinium* north of the Thames. At the time this was an area of around 65 ha. Perring (2017, 47) continues that the destruction from this fire can be traced to the *pomerium* limits of the pre-Hadrianic settlement in every direction. It is particularly well attested either side of the approaches to London Bridge where the quays and warehouses were damaged to the river's edge, leading some to speculate that the fire actually began here. Interestingly, given the scale of the configuration the Walbrook failed to act as a firebreak and destruction is evident on Ludgate Hill as well as Cornhill. In fact the only areas of *Londinium* that seem to have been largely untouched by the conflagration are the upper Walbrook valley and Southwark. This is interesting in itself because, as detailed above, they were the two industrial zones of the Roman town at the time. The fire event therefore seems to have been concentrated in the residential and administrative areas. Additionally of interest, many of the timber-and-clay buildings appear to have caught fire on the street front first, indicating they were deliberately torched. Perring is instructive here, saying (2017, 50):

> In an accidental fire one would expect to find areas of buildings saved downwind of the fire's starting point and in peripheral areas where reduced building densities left natural fire-breaks, as was evident in the Great Fire of 1666. This was not the case and the nature of the destruction is therefore more consistent with arson. This might also account for choices made over what to save from the disaster. While most valuables appear to have been removed, the sheets of a bronze diploma granting Roman citizenship were fused together in fire damage to a town-house at Watling Court. This was an odd thing (for the owner) to have abandoned, since it

was easily portable and precious to the recipient and his heirs, but more easily overlooked by looters. Disturbed human remains were also found in fire debris at Watling Court.

All of this evidence combines to indicate that the destruction of London north of the Thames at this time was unusually comprehensive and deliberate. Using the Boudiccan fire as an analogy, what is today dubbed the Hadrianic fire seems to have been the consequence of war destruction.

The fire is usually dated to around AD 125 based on the assemblage of over 600 samian vessels found at Regis House on the Thames waterfront, though some have argued it could be earlier. In that regard, coins of Trajan have been recovered from floor surfaces beneath the fire horizon, for example at One Poultry and Lime Street, while no coins of Hadrianic issue have been found in or below the burnt layer. Fire debris in the town also contained Thames-Estuary-made Black Burnished Ware 2 pottery and Cologne colour-coated ware, both dated to between AD 100 and AD 140. Dendrochronological dating of structures pre-dating the fire also indicates that the fire occurred in the AD 120s. A well destroyed in the conflagration at Gresham Street featured timbers dated to AD 108/109 while a warehouse destroyed on the Pudding Lane waterfront was built with timbers felled between AD 94 and AD 129. Archaeomagnetic samples from fire debris at this site also provide dates between AD 110 and AD 180, though it should be noted that the tolerances of archaeomagnetic dating are insufficiently precise for this to be treated as absolute. It is also evident that the fire event damaged the huge *basilica* and *forum* given significant modifications were made to them in the AD 120s, these presumably being post-fire repairs. There are also indications that the timber quays on the waterfront were also rebuilt in the early Hadrianic period, replacing earlier second-century revetments such as those found at Regis House which were built around AD 102. Again this was likely to replace the originals damaged by the Hadrianic fire. Further, this post-fire quay was built around AD 128, indicating that the fire occurred in the earlier AD 120s. A final piece of evidence in this regard is the substantial jetty built over the Roman Thames foreshore, which was found in the innermost ward of the Tower of London in 1977. This used timbers felled in the winter of AD 126/7. This is somewhat downriver from the Roman port of London and has been interpreted as a jetty built to exploit a location convenient for shipping coming upriver during a period when London's port remained damaged beyond use by the fire.

For balance, in recent years some have speculated that the Hadrianic burning event in London was not a single event but the misinterpretation of a variety of separate fires that occurred in London throughout the reign of Hadrian. However, the most recent research suggests this was not the case. In that regard, Hingley (2018, 120) says: 'Recent excavations have carefully assessed the Hadrianic fire and have now suggested that at least one substantial fire engulfed part of the western and central area of Londinium at some stage during the AD 120s or early AD 130s.'

I now move on to consideration of the Cripplegate Fort and its association with the Hadrianic War in London hypothesis, with the starting point once more analogy with the Boudiccan Revolt. After the latter had been defeated the Romans decided to make London the provincial capital, this triggering the major building programmes detailed at the beginning of this chapter. However, the first manifestation of *Londinium*'s revival was the building of the 1.5 ha Neronian fort at modern Plantation Place on Fenchurch Street, found during rescue excavations by MOLA in the early 2010s. This was a timber and earthwork structure, similar in design to a standard Roman marching camp though more robust in its construction, enclosed by double ditches each 1.9m wide and 3m deep. Hingley (2018, 62) provides more detail, saying:

> Dominating a strategic point of high ground, the fortification was close to the major road junction and the early marketplace above the bridgehead. Its northern ditches cut through the main north-west road of early Roman Londinium and it is unclear why this road was put out of use. This fortified enclosure overlay timber buildings…burned during the Boudiccan uprising and the rampart itself contained charred timbers and burnt mud bricks that were reused from destroyed buildings.

The fort could accommodate 500 troops and was occupied for around ten years. Within its walls were located a granary, latrine and cookhouse, with the soldiers housed in tents rather than permanent wooden or stone-built structures.

Moving forward in time to the AD 120s, exactly the same thing happened in London after the Hadrianic fire, with the building of the Cripplegate Fort that Perring (2017, 52) says is evidence of the town's Hadrianic military occupation. This stone-built playing-card shaped fort was much larger than its Fenchurch Street predecessor, measuring 220m by 215m and occupying an area of 4.7 ha. The site chosen was the high ground north-west of the Roman town, with construction beginning around AD 120 (based on Samian Ware finds there). Perring adds that there are indications the site had already been earmarked for public use in the Flavian period, this suggested by the awkward insertion into early Roman London's urban topography of the road that led to the later fort's south gate.

Unlike the Neronian fort with its reused Boudiccan fire debris, no Hadrianic fire reuse is evident in the Cripplegate fort, though layers of charcoal and burnt daub were observed beneath parts of its walls when excavated. This shows it was built shortly after the Hadrianic fire. The fort's construction is unusual since urban garrisons were a rarity in the Roman Empire, with the few examples including Rome's legionary fort-sized *Castra Praetoria* camp which housed the Praetorian Guard and the fort at Lyon (Roman *Lugdunum*) where troops were based to protect the mint there.

London's stone-built fort presented a very powerful symbol of Roman authority and Perring (2017, 53) says it could indicate that London was also considered unusually important. The most common theory regarding its presence suggests it housed soldiers serving the governor, procurator, or those otherwise seconded to London. These would have included the governor's *singulares consularis* guard of auxiliary cavalry and infantry, and also the *beneficiarii consularis* or *beneficiarii procuratoris* serving on the staffs of the governor or procurator. The total number of these guards and *beneficiarii* would have fluctuated, but up to 1,600 could have served in such capacities in London at various times, with many travelling around the south-east of the province on their various Imperial duties.

However, it should be noted that this substantial fort was also of a similar size to those on the German frontier where they served a purely militaristic function. These housed *milliary alae* of 768 auxiliary cavalrymen, *milliary* cohorts of 800 auxiliary foot troops, and often both. Further, objects found within the Cripplegate fort suggest that it housed not only auxilia (both cavalry and infantry) but also legionaries. This reinforces the view that, at least at the beginning of its use, the fort contained a composite garrison placed there with military action in mind rather than administration. In that regard, parts of eight buildings identified as barrack blocks have been investigated in the southern part of the fort. Assuming symmetry elsewhere within the walls, this would allow for between eighteen and twenty-two buildings overall. Most of the barracks probably housed infantry, with as detailed in Chapter 1 each century of eighty men accommodated in one such block (their centurions housed in separate quarters at the end of each block). Those that housed cavalry featured two units of troopers, each of around thirty-two men, who would have occupied similarly sized blocks that included integrated stabling.

Taking the view that the fort was at first built with conflict in mind, Perring (2017, 54) adds that in pre-Hadrianic London there is evidence from across the town that the personnel serving the governor and procurator were housed in a civilian context, as was the case in most places elsewhere in the Empire. He continues that the fort was also larger than needed to house the full complement of such soldiers routinely based in London, either in the pre- or post-Hadrianic fire periods. He continues:

> In sum there was no evident need to build a fort to house the soldiers serving the governor (and procurator) and his administration, who could easily have lived elsewhere as they did in earlier and later periods. The fort was larger than needed and failed to include facilities for higher-ranked officers (for example a commanding officer). The exercise also runs counter to normal Imperial preference. The decision to station troops within a fort at London finds direct parallel, however, in arrangements after the Boudican revolt (as detailed). The Cripplegate fort could have been built in response to post-fire political circumstance, involving the settlement of a new garrison of occupation, rather than in anomalous administrative display.

In the most recent consideration of the construction of the fort, Hingley agrees. He says (2018, 120):

> The fort at Cripplegate was constructed soon after (the Hadrianic fire) and this could suggest, as in the case of the earlier (Boudiccan) burning of AD 60/ 61, the fire was the result of a deliberate attempt to destroy Londinium after which a military unit was stationed at Londinium to supervise the reconstruction.

To the east of the fort lay the upper Walbrook valley, open land on the north-west margins of the Flavian city which was crossed by small tributaries of the Walbrook. In the pre-Hadrianic period this had attracted little attention except for the building of the original wooden amphitheatre. However, with the building of the Cripplegate fort a grid of streets was imposed on the area, which was a significant engineering exercise involving the drainage and reclamation of marshy areas and the laying of gravelled road-surfaces on timber-and-turf causeways flanked by timber drains. This new district seems to have been the fort *vicus*, with the upper Walbrook valley particularly suited to military activity given the stream's north-western tributaries separating the domestic and military spheres of activity as was traditional in Roman settlements. The presence of a *vicus* is more evidence that this fort was, at least initially, militaristic in nature rather than a residence for guards, *beneficiarii* and similar.

Of particular interest here, there is a marked concentration of head-pots in the archaeological record dating from the late first century AD through to around AD 160. Elsewhere in the Empire head-pots have been linked with the presence of auxiliary troops recruited from the Rhine delta and northern Belgium, an interesting coincidence given the commentary above about the Walbrook skulls and headhunting. The fort and its *vicus* suggest that London witnessed an increased military presence following the Hadrianic fire, this coinciding with a significant increase in the ritual deposition of human crania in the upper Walbrook detailed earlier, and also the appearance of head-pots in the fort's civilian settlement.

London's military occupation as presented by Perring and indicated by the construction of the Cripplegate fort lasted for around forty years. The town appears to have witnessed a severe contraction in the Antonine period, a process that may have been exacerbated by the plague, which hit Roman Britain around AD 165. The arrival of this pestilence may have hastened the evacuation of troops no longer needed for policing duties in the province, this then exaggerating the process of urban contraction in towns such as London. Whatever the cause, the Cripplegate fort was evacuated in the late second century, with a date of AD 165 being a good fit for the surviving archaeological evidence. Activity did initially continue in the area. For example ritual corpse abuse (alluded to earlier in this Chapter), sometimes involving the decapitation and display of heads associated with a military presence, did still occur in the region of the former fort *vicus* on rare occasions until the later second century AD. The ideas involved here perhaps influenced those who much later violently decapitated and then buried the stone head of Mithras and other deities when London's Mithraeum was decommissioned and reused as a temple of Bacchus in the early fourth century AD (Hingley, 2018, 215). Practices involving the disposal of human remains were, however, largely expelled from the upper Walbrook valley by the end of the second century AD when it was formally incorporated into the city with the construction of the Severan land wall.

To conclude this section, based on the above analysis of the Walbrook skulls phenomenon, Hadrianic fire and subsequent building of the Cripplegate fort, Perring's theory of a Hadrianic War of some kind in London in AD 120s is compelling. However, there is one important thing missing from the narrative, namely definitive proof regarding who the protagonists were. Whose skulls are found in the Walbrook, who burnt pre-Hadrianic London and whom was the Cripplegate fort built to send a message to in order to prevent any future insurrection? Perring believes the culprits were members of the local community driven to rebellion by some unknown factor, stating (2017, 61):

> The absence of equivalent destruction horizons at other towns in the South-East might indicate that the troubles, if such they were, remained local to London. Continuing with this line of speculation, it could be argued that Southwark avoided extensive destruction because the rebels failed to cross the Thames. The large numbers of heads brought to the Walbrook could indicate that victory was obtained nearby, since although trophy heads could be transported long distances, this was for the public humiliation of eminent individuals rather than the fate of entire hosts. Similarly, large numbers of hostile prisoners bound for execution in the amphitheatre are unlikely to have been marched long distances and are more likely to have been captured locally. A rebellion that drew on local support would, in turn, have added to the case for the visible military response represented by the Cripplegate fort. This was much larger and more imposing than the Fenchurch Street fort built in London after the Boudiccan revolt, influenced in part by a shift from earthen to masonry construction that characterised the architecture of the second century, and built as much to intimidate as to reassure.

He continues that the evidence for decapitation and denial of burial witnessed by some of the Walbrook skulls suggests exceptional punitive retribution. Such brutality is a treatment often set aside for those who betrayed Rome. Further, if a rebellion had found local support this need not have been exclusively British given the very cosmopolitan nature of *Londinium*, the town a thriving provincial capital and emporium. DNA and stable isotope analysis from one of the London Wall skulls indicates that this individual was a black-haired and brown-eyed male who was probably not born in Britain, and that his mother's family came from Eastern Europe or the Near East. It should therefore come as no surprise if a revolt in London drew slaves and disaffected soldiers to its cause. The latter point then naturally leads to another question given the central subject of this book. If it still existed and was in the province, what was the *legio* IX *Hispana* doing at the time of the Hadrianic War in London?

The IXth Legion and London's Hadrianic War

To be clear, what follows is pure speculation given there is no evidence at all of the IXth legion's involvement at any stage during any Hadrianic War in London. However, as detailed earlier, there is also no evidence at all that it served in the region of modern Scotland, even though as the most northerly legion it must have done, nor any evidence regarding a dramatic fall from grace in the far north as discussed in Chapter 4. Therefore this hypothesis deserves our attention, if only to provide balance regarding the various other theories regarding its demise. Two principal scenarios are covered here, one with it being the victim and one the protagonist, both assuming that *legio* IX *Hispana* survived into the AD 120s.

In the first instance, we have the IXth legion (or a significant part thereof) being called down from its legionary fortress in York to deal with a major incident in the provincial capital and suffering so badly at the hands of the rebels that it disappears from history. This might seem unlikely given the distance from Roman York to London along Ermine Street is some 325km, especially as it would also have left the northern border significantly understrength. At the time the other two British legions were actually closer as the crow flies, with *legio* II *Augusta* at Caerleon 275km away and *legio* XX *Valeria Victrix* at Chester 317km away. However, the Ermine Street route was effectively a direct trunk road down to *Londinium*, while both the other two legions would have had to travel to Wroxeter in the Welsh Marches before they could pick up Watling Street and then head south-east. One short cut open to the Caerleon-based *legio* II *Augusta* was to pick up Akeman Street at Gloucester and then head to St Albans, but even this route was more circuitous than Ermine Street, the route the IXth legion would have taken. Further, the two legions on the west coast were almost certainly engaged in policing operations in Wales, its interior always a recalcitrant part of the province. In this scenario the majority of the Walbrook skulls (in the context of headhunting or mass beheading) would then be either those of slain legionaries, or those of the rebels after they had been later defeated, presumably (at least in part) by auxiliary cavalry with Gallic or German ancestry. The arrival of Sabinus' *expeditio Britannica* might then be considered a response to any disaster in London, or as detailed in the previous chapter a short-term stopgap to secure the northern border before the arrival of *legio* VI *Victrix* with Hadrian in AD 122. However unlikely this all sounds, it should be pointed out that *legio* IX *Hispana* had form here, this again harking back to the Boudiccan Revolt of AD 60/61. This was the defeat of its then *legate* Cerialis with a significant part of the legion when failing to prevent the sack of Colchester. Such was the scale of this disaster that Cerialis fled with his guard cavalry, leaving the surviving legionaries to their grim fate, he remaining holed up in a nearby fort until the defeat of the revolt (Elliott, 2018b, 81).

The second scenario is in my opinion the more interesting, and more likely of the two. This sees the IXth legion being deployed to London once more, but this time participating in or even leading the rebellion. The Walbrook skulls would then be those of legionaries slain by the auxiliaries who put the rebellion down. It should be remembered that *legio* IX *Hispana* also had form here. As detailed in Chapter 1, it rebelled around the time of Augustus' death in AD 14 while based with two other legions at a legionary fortress on the River Danube in the then province of Pannonia. By way of analogy, there are also other examples of legions rebelling, for example *legio* I *Germanica* and *legio* XVI *Gallica*, both of which sided with Civilis during the Batavian Revolt as detailed in Chapter 4.

Further, given the very large military presence in Britain needed to maintain the northern border, and its distance from Rome, the province also had its own form regarding the volatility of its legions. Later in the Empire they regularly supported those usurping the Imperial throne. Notable among the numerous examples were Clodius Albinus who usurped against Septimius Severus in AD 196 (the British legions suffering greatly here in his defeat by Severus at the Battle of Lugdunum in AD 197, Elliott, 2020, 26), Postumus and his Gallic Empire which lasted from AD 260 through to AD 274, the North Sea Empire of Carausius and Allectus from AD 286 to AD 296, the famous usurpation of Constantine in York in AD 306 (the only one that ultimately succeeded in the long run), the north-west European Empire of Magnetius from AD 350 to AD 353, the similar

Empire of Magnus Maximus from AD 380 to AD 384, and finally the usurpation of Constantine III in AD 407 which ultimately played a key role in Britain leaving the Empire.

However, earlier, we have an example of a full revolt by the British legions in their own name. This is in the reign of the mad and bad Commodus (AD 161 to AD 192), when at the time of his accession trouble had broken out among the newly formed Maeatae and Caledonian confederations north of Hadrian's Wall (Dio, 77.12). This was serious enough for the forts at Halton, Chesters, Rudchester and Corbridge within the province itself to be destroyed, with a Roman general and his bodyguard killed in the process. Commodus responded by ordering the British Governor Ulpius Marcellus to counter-attack in force. His two-year campaign north of the border was a great success, with three epigraphic inscriptions (one at Corbridge and two in Carlisle) referencing successful military action (Southern, 2013, 229). Commodus then received his seventh acclamation as *Imperator* and took the title *Britannicus* in AD 184. However, success came at a price among the three legions (still *legio* II *Augusta*, *legio* XX *Valeria Victrix* and *legio* VI *Victrix*). In AD 180 Marcellus had to put down some kind of military revolt when they were campaigning in the north, he earning a reputation as a strict disciplinarian in the process. Worse then followed after his ultimate victory, with the legions breaking out in a full rebellion against him in AD 184. Overthrown, he was recalled to Rome in disgrace, with the legions then trying to appoint a *legate* called Priscus as a usurper governor. He refused, with Dio (73.9) having him say 'I am no more an emperor than you are soldiers'. At this point Dio adds the legions then appointed a delegation of 1,500 legionaries (he calls them 'javelinmen') to travel to Britain to denounce the Praetorian Prefect Sextus Tigidius Perennis to Commodus over some slight they felt he had caused them. Dio (73.9) says they accused the Praetorian Prefect of plotting against the emperor, and after some convincing by his advisors, Commodus believed them. Perennis was handed over to the British soldiers who killed him along with his wife, two children and sister. It should be said that this sounds a most unlikely tale, though Birley (2005, 169) believes one explanation is that the legionaries were part of a task force set up to round up the deserters that were becoming endemic at the time in Gaul and Spain. He adds that this may have seemed a good way of dealing with some of Britain's most mutinous legionaries, and the whole story does fit the narrative of Britain's often-troublesome legions. A further hypothesis is that the troops were the *beneficiarii consularis* or *beneficiarii procuratoris* seconded from the legions in Britain to serve on the staff of the governor and procurator in London, in which case the delegation may have had some kind of official capacity.

Whatever the truth, the emperor quickly moved to restore order in Britain. First he ordered the *legates* of the three British legions to be cashiered, and then unusually replaced them with equestrian-rank officers promoted from within their own ranks (Kulikowski, 2016, 63). He then, as a stopgap, appointed Marcus Antius Crescens Calpurnianus as a temporary governor. Birley (2005, 171) argues this may have been because, with the three legionary *legates* deposed, he may have been the only Senatorial level aristocrat left in the province. Unsurprisingly, the Maeatae and Caledonians decided to take advantage of the disruption in the province and attacked the frontier again in early AD 185. However, they were once more defeated, showing the legions were still more or less intact, with more coins being minted to celebrate victory in Rome. This is interesting in itself as its shows that, even when mutinous, the British legions were still highly effective military units.

Commodus now turned to his ultra-reliable Imperial troubleshooter Publius Helvius Pertinax, later the first to sit on the Imperial throne in the AD 193 'Year of the Five Emperors', to settle matters once and for all in Britain as its new governor. Once in post, Pertinax got to work straight away. His top priority was to bring the legions to heal, and like Marcellus he followed a very strict line in discipline. Again this seems to have backfired, for although he won over two of the legions, the other mutinied again. The *Historia Augusta* (Pertinax, 3.6) says the trigger was actually his turning down an offer to usurp Commodus. It details: 'they wished to set up some other man as emperor, preferably Pertinax himself.'

Whatever the cause, the mutiny was a serious event, the troops ambushing him and leaving him for dead with his *singulares consularis* bodyguard slain. The *Historia Augusta* (3.9) then says that, after recovering, he punished the legion very severely, perhaps by ordering a decimation whereby one legionary in ten was executed by his fellow soldiers. This seemed to work as Dio (73.9) says Pertinax eventually 'quelled' the mutiny.

While the above is clearly not related to the earlier disappearance of *legio* IX *Hispana*, the analogy is sound given the clearly troubled relationship the British legions often had with the Imperial centre, whose principal representative in a province was the governor himself. One gets the impression from the primary sources that they were ready to support a serious usurper at the first opportunity, and when unhappy often took matters into their own hands. In fact both of the above scenarios would be believable if there was a single piece of evidence regarding the Hadrianic War and loss of the IXth legion hypothesis. However, as pointed out earlier, there isn't.

If for whatever reason *legio* IX *Hispana* met its demise as part of a Hadrianic War in London, then we can almost certainly date the event to the early AD 120s given *legio* VI *Victrix* arrived to replace it in AD 122 together with Hadrian and the new governor, Nepos. However, I add a note of caution here, this concerning the two potential governors in Britain at the time of any potential Hadrianic War in London in the early AD 120s. These were Nepos himself (if for some reason the IXth legion were still in the province when he arrived in this scenario, which I believe highly unlikely) and his predecessor, Falco. If either had been associated with such a dramatic reversal during their term as governor it would have had a serious impact on their future position in Roman society, as for example with Ulpius Marcellus detailed above who was recalled to Rome in disgrace after the later second century AD legionary revolt in Britain. The reality for both though is the opposite in that each, in their own ways, thrived. The Imperial troubleshooter, Falco, who seemingly resolved matters in the north as detailed in the previous chapter, was afterwards promoted to an even more prominent governorship. This was to the plum Senatorial posting in western Anatolia of Asia, deemed alongside Africa Proconsularis and Achaea one of three key posting for the most eminent and richest Senatorial families. Afterwards he happily retired to his family estates near the Roman city of Tusculum in the Alban Hills. He is last recorded hosting the then emperor Antoninus Pius and a young Marcus Aurelius on one of his farms where he showed them his experiments in arboriculture, the study, cultivation and management of trees, shrubs and vines (Birley, 2005, 119). Meanwhile Nepos proved a highly effective governor in Britain, his legacy to this day secured through his overseeing the building of Hadrian's Wall where his successful governorship is attested by the copious number of military inscriptions in his name. He chose not to hold another senior position and happily retired to his house on the fashionable Esquiline Hill in central Rome, an easy walk away from the *Forum Romanum*. During his retirement he was made one of the *augures publici* priests who practised augury, the interpretation of the will of the gods by studying the flight of flocks of birds. He also had a stake in a major brickworks in the Imperial capital given many bricks used there in this period feature the stamp of his family. The only blot on his otherwise impeccable lifelong career along the *cursus honorum* was when, late in life, he fell out for some reason with his former great friend Hadrian, though this was in no way related to his time in Britain.

Closing Discussion

Above I have set out Perring's compelling argument that there was some kind of major event in Roman London in the AD 120s, which he dubs the Hadrianic War, based on his interpretation of the Walbrook skulls, Hadrianic fire and building of the Cripplegate fort. I believe he makes a very strong case that this did indeed occur. In this context I have reviewed in this chapter whether the disappearance of *legio* IX *Hispana* could have been linked to such an event, either as a victim of the revolt, or as its protagonist (or at least one of them). Sadly, as mentioned and like so many things regarding the IXth legion's demise, there is not a shred of evidence for this. However, as discussed, analogously and anecdotally it still remains a possibility that should be taken seriously, especially in the context of a subsequent *damnatio memoriae*.

Chapter 5

The Rhine and Danube Frontier

B efore the 1960s Britain was the sole focus of any research, academic or otherwise, regarding the mysterious fate of legio IX *Hispana*, with no serious archaeologist or historian looking elsewhere in the Empire for an answer. Then, in 1967, the leading Roman historian of his day published a new book that included a tantalizing new piece of evidence. This was Sheppard Frere, then Professor of the Archaeology of the Roman Empire at Oxford University, with the first edition of his groundbreaking *Britannia: A History of Roman Britain*. In an almost throwaway comment, he wrote a most iconoclastic sentence regarding the fate of the IXth legion, saying (1967, 139):

> ...there remains also the probability that the legion was withdrawn
> from Britain at some date between AD 108 and AD 122 and that it
> perished unrecorded later on, either in Judea in (AD) 132 – (AD)
> 135 or later still [see Chapter 6 for discussion in this regard] or later
> still. Evidence which might support such a view is the discovery
> of a tile-stamp and a mortarium stamp of legio IX (Hispana) at
> Nijmegen (Roman Noviomagus Batavorum) in Holland...these
> finds certainly suggest that the Ninth may have been stationed
> in Nijmegen for a short period after (AD) 108, the latest date
> for its presence at York, and perhaps from about (AD) 121.

Given the finding of the IXth legion stamps in the Netherlands was until then only known to a few local academics, the publication of their existence in what became the generation defining and best selling book about Roman Britain opened up a whole new world of possibilities concerning its demise. Therefore, in this chapter I follow the evidence trail to the northern continental frontiers of the Empire to test the hypothesis that the legion may have been lost there. To do that, I first examine the *legio* IX *Hispana* stamps found in the Netherlands, before detailing the Empire's provincial structure from the North Sea to the Black Sea along the Rhine and Danube to provide context. I then consider the Germanic tribes north of the continental frontier who would have been the legion's opponents if based there. Next, I look at Roman military activity in the continental north in the early and mid-second century AD to determine whether *legio* IX *Hispana* was presented with opportunities for martial glory on a scale anywhere near the legions in the north faced there in the previous century. That was certainly the case later, with the Marcomannic Wars that broke out north of the Danube in AD 166. This is the subject of the last section in this chapter, before I once more finish with a closing discussion.

The Netherlands Tile Mystery

Frere's mention of the Netherlands IXth legion stamps would have gone unnoticed if one reviewer had not alighted on it. This was Denis Henry, then assistant Master at Stonyhurst College in Lancashire. His review in the *Classical Philology* academic periodical was soon picked up by others, and before long many researchers were turning to the Rhine frontier as a new location to look for evidence of *legio* IX *Hispana*'s disappearance (Campbell, 2018, 122).

The new evidence of the legionary stamps that Frere had come across was first locally publicized in 1964 at the Sixth International 'Limes-Kongress' forum for Roman frontier studies. Here attendees were shown a fragment of a Roman *tegula* roof tile. This had been excavated in 1959 in the final occupation layer of the barrack blocks of the Roman legionary fortress in the Hunerberg region of the city of Nijmegen on the lower Rhine. To the amazement of all this featured the stamp of the IXth legion.

Such ceramic building materials (CBM) were a ubiquitous feature of the experience of *Romanitas* across the Empire, with a wide variety of different types of tile and brick used as key components in many diverse construction techniques. One of the most common types of CBM found on Roman archaeological sites are *tegulae* (as with that in Nijmegen) and *imbrex* roof tiles. These designs originated in Classical Greece and were adopted by the Romans to replace the previously used wooden shingles. They were used to roof every type of structure in the Empire, from private dwellings to the finest palaces and temples, the design so simple yet effective that on many of these latter fine public buildings the clay originals were replaced with tiles made from marble and even bronze.

The *tegula* (after the Greek *solenes*) was a plain flat tile of variable size, sometimes as large as one metre square, with a raised flange along two parallel edges. These were laid flat side-by-side on the roof, with the two flanges from adjacent tiles set next to each other. Meanwhile the *imbrex* (after the Greek *kalupter*) was a semi-cylindrical roof tile that was half-pipe in shape. This tapered gently from a larger end to a narrower end and was laid vertically over the *tegulae* flanges, with the narrow lower end of one fitting into the larger end of the *tegula* immediately below. When this dual tile arrangement was suitably imbricated in place there was little need for any further waterproofing or the use of a sealant. Roofs featuring *tegulae* and *imbrices* were often surrounded by *antefixae* (from the Latin for fasten before or below). These were vertical blocks that terminated the rows of *imbrices* on the roof and were often finely carved, particularly on grand stone built structures where they could form part of the *anthemion* ornamental surround.

The Romans manufactured a wide variety of other different types of CBM, including building bricks by the million (such as those manufactured in the brickworks in Rome owned by the Nepos family as detailed in Chapter 4), hollow voussoir box tiles used to build roof arches, floor tiles, small square *tesserae* for use in tessellated floors and mosaics, *pilae* tiles used in hypocaust stacks to support floors in underfloor heating systems, and box-flue tiles used within wall cavities to allow heat to circulate upwards, once again as part of a hypocaust system.

It was common across the Empire for the manufacturers of all kinds of CBM to stamp them, this identifying the brickyard where they were made. In the case of private manufacturers an excellent example can be found in Kent in Britain. Here, at Plaxtol in the west of the modern county a family by the name of *Cabriabanu* stamped tiles which were then used down the Darent Valley through to the Thames Estuary, and then into London. Examples have been found at sites including Lullingstone and Darenth in Kent, and at Bishopsgate in the provincial capital (Davies, 2009, 262). Nearby, on a far larger scale, a huge Imperially-owned brickyard was operated by the *Classis Britannica* regional fleet in Britain at Fairlight in the coastal region of the Weald. This produced all of the brick and tile needed to facilitate the enormous iron-manufacturing operation in the Weald, also operated by the *Classis Britannica* as a giant *metalla* extractive industry that supplied all of the iron to the Roman military in the north of the province from the later first century AD to the mid-third century AD. Hundreds of examples of CBM stamped with the acronym CLBR have been found across the region, and indeed throughout the South East, including in London. Brodribb (1979, 141) argued that the official stamp of the regional fleet was used on these State-produced tiles for prestige reasons, and to ensure their quality. In that regard it is noteworthy that the stamps always appear on the upper sides of *tegulae*, *imbrices* and floor tiles (the stamp also appearing on brick, hypocaust *pilae* and box-flue tiles) rather than their underside, and would thus have been externally visible.

Coming back to the IXth legion, they similarly stamped the tiles manufactured by the specialist tilers who served within the ranks of its legionaries. The process of brick and tile manufacture was standardized across the Empire, with only a few regional variations. McWhirr and Viner (1978, 360) summarised the Roman tile manufacturing process as detailed below:

- Clay excavated, usually in the autumn.
- Clay allowed to weather over the winter, being broken down by frost and rain.
- Clay prepared for manufacture, with aggregate sometimes being added and then the finished product being covered until needed.
- Tiles made using a wooden frame, mold or former, when any modifications such as the flange on *tegulae* would be added.
- Tiles left to harden in the open air, sometimes being stamped. Given the tiles were left in the open at this stage of the process, this often led to them featuring footprints of wild animals and birds.
- Tiles fired or burnt in a kiln or clamp and then stored. The iron oxides in the clay, and the conditions of firing, determined their colour.
- Tiles transported to buyer and used.

Back to the Netherlands on the trail of the IXth legion, in the late 1950s and early 1960s the excavations at Nijmegen had revealed a large part of the 16 ha legionary fortress there. This was first constructed around AD 70 following the defeat of the Batavian Revolt in the Rhine Delta. The initial fort was built with a timber palisade atop an earthen rampart, with a surrounding double ditch. However, within a generation this was replaced with a far grander stone-built fortress, analogously similar in manner to the replacement of York's timber original with its own stone walled fortress. Both the wooden and later stone-built fortresses at Nijmegen were home to *legio* X *Gemina*, one of the most famous legions in Roman history. This had been founded by Julius Caesar when governor of the province of Hispania Ulteriro in 62 BC, later becoming his personal elite legion. We know that the legionaries themselves participated in the building of the stone fortress because they left inscriptions dated to AD 101 and AD 102 in the nearby quarries at Brohltal, with other inscriptions there showing they were joined in the task by the legionaries of two other legions, *legio* I *Flavia Minervia pia fidelis* and *legio* VI *Victrix*. However, change was on the way and within two years the Xth legion had been called away eastwards to the Danube frontier where it later participated in Trajan's Second Dacian War from AD 105 to AD 106. It was never to return to Nijmegen, the fortress there instead occupied by a composite force comprising *vexillations* from the three legions based in Britain as a stopgap, these including legionaries from *legio* IX *Hispana*.

The finding of the initial IXth legion stamped *tegula* from the site was quickly followed by over 100 more being identified, these on various types of brick and tile, with others being found at the nearby Roman brick works at De Holdeum. These were all found with contemporary coins and pottery that enabled them to be dated to the reigns of Trajan and the early part of Hadrian's (Campbell, 2018, 124). Of note here, the stamps on the Nijmegen brick and tile were all styled *legio* VIIII *Hispana*, while all the stamped CBM from the legion's home in York is stamped *legio* IX *Hispana*. The only places in Britain which feature the VIIII stamp are at the Roman brick works at Scalesceugh in Cumbria, and the nearby northerly forts at Carlisle and Stanwix (Roman *Petriana*). Given the similar use of the numeral format VIIII there, it seems more than likely that it was a vexillation from this location in the far north west of Britain that travelled to the Netherlands. Interestingly, we can place this vexillation back in its home base of York at least for a short time in AD 108 given the famous inscription from the *Porta Principalis Sinistra* also styles the legion VIIII Hispana. Back to Nijmegen, we can also put a definitive closing date on the composite force staying there. This was around AD 120 when legio XXX Ulpia Victrix arrived to take over occupation of the fortress. It was to remain there until the legionary base was abandoned five years later.

For completeness here, it should be noted that British archaeologist Miles Russell has claimed that the tile stamps found at Nijmegen date to much earlier. He says (2011, 40) that they 'seem to date to the 80s AD, when detachments of the IXth were indeed on the Rhine fighting Germanic tribes.' I personally have found no datable evidence to place the IXth legion at or near Nijmegen at this time.

The other piece of archaeological evidence presented at the 1964 Sixth International 'Limeskongress' regarding *legio* IX *Hispana* was the rim of a coarseware Roman *mortarium* mixing bowl. Originally found at the site of the de Holdeurn Roman tile-works in 1938, this had gone missing during the Second World War and was only re-found two year's before the conference took place. The bowl also featured the stamp of the IXth legion on its rim, again in the VIIII format. No similar item has been found in Britain, where the Roman military relied on civilian manufacturers for most of their ceramic day-to-day requirements including *mortarium* (Campbell, 2018, 126).

Meanwhile, in 1957 more evidence had emerged of the presence of the IXth legion in Germania Inferior, but again this didn't come to light until much later. This was in the form of an altar to Apollo found at Aachen-Burtscheid (Roman *Aquae Granni*) in the west of the province, where the local sulpher springs were exploited as a Roman health spa. The inscription on the altar named Lucius Latinius Macer, *praefectus castrorum* camp prefect of the IXth legion (interestingly not styled VIIII *Hispana,* indicating he was unlikely to have been part of the Cumbrian vexillation deployment), as the man who had set it up to celebrate the healing powers of the waters there. However, we have no dating evidence for the altar and it seems likely this was an individual officer travelling there with a health condition. Meanwhile, another memorial to an officer of the IXth legion has also been linked to Germania Inferior. This was Marcus Cocceius Severus, *primus pilus* senior centurion of the legion. His commemoration is today in Turin Museum, though I can find no evidence to link him to the Rhine frontier.

Finally in the region, most recently a silver-plated bronze pendant was found in the 1990s that was originally part of a *phalera* Roman military medal. On its reverse was inscribed *legio* IX *Hispana* (again not VIIII *Hispana*), though once more there is no context to explain how it came to be lost in Germania Inferior.

Taken together, the archaeological evidence from all of the above seems to show that a specific vexillation of the IXth legion, probably one based near Carlisle and using the legionary numeral form VIIII, was deployed to Nijmegen between AD 104 at the earliest and AD 120 at the latest, as part of a composite force sent there to replace the Xth legion. To date, there is no evidence at all to suggest that this was the entire IXth legion, or even a significant part of it. Therefore, to determine if there was a possibility that the whole legion was deployed in this way (either at this time or later), I now move on to consider the northern *limes* along the Rhine and Danube where any legionaries of *legio* IX *Hispana* would have operated.

The Rhine-Danube Frontier

Gaul and Germany featured rich provinces, especially during the Principate Empire, which illustrated how quickly indigenous territories could be culturally assimilated into the Roman way of life. Real Roman interest here began in the mid-second century BC through mercantile engagement with the Greek colony of Marseille (Greek and Roman *Massilia*). Soon a treaty was signed to protect the town from Gauls to the north, Iberians to the west and Carthaginians across the Mediterranean. Further Roman interest in the region led to the creation of a new province in 122 BC along the Mediterranean coast called Transalpine Gaul (also known as Provincia Nostra, this translating as 'our province'), it later being renamed Gallia Narbonensis after its regional capital of Narbonne, founded by the Romans in 118 BC.

This large province then became the springboard for Julius Caesar's conquest of Gaul when he became its governor in 58 BC, he also taking the role in Cisalpine Gaul (the far north of Italy either side of the Po River). In pursuit of glory and wealth, Caesar lost no time in campaigning north and by the end of the decade had reduced the Gallic kingdoms there to Roman vassalage. From that time they became new Roman provinces, these revised by Augustus in 22 BC, with more territory to the north and east being added later. By the beginning of the second century AD there were nine provinces in the region, these being:

- Germania Inferior in the Rhine Delta and lower Rhine valley.
- Germania Superior in the upper Rhine valley.
- Gallia Belgica, broadly the area of modern Belgium.
- Gallia Lugdunensis, a broad strip through modern central France ranging from Brittany in the west to the provincial capital of Lyon (Roman *Lugdunum*) in the east.
- Gallia Aquitania along the Bay of Biscay.
- Gallia Narbonensis in modern Provence, a Senatorial province.
- Three small provinces bordering Gallia Narbonensis and Italy, from north to south Alpes Graiae et Poeninae, Alpes Cottiae and Alpes Maritimae.

This large region featured distinct cultural and economic differences across its wide geography. The far north and east were more militarized given the provinces there featured the *limes Germanicus* separating the world of Rome from *barbaricum* (as viewed by contemporaries) to the north. The legionary fortress at Nijmegen detailed above was for a time a key component of this.

Further south, the northern Gallic provinces were nicknamed Gallia Comata, meaning 'long haired Gaul'. This territory featured fine quality agricultural land heavily exploited for arable and fruit crops, including the fine quality wines associated with the region to this day. It was also the home to a dense network of *fabricae* state-run manufactories around Autun (Roman *Augustodunum*) in the modern Bourgogne-Franche-Comté region of modern France. These produced much of the equipment for the military in the region. As the Principate progressed, this region of non-Mediterranean Gaul also developed a reputation for social conservatism in its arts and culture, and was home to a substantial commercial class whose goods were traded across the Empire. Pre-eminent among these at the time of *legio* IX *Hispana* were the Samian Ware ceramic works at La Graufesenque near Millau, Lezoux and Clermont-Ferrand. These made high-quality tablewares using a glossy red surface slip which was popular across the Empire. Much of this fine pottery has been found in early York from the period when the IXth legion was resident, and also across the Ouse in the *canabae* civilian settlement there.

By way of contrast the far south of Gaul was far more urbanized, reflecting the longevity of large-scale stone-built settlement there dating back to the early period of Greek expansion in the western Mediterranean (Cornell and Matthews, 1982, 128).

In addition to Lyon, key cities in Gaul and Germany included Cologne (Roman *Colonia Agrippina*) with its major legionary fortress that later became the provincial capital of Germania Inferior, Mainz (Roman *Mogontiacum*) with its legionary fortress which was the provincial capital of Germania Superior, Reims (Roman *Durocortorum*) which was the provincial capital of Gallia Belgica, Narbonne (Roman *Narbo*) which was the provincial capital of Narbonensis, and the key Mediterranean port city of Marseille (Roman *Marsilia*).

The Rhine frontier featured a dense chain of fortifications to maintain the northern *limes* that ran for over 570km from the Rhine Delta to the Danube. The key bases were its legionary fortresses, with sites at Nijmegen (until abandoned, see above), Xanten (Roman *Vetera*) and Neuss (Roman *Novaesium*) joining those already detailed at Mainz and Cologne. A further 55 other forts of various sizes, and over 1,000 watchtowers completed the defensive frontier here.

The *limes Germanicus* was divided into three sections, these being:

- The Lower Germanic *limes* extending from the North Sea coast to the Rheinbrohl municipality in the Rhineland Palatinate of modern Germany.
- The Upper Germanic *limes* from Rheinbrohl to Lorch am Rhein near Darmstadt in Hesse.
- The Rhaetian *limes*, with only the section on the Rhine detailed here, the Danubian length covered in the next section.

As the second century AD progressed the *limes* of the first two sections became home to some of the crack legions of the Roman Empire. These included *legio* XXX *Ulpia Victrix* (which moved from Germania Superior to eventually replace *legio* X *Gemina*), *legio* VIII *Augusta* and *legio* XXII *Primogenia pia fidelis* in Germania Inferior, and *legio* I *Minervia pia fidelis* in Germania Superior. The military establishment here also featured the usual complement of auxiliaries, and the *Classis Germanica* regional fleet. This navy was responsible for patrolling the Rhine from deep within the continental interior at its confluence with the Vinxtbach stream in the modern Rhineland Palatinate through to the Zuiderzee and the North Sea coastlines in the Rhine Delta area. It also had responsibility for the Rhine's many tributaries, and was later tasked with patrolling the Rivers Meuse and Scheldt. Together the legions, auxiliaries and fleet faced off against multiple threats to the north, including the Germanic Saxons, Thuringii and Alamanni (see below).

Moving eastwards to the Danube frontier, this was another key military border zone that featured nine provinces, these being (west to east):

- Raetia, the province linking the Rhine and Danube.
- Noricum.
- Pannonia Superior.
- Pannonia Inferior.
- Dalmatia.
- Moesia Superior.
- Dacia.
- Moesia Inferior.
- Thracia.

This region of the Empire was particularly complex in terms of wealth and culture, with Cornell and Matthews (1982, 140) explaining that:

> The Danubian provinces, taken together, span the whole range of Roman civilization, from the settled Celtic tribes of the west and the urbanized seaboard of Dalmatia to the ancient Greek cities of the Black Sea coast. The Thracian regions east of the pass of Succi were Greek-speaking and their cities have Greek names. (Meanwhile) the 'latinisation' of Dacia, after an occupation of 150 years, is actively attested by modern Romanian.

The key cities of the region included Augsberg (Roman *Augusta Vindelicorum*) which was the provincial capital of Raetia, Wels (Roman *Ovilava*) which was the provincial capital of Noricum, Vienna (Roman *Vindobona*), Roman *Carnuntum* which was the provincial capital of the vital province of Pannonia Superior where Septimius Severus was later proclaimed Emperor (Elliott, 2018a, 100), Split (Roman *Aspalathos*) on the Adriatic coast where Diocletian later built his palace when he retired, Budapest (Roman *Aquincum*) which was the provincial capital of Pannonia Inferior, Kostolac (Roman *Viminacium*) which was the provincial capital of Moesia Superior, Roman *Ulpia Traiana Sarmizegetusa* which was the provincial capital of the redoubt province of Dacia following Trajan's two wars of conquest there, Constanta (Roman *Tomis*) which was the provincial capital of Moesia Inferior, and Roman *Perinthus* which was the provincial capital of Thracia.

As with the Rhine, the Danubian provinces were defined by the northern *limes* here which ran for much of the river's 2,860km length. Cornell and Matthews (1982, 140) call these the backbone of the Empire, with the lengthy fortifications there divided into four sections:

- The Rhaetian *limes*, here only the section on the Danube.
- The Noric *limes* in Noricum.
- The Pannonian *limes* in Pannonia Superior and Inferior.
- The Moesian *limes* in Moesia Superior and Inferior, running down to the Black Sea. From AD 106 after Trajan's Dacian conquests until the province was abandoned during the reign of Aurelian (AD 270 to AD 275) this section actually ran far to the north, encompassing the whole Dacian salient standing proud to the north of the Danube.

As the second century progressed the Danubian *limes* was home to some of the most experienced legions of the Empire, these all later battle-hardened during the Marcomannic Wars (see below). These were based in a string of legionary fortresses along the frontier, ranging from Vienna in the west to *Troesmis* in the east. By the late second century AD the legions here included *legio* III *Italica concurs* in Raetia, *legio* II *Italica* in Noricum, *legio* XIV *Gemina Martia*, *legio* I *Adiutrix pia fidelis* and later *legio* X *Gemina* in Pannonia Superior (which stayed on the Danube frontier after its deployment from Nijmegen in Germania Inferior, see above), *legio* II *Adiutrix pia fidelis* in Pannonia inferior, *legio* IV *Flavia felix* and *legio* VII *Claudia pia fidelis* in Moesia Superior, *legio* XIII *Gemina pia fidelis* in Dacia and *legio* I *Italica*, *legio* V *Macedonia* and *legio* XI *Claudia pia fidelis* in Moesia Inferior. As with the Rhine frontier, they were joined by an equivalent number of auxiliaries, while the two regional fleets here were the *Classis Pannonica* on the upper Danube and the *Classis Flavia Moesica* on the lower Danube. The latter also had responsibility for the western and northern stretches of the Black Sea and controlled access from there to the Mediterranean.

These legions faced off against yet more aggressive northern neighbours. These included the Germanic Marcomanni, Juthungi and Quadi, various Sarmatian tribes including the Iazyges and Roxalani, remnant Dacians and Bastarnae, and later various Gothic confederations. All proved tough opponents in the Marcomannic Wars.

The Germans and Sarmatians

The Germanic peoples of continental northern Europe were a major opponent of the later Roman Republic and Empire, and were identified by the Romans themselves as a distinct ethnic group when compared to their southerly Gallic neighbours. The Germans originated in the westward Indo-European migrations from the Pontic-Eurasian steppe and by 3,300 BC had split off from the main migratory group to head north-west towards the southern coastline of the Baltic Sea. They are often referred to as Teutonic, Suebian or Gothic in antiquarian literature, with the latter two terms coming to refer to specific Germanic peoples.

Writing at the end of the early first century AD, Strabo (7.1.2/ 3) provides contemporary insight into how the Romans viewed the Germans, saying:

> Now the parts beyond the Rhenus (Rhine), immediately after the country of the Gauls, slope towards the east and are occupied by

the Germans, who, though they vary slightly from the Celtic stock in that they are wilder, taller, and have yellower hair, are in all other respects similar, for in build, habits, and modes of life they are such as I have said the Gauls are. And I also think that it was for this reason that the Romans assigned to them the name Germani, as though they wished to indicate thereby that they were 'genuine' Gauls, for in the language of the Romans germani means genuine.

The last point above, referencing the Germans as 'genuine' Gauls, is most likely a literary device by Strabo reflecting what he believed was their superior martial prowess following the sanguineous conquest of Gaul by Caesar in the 50s BC and the ease with which the Gallic provinces were later incorporated into the Empire.

The Germanic tribes known to the Romans originated in homelands in southern Scandinavia and the far north of Germany where they had been settled for over 2,000 years following the earlier Indo-European migrations. The later Republican Romans described four broad Germanic groupings, the first being the Ingaevones. These comprised the Cimbri, Teutones and Chauci tribes. These were based in the Jutland Peninsula, Frisia and northern Saxony. Another early Germanic grouping were the Irimones, these situated further to the east between the Oder and Elbe rivers. A third grouping were called the Istvaeones, later located on the Rhine and around the Weser. The final group were called the Herminones, comprising the Suebi (from whom the Marcomanni were descended, see below, as well as the Quadi, Semnones and Lombards), Chatti and Herunduri tribes, these later dominating the Elbe region. All four of these early terms for the large tribal collectives gradually fell out of use as individual tribes came to be known to the Romans.

Once the German tribes began their migrations south from their original southern Scandinavian and north German homelands they carved out new territories between the Rhine and the Pripet Marshes in modern Belarus. There they slowly consolidated until they eventually coalesced into the huge confederations which caused so much trouble to the later Roman Empire, particularly after the Hunnic expansions westward from the Central Asian steppe drove them increasingly against the Roman *limes* along the Rhine and Danube. By then six major confederations had emerged, these being the western Visigoths, eastern Ostrogoths, Vandals, Burgundians, Langobards and Franks, all playing a key role in the fall of the Roman Empire in the west.

Rome's first real engagement with the Germans was in the Cimbrian Wars. This began in the later second century BC when the Cimbri, Teutones and their Ambrones allies migrated south into Gaul where they fought a series of wars with the Gallic tribes there. In 113 BC they invaded the lands of the Taurisci, a confederation of Gallic tribes in Noricum. These were Roman allies and the Senate decided to send an army to their aid. The Roman force was commanded by the consul Gnaeus Papirius Carbo who requested the Cimbri retreat. They did so but were deceived by the Romans who set an ambush for them. The Cimbri found out and attacked the Romans first at the Battle of Noreia. Carbo's treachery backfired spectacularly with the Romans suffering a huge defeat.

This engagement marked the beginning of the Cimbrian War that lasted until 101 BC. The Germans could have attacked Italy at this point but chose instead to head west to invade Roman Transalpine Gaul in 109 BC. A new Roman army under Marcus Junius Silanus was sent to intercept, but again the legions were comprehensively defeated. Next, in 107 BC, the Romans were again defeated, this time by the Gallic Tigurini tribe who were allies of the Cimbri. The name of this battle is unrecorded, but shortly afterwards the Romans again engaged the Tigurini, this time at the Battle of Burdigala (modern Bordeaux). The result was the same, total defeat, with the consul Lucius Cassius Longinus Ravalla killed.

Much worse was to follow. In 105 BC the Romans resolved to settle matters with the Cimbri once and for all. The new consul Gnaeus Mallius Maximus gathered a huge force of 80,000 legionaries and allies. However, when the two sides met on the banks of the Rhône at Arausio this was also crushed, with the river choked with dead legionaries for many days afterwards. Here the Romans lost an enormous 60,000 legionaries, their largest loss since Cannae against Hannibal in the Second Punic War.

Panic now gripped Rome, with the phrase *terror cimbricus* being used to describe the mood of the people. Roman grit showed through, however, this time in the form of the great political and military leader Marius. Elected consul in 104 BC, he gathered a new army to counter any Cimbri invasion of Italy, basing it in southern Gaul. There he waited, training new legions and being elected consul again in 103 BC and 102 BC. In the latter year he finally confronted the Cimbri's allies who had started to move south. At the Battle of Aquae Sextiae in Aix-en-Provence he destroyed a combined force of Teutones and Ambrones, inflicting 90,000 casualties on the Germans and capturing 20,000 including the Teutones king Teutobod.

Marius was elected consul again in 101 BC and in that year was able to tackle the Cimbri head on. The enormous tribe had begun to move south and for the first time penetrated the Alpine passes, entering Cisalpine Gaul. The Roman force there of 20,000 withdrew behind the Po River, allowing the Cimbri to devastate the fertile countryside to its north. However, this gave Marius time to arrive with his legions which he positioned to the Germans' rear, blocking their escape routes back to Gaul. With 54,000 men at his disposal he then led the combined Roman army to an immense victory at the Battle of Vercellae near to the confluence of the Po and the Sesia rivers. Here his newly reformed legions, detailed in Chapter 1, proved to be superior to the Cimbri warriors. Defeat for the Germans was total, they allegedly losing up to 160,000 men, with 60,000 captured including a large number of camp followers. Soon the slave markets of Rome were overflowing.

The Romans next encountered the Germans during Caesar's conquest of Gaul, in which the original IXth legion played a full part (see Chapter 1). In the first instance he campaigned against the Suebi in his second campaign of 58 BC after defeating the Helvetti. The native Gauls presented him with his opportunity for more glory when their tribal leaders gathered to congratulate him over his earlier successes. When this meeting took place a number from eastern Gaul tearfully begged him to intervene against a huge group of Suebi who had crossed the Moselle at the request of the Gallic Sequani tribe. The latter had asked for help from the Germans when fighting a neighbouring tribe. Once this conflict was resolved, however, the Suebi then refused to return home. Some 120,000 were now camped in eastern Gaul where they were exacting tribute and taking hostages from all of the regional tribes.

Caesar jumped at the chance for another victory. In the first instance he sent word to the Suebi king Ariovistus that he wanted to meet with him to discuss the situation, suggesting they gather halfway between their two locations. The German king declined. Caesar then sent another message, this time with clear instructions for Ariovistus. This included not bringing any more Germans into Gaul, refraining from any further raiding and returning the Gallic hostages to their tribes. He threatened to use force if his demands were not met. Unsurprisingly, Ariovistus refused again, with the Germans raiding further into Gaul to reinforce the message. Caesar also received word that thousands more Suebi were now massing further east, waiting to cross the Rhine and Moselle to join the Germans already in Gaul. He decided to act quickly, marching his whole force eastwards at a rapid pace. The Suebi countered by moving on the Sequani capital of Besançon (Roman *Vesontio*), prompting Caesar to move even more quickly in a series of day and night marches. He arrived there first and installed a garrison before allowing his troops a few days rest.

Eventually, after much marching and counter marching trying to bring the Suebi to battle, Caesar forced a meeting engagement, today known as the Battle of Vosges. Here he won a huge victory, with no quarter given and the German army massacred. Ariovistus was one of the few to escape, only to disappear from history. The additional Suebi waiting to cross the Rhine and Moselle now returned home, with the slave markets in Rome again overflowing with German captives. Caesar later campaigned at least twice more against the Suebi and their allies during his Gallic conquests, twice famously building fine military bridges across the Rhine to raid their territory, but each time met little real resistance (Elliott, 2019, 112). After his final conquest of Gaul in 52 BC the Germans then showed little interest in interfering in the region again as the Romans created their new provinces there, often serving as mercenaries in Roman armies as the Republic spiralled into its final series of civil wars that saw Octavian emerge the victor.

Prior to the IXth legion's time in Britain, the final major Roman engagement with the Germans was the disastrous defeat of Varus and his three legions in AD 9 while campaigning in the Teutoburg Forest, the vast range of low, forested hills in the modern German states of Lower Saxony and North Rhine-Westphalia. Roman historians specifically noted here the brutality shown to the legionary and auxiliary captives after this epic defeat, in particular to senior Roman officers.

The Romans believed the Germans were more democratic than their Gallic neighbours, with their armies largely comprised of part-time foot warriors led by a mounted aristocrat elite who often fought as cavalry. These mounted troops were viewed by the Romans as being just as fierce as their Gallic counterparts. At the time of *legio* IX *Hispana* most German cavalry carried only short spears, javelins and a square shield, the very well off also having long iron slashing swords, a helmet and perhaps armour (most often a chainmail hauberk). However, German mounted troops were most feared by the Romans due to a particular innovation they were known for in the ancient world. This was the deployment of picked light infantry armed with bows and javelins among their ranks to disrupt opposing cavalry and foot formations, continually harassing their opponents once the German cavalry engaged in combat.

Meanwhile, German line-of-battle infantry were even more feared by the Romans than their cavalry, with contemporary authors noting they fought in closer formation than the Gauls, with less emphasis on individual verve and more on cooperation. Most German foot troops were armed with short spears, long daggers and axes. Some were famed in the Roman world for specific types of weaponry only associated with one confederation or tribe, for example the Franks with their fearsome *francisca* throwing axe. This was used in much the same way as a Native American tomahawk. In terms of their defensive panoply, in Roman sculpture German foot troops are most often shown carrying a square shield, and almost never wearing armour or a helmet.

The Germans proved pragmatic opponents, often withdrawing in the face of stiff opposition, as Caesar experienced when trying to bring the Suebi to battle. They also proved experts at picking terrain to suit their strengths, as shown by Arminius against Varus. When they did eventually engage, both cavalry and infantry relied on a fierce charge to break the enemy's battle line. In this regard, German troops of all kinds were known for their blood chilling war cry called the *barritus*. This started in a low voice and rose to a high-pitched chilling scream. Many Roman units later adopted this in the Dominate phase of Empire when large numbers of Germans were recruited into the legions and auxiliary units, and German leaders came to dominate the Roman officer class.

The Germans campaigning along the Danube in the second century AD were often joined by their Sarmatian neighbours in battle. These peoples were originally of Iranian stock who migrated from Central Asia through the Ural mountains between the sixth and fourth century BC. They eventually settled across most of southern European Russia, the Ukraine and the eastern Balkans. Like the Scythians with whom they were closely related, the Sarmatians were best known for their skilled horsemanship which came to dominate their style of warfare. This featured highly mobile columns of lance-armed shock cavalry, their principal weapon the *kontos* lance 4m long that was held two-handed. This was so long it had to be braced across the rider's thighs and was much feared by the Romans. The mounted warriors were also frequently armed with powerful composite bows, with the better-off warriors clad in long coats of scalemail and chainmail armour. Key tribes faced by the Romans included the Iazyges and Roxalani who played a major role in the Marcomannic Wars (see below).

Roman Foreign Policy in the Mid-Second Century AD

A key consideration in looking at opportunities for *legio* IX *Hispana* to campaign beyond the Rhine and Danube is Hadrian's abrupt switch from Trajan's expansionist foreign policy to one of consolidation, this continuing through the long reign of Antoninus Pius (who never left Italy while emperor). As Cornell and Matthews (1982, 103) detail:

> In temperament Hadrian was very different from his predecessor. Trajan was a plain soldier, Hadrian a restless, inquiring intellectual with a deep love of Greek culture.

In effect, from this point until the accession of Marcus Aurelius and Lucius Verus in AD 161, it was the norm for the legions and auxilia to remain within the borders of the Empire. Up to this point the policy of basing each Principate legion in legionary fortresses at intervals around the fringes of the Empire had had a dual purpose, namely to provide a springboard for campaigns of Imperial expansion as with Trajan's Dacian and eastern campaigns, and to defend Roman territory (Cornell and Matthews, 1982, 81). However, from now until the Roman-Parthian and Marcomannic Wars of the AD 160s and 170s detailed below, the focus was purely on the latter. Such passivity had serious implications for the military through the middle of the second century AD, with Kean and Frey (2005, 83) explaining:

> The obvious flaw in Hadrian's policy of staying within the borders of the Empire and avoiding engagement in foreign wars was that a static army loses its edge, grows demoralized, and becomes a potential source of trouble. Further, that the warlike tribes massing against the frontiers might interpret the Romans hiding behind their fortifications as a sign of weakness.

However, both Hadrian and Antoninus Pius were lucky in that Trajan's earlier martial prowess was such that the tribes north of the Rhine and Danube, and the Parthians in the east, remained relatively passive during both of their reigns. In fact the only parts of the Empire where we still see large-scale military campaigning in the mid-second century AD is in Judea, where the 'bar Kokhba' third Jewish Revolt broke out in AD 132, and in Britain. The former is covered in detail in Chapter 6, but the latter deserves further explanation here given the context provided regarding the province in the aftermath of *legio* IX *Hispana*'s destruction or departure, and also as a comparator to the relative inaction in the continental north elsewhere.

Britannia was relatively peaceful in the immediate aftermath of the events of the AD 110s in the north and potentially the AD 120s in London. However, when Hadrian died in AD 138 trouble broke out again almost immediately and the new emperor Antoninus Pius ordered renewed campaigning in the province yet again. Thus within a year the new Governor Quintus Lollius Urbicus was in the north, there to oversee a significant upgrading of the logistical infrastructure in the region to support a new northern campaign. This included the refurbishment of key fortifications at sites such as Corbridge, Risingham and High Rochester. We have little visibility of the campaigns north of Hadrian's Wall that followed but they were over by AD 142, with coins being minted to commemorate a famous victory. The route taken in this campaign above the Solway Firth-Tyne line can be tracked through the rebuilding of the old Flavian forts, for example Newstead near Melrose, and the additional building of new ones, the advance clearly being rapid and decisive. Any native opposition was easily overcome, perhaps indicating that the reason behind this particular venture north was more for Imperial aggrandizement than because of a renewed and dangerous threat. The advance northwards was also accompanied by the renovation of the Flavian military harbours that had supported the campaigns of Agricola, and again also the construction of new ones. In the Clyde these included Dumbarton on the north shore and Lurg Moor and Bishopton on the south shore, while in the Forth they included Inveresk, Cramond and Carriden. Inveresk, where Dere Street crosses the River Esk before heading westwards to Cramond, is particularly important in the context of this campaign as two contemporary pieces of epigraphy in the form of altar dedications have been found there (one to Apollo Grannus, the deity of mineral and thermal springs who was associated with healing), these placed by Quintus Lusius Sabinianus, the British procurator at the time. The presence here of the official tasked by the emperor with making the province pay is a big deal in that it could indicate a desire to maintain a permanent presence in the north of Scotland, and indeed it is at this time that the Antonine Wall was constructed on the Clyde-Forth line, bringing the Scottish Borders within the province of Britain.

The events of the campaign and the building of the wall were significant enough to have an entry in the *Historia Augusta* (Antoninus Pius, 5.4), which says the Emperor 'defeated the Britons through his legate Lollius Urbicus, and having driven back the barbarians, he built another wall, of turf.'

The wall seems to have been constructed in haste, with the whole of *legio* II *Augusta* and *vexillations* from the *legio* VI *Victrix* and *legio* XX *Valeria Victrix* involved (note again no mention of *legio* IX *Hispana*). Called the *vallum Antonini* during the Roman occupation in Britain, as the *Historia Augusta* indicates this was a turf fortification built on stone foundations, it representing the most northerly frontier in Roman history. At 63km in length, it was 3m in height and 5m in width. The wall featured a deep ditch on the northern side, while the turf wall itself was topped with a wooden palisade. Construction began after the military successes celebrated in AD 142 and took about twelve years to complete, with the final wall protected by sixteen forts (two of which were, at least in part, stone built), with small fortlets between them in a similar manner to the system used along Hadrian's Wall.

While the Antonine Wall was occupied some 7,000 troops remained in the north to garrison the new frontier, with Hadrian's Wall on the Solway Firth-Tyne line being abandoned for the most part. These troops were soon in action as trouble erupted again in the AD 150s, and on such a scale that once more reserves were urgently summoned to the province from the legions and auxilia in Germania Inferior and Superior. We know about this military activity in the north from dedications the troops themselves erected to the Emperor in a shrine next to the bridge over the River Tyne, which also mention *vexillations* from the three resident British legions. Such trouble in the north is also attested by the minting of coins in Rome dating to AD 154–155 which show the image of Britannia in mourning. Further, the Greek geographer and traveller Pausanias (Guide to Greece, 8.43.4) also mentions Antoninus Pius depriving the Brigantes of territory. This may indicate that the trouble in the north at this time was from a threat at least partly much further south than the Antonine Wall, perhaps reflecting more native discontent there regarding the high cost of maintaining the exponentially large military presence in the north (though noting some argue this was a misunderstanding by Pausanius, with the Brigantes he references actually being located in Raetia near modern Bregenz in Austria). While we have no further insight regarding the military activity at this time, we do know that by AD 158 the Antonine Wall had been abandoned, only sixteen years after its construction had begun and perhaps acknowledging Pausanias' southern threat. It was later renovated during the Severan attempts to conquer Scotland in AD 209 and AD 210, though abandoned once more after this emperor's death in York in February AD 211.

The evacuation of the north above the Solway Firth-Tyne line at the end of Antoninus Pius' reign was carried out by the new governor Gnaeus

Julius Verus, he re-establishing the northern border along the line of Hadrian's Wall that was extensively renovated at this time. Interestingly, during the Governorship of Verus' next but one replacement Sextus Calpurnius Agricola, the *vallum* to the rear of Hadrian's Wall was also filled in, indicating that any internal threat from the Brigantes had been overcome. Some military presence did remain further north for a while, as happened in the immediate period following the post-Agricolan Scottish withdrawal, with some of the forts perhaps remaining garrisoned as late as the AD 190s, when it has been argued troops from the *legio* VI *Victrix* dedicated an altar to the god Mercury at the fort at Castlecary on the line of the old Antonine Wall, although this dating is problematic. Further military activity is then evident in AD 169 at the time of the death of co-Emperor Lucius Verus, with the *Historia Augusta* (Marcus Aurelius, 22.1) again referencing trouble in Britain, although giving no further details. Then, six years later we have references showing the *Classis Britannica* regional fleet in Britain transporting 5,500 Sarmatian heavy cavalry to the north of the province, perhaps indicating that reserves were required once more.

In the context of this book, there is one key point to be made here about trouble in Britain in the mid-second century AD. This is that, clearly given the arrival of *legio* VI *Victrix* in York in AD 122 to replace it, *legio* IX *Hispana* took no part in these campaigns as it had already left the province, if it still existed at all. However, with the advent of the diarchal emperors Marcus Aurelius and Lucius Verus, trouble was about to break out in the Continental north again, and so I now travel there in an effort to pick up the trail of the IXth legion.

The Marcomannic Wars

After the Imperial conquests of Trajan's reign, when the Principate Empire expanded to its greatest extent, most of the Roman world experienced the long peace detailed above in the reigns of Hadrian and Antoninus Pius. This came to a shattering end almost as soon as Marcus Aurelius and Lucius Verus became joint emperors in AD 161. In the first instance, trouble broke out in the east with the start of the Roman-Parthian War which lasted until AD 165. This is fully detailed in Chapter 6 as a candidate conflict for the loss of *legio* IX *Hispana*.

However, a far more dangerous war then broke out in the mid-AD 160s, with the start of the Marcomannic Wars along the Danube. Now, for the first time since the Cimbrian Wars, Italy itself was threatened as 'barbarian' invaders penetrated deep into the Imperial centre, and I now attempt to pick up the trail of the IXth legion in this conflict.

The principal opponents in these wars were the Germanic Marcomanni, Juthungi and Quadi in *Magna Germania*, as the unconquered lands north of the Danube were known, and their Sarmatian Iazyges allies. All were being driven hard against Rome's Dacian and Danubian frontiers by the westward expansion of the Visigoths and Ostrogoths, the German peoples to their east, who themselves were being driven westwards by the initial expansion of the Huns as detailed above.

The Marcomanni were descendants of the Suebi who'd fought Julius Caesar in his Gallic campaigns. By the AD 160s they had long migrated away from Roman Gaul to settle in the region of modern Bohemia. The Juthungi were also of Suebi descent, though resided nearer their original homelands in modern Bavaria, while the Quadi (again with Suebi ancestry) were located further east in modern Moravia. The fearsome Iazyges were also now settled near the Danubian Roman *limes*, by this time having travelled to the region of modern Hungary and Serbia from the Pontic steppe.

The wars on Rome's northern frontier had actually begun slightly earlier, with invasions across the upper reaches of the Rhine and Danube into Germania Superior and Raetia by the Germanic Chatti and Chauci who took advantage of Rome's distraction while campaigning in the east against Parthia. These disruptive incursions lasted from AD 162 to AD 165. Both were eventually repulsed. The Marcomannic Wars proper then began in AD 166 when 6,000 Germanic Langobard and Lacringi warriors fought their way over the Danube into Pannonia Superior (Heather, 2009, 96). Though soon defeated by *vexillations* from *legio* I *Adiutrix pia fidelis* under a *legate* called Candidus and the auxiliary cavalry *ala Ulpia Contariorum* under the Senator Marcus Macrinius Avitus Catonius Vindex (a veteran of the *legio* VI *Victrix* in York), this set a trend that lasted for the next fourteen years.

After these initial incursions, the Romans at first tried to buy off the German tribes causing trouble along the Danube. Marcus Iallius Bassus, governor of Pannonia Superior (a noted literary figure and adopted member of Marcus Aurelius' family) started negotiations with the eleven most aggressive tribes. A truce was soon agreed with the help of the Marcomanni overking Ballomar, after which any Germans remaining on the south side of the Danube withdrew.

However, no permanent peace deal was reached and later in AD 166 the frontier was tested again when the Sarmatian Iazyges and their Germanic

Vandal allies invaded the province of Dacia in force. Here the frontier defences failed, with the governor Calpurnius Proculus killed leading a hastily assembled army trying to stem the incoming tide of invaders. These then penetrated deep into the provincial interior, with the emperor forced to deploy the veteran *legio* IV *Macedonia* from Moesia Inferior to drive them out of Dacia. An uneasy peace then settled on the region.

Marcus Aurelius and Lucius Verus clearly viewed the ongoing threat from north of the Danube as serious and determined to carry out a major punitive expedition against the Iazyges and their German allies. It is unclear if they intended to conquer new territory, particularly in *Magna Germania* (with the subsequent creation of new provinces), or whether their main aim was a punitive expedition on a grand scale. Whichever, it was not to be in AD 167. A serious outbreak of plague across the Mediterranean put their plans on hold for that year. This was so serious that they were forced to recruit gladiators, bandits and Germans to fill the depleted ranks of the Roman military (*Historia Augusta*, Marcus Aurelius, 21.6).

By AD 168 things had stabilized in the Imperial capital and the emperors headed north to Aquileia on the north-eastern Adriatic coast where they established their forward headquarters. Orders were then dispatched along the northern frontiers to gather an enormous force to campaign across the Danube which they planned to lead in person. This included the two newly raised legions, which have enabled us today to date the legionary list on the Collonetta Maffei pillar, *legio* II *Italica* and *legio* III *Italica*. Their first targets were marauding Marcomanni, Quadi and Victohali tribesmen who'd taken advantage of the disruption caused by the plague in AD 167 to attack Pannonia Superior. However, as the Imperial force approached the key legionary fortress of *Carnuntum* (also headquarters of the *Classis Flavia Pannonica*) the Germans withdrew, giving assurances of their future good conduct. The emperors then returned to Aquileia for the winter, leaving the army poised for further campaigning in AD 169. However, the death of Lucius Verus in January that year set back military operations again, with Marcus Aurelius returning to Rome to supervise his funeral.

The now sole emperor returned to the offensive in the autumn of AD 169. His first target was the Iazyges, though the war at first went badly. The Sarmatians struck first, targeting the Roman gold mines at Alburnum in Dacia. The emperor ordered Claudius Fronto, the governor of Moesia Inferior and an Imperial favourite, to gather a local force and intercept them. In the ensuing battle the governor was killed and his force scattered. Meanwhile, with the emperor's attention focused on this crisis, several German tribes along the Danube used the opportunity to launch their own raids deep into Roman territory. In the east, these included the Costoboci who, from their Carpathian mountain homelands, struck the province of Thracia with savage ferocity. Pillaging all before them, they soon reached Greece proper where they destroyed the ancient Temple of the Eleusinian Mysteries near Athens.

However, this wasn't the emperor's biggest problem. Across the Danube the one time mediator Ballomar now seized his chance to launch a strike deep into Pannonia Superior. Gathering his own Marcomanni warriors and Quadi allies, he headed directly for *Carnuntum* to force a decisive meeting engagement. This he got in AD 170, mauling a Roman force there comprising *legio* XIV *Gemina Martia Victrix* and 14,000 auxiliaries. Ballomar's army then split into two, one column heading west to ravage the province of Noricum, while the other continued south, razing the city of Oderzo (Roman *Opitergium*) in north-eastern Italy and then besieging Aquileia. This sent shock waves through the Roman world of a kind last experienced in the Cimbrian Wars. The emperor, still on the Danube in the north, quickly ordered the Praetorian Prefect Titus Furius Victorinus to lead a hastily gathered force to repel them, but his army was promptly defeated and he was killed, the third senior leader to die since the troubles had begun.

Realizing the serious position now faced by Rome, Marcus Aurelius now turned to the up-and-coming troubleshooter Pertinax, later governor in Britain (see Chapter 4) and briefly emperor in AD 193, promoting him to the post of procurator in both Dacia and Moesia Superior. The timing of his move couldn't have been better given the shambles elsewhere in the region. Pertinax immediately set to work reordering the economy of the Dacia. This had been severely dislocated by the earlier incursion of the Iazyges. With taxes from the region's industry, agriculture and population once more flowing into the imperial *fiscus* treasury, new troops were raised and the frontiers and fortifications there strengthened. Then, in the Spring of AD 171, Marcus Aurelius was at last ready to strike back against the Marcomanni and Quadi. First he quickly redeployed the legions from the border to the Imperial interior to challenge the raiding Germans, who by this time were running out of provisions. He then appointed the highly experienced Tiberius Claudius Pompeianus commander in chief, who immediately recruited Pertinax to be his aide. Pertinax served with Pompeianus for a short time while preparations were made to go back on the offensive, then being elevated again to become an adlected Senator which allowed him to take command of *legio* I *Adiutrix pia fidelis* in Pannonia Superior as part of Pompeianus' much wider military reorganization in Europe. This included bolstering the *Classis Flavia Moesica* on the lower Danube and the building of a new series of fortifications in northern Italy called the *praetentura Italiae et Alpium*. Pompeianus then divided his force into legionary spearheads, each supported by their own auxiliaries. He himself quickly relieved Aquileia, routing the Marcomanni and Quadi there who fled back north across the Danube, suffering heavy casualties in the process. Meanwhile, another column under Pertinax struck out for the second German force which was still ravaging Noricum and had even reached Raetia. Total success followed, with this German force also driven beyond the Danube with heavy casualties. Marcus Aurelius himself publicly praised Pompeianus and Pertinax for their service.

The emperor now realized the Romans were still in no position to go on the offensive across the Danube and consolidated his forces along the northern *limes*, rebuilding and reinforcing the defences where they had been overrun. Intense diplomatic activity then followed as he attempted to win over as many of the German and Sarmatian tribes as possible before going back on the counter-attack. In particular, peace treaties were signed with the Quadi and the Iazyges, with the Lacringi and Hasdingi Vandals also becoming Roman allies and agreeing to provide warriors for his next campaign.

In the Spring of AD 172 Marcus Aurelius was finally ready to go on the offensive and launched a massive assault across the Danube from Pannonia Superior and Noricum against the Marcomanni and any German and Sarmatian tribes still allied with them. Ballomar's loose confederation was shattered and the Marcomanni quickly sued for peace, with the emperor taking the title 'Germanicus' and coins being minted featuring the term 'Germania Capta'. Pertinax was again in the vanguard, though another *legate* gained the greatest fame. This was Marcus Valerius Maximianus who, leading the Pannonia Inferior-based *legio* II *Adiutrix pia fidelis*, killed the chieftain of the German Naristi tribe in single combat. The emperor granted the *legate* the chieftain's fine stallion as a reward.

The Romans again campaigned north of the Danube in AD 173, this time against the Quadi after they predictably broke their earlier treaty commitments. Victory again followed, though the campaign is best known for the 'miracle of rain' incident recorded on the Column of Marcus Aurelius in Rome and coins. Here, *legio* XII *Fulminata* and perhaps Pertinax with his *legio* I *Adiutrix pia fidelis* had been trapped by a larger force of Quadi and was on the brink of surrendering because of thirst and heat. However, a sudden thunderstorm provided a deluge that refreshed the legionaries and auxilia, while a lightning strike on the Quadi camp sent the Germans fleeing in terror.

Roman military attention now switched to the Rhine frontier. Here, the future emperor Didius Julianus (later the brief successor to Pertinax in the 'Year of the five Emperors') had been the governor of Gallia Belgica since AD 170. As detailed above, this province, once home to some of Julius Caesar's fiercest Gallic opponents, stood just south of the northern border provinces of Germania Inferior and Germania Superior. In AD 173 it suffered a major incursion from the Germanic Chauci. Taking advantage of the Roman tribulations on the Danube, they smashed through the *limes* along the lower Rhine and penetrated deep into the rich farmlands of modern Flanders. The legions in the two German provinces struggled to contain the threat and Didius Julianus was forced to raise a force of local recruits, probably veterans settled in *coloniae*, which he led to great effect. Soon the Germans had been forced back over the Rhine. The governor then began a programme of fortification along the English Channel coast of his province before returning triumphant to Rome to celebrate a triumph.

With the *limes* along the Rhine now stabilized, in the spring of AD 174 Marcus Aurelius was now ready to go on the offensive once more. He quickly crossed the Danube with a huge force, targeting any Quadi still holding out against Rome. Over the winter a number of tribes there had deposed the pro-Roman king Furtius and replaced him with his arch rival Ariogaesus. Marcus Aurelius refused to recognize the latter and forced him to stand down, sending him to Alexandria in exile. By the end of the year the whole of the Quadi were subjugated, with the leading nobles sending hostages to Rome, warriors being recruited into the ranks of the Roman auxiliaries for assimilation, and Roman garrisons being installed in fortified camps throughout their territory.

Marcus Aurelius had one more piece of unfinished business along the Danube, to punish the Iazyges for the death of his friend Fronto in AD 169. In AD 175 he again gathered a mighty force and launched an assault from Pannonia Inferior and Dacia deep into their homelands. For this *expeditio sarmatica* the emperor targeted the plain of the River Tizsa in modern Hungary, winning a number of victories after which the leading Iazyges king Zanticus surrendered and a peace treaty was agreed. Captured Roman prisoners were then returned and the Iazyges supplied Rome with

8,000 of their *contos*-lance armed cavalry. Around 5,500 of these were those deployed to Britain as detailed above, where they were based at Ribchester in modern Lancashire (Roman *Bremetennacum*). The emperor then took the title 'Sarmaticus' and once more minted coins to celebrate victory. This brought to an end the First Marcomannic War.

We have remarkable insight here into the true jeopardy faced by the Empire in this conflict through the words of the emperor himself. This is in the form of a series of philosophical, somber observations written down in Greek by Marcus Aurelius when on campaign which he styled 'To Himself' (Cornell and Matthews, 103, 1982). They have survived to this day as his 'Meditations', and given the unpredictable nature of the first conflict in the Marcomannic Wars, one observation is particularly prescient (5.9):

> Do not be distressed, do not despond or give up in despair, if now and again practice falls short of precept. Return to the attack after each failure, and be thankful if on the whole you acquit yourself in the majority of cases as a man should.

Soon the emperor's resolve was tested once more, for early in AD 177 the Quadi reneged on their peace agreements with Rome. The Marcomanni soon followed and so began the Second Marcomannic War. This new insurrection spread rapidly along the upper Danube and soon the Germans had penetrated the *limes* and began raiding Imperial territory. Marcus Aurelius reacted swiftly, calling his new campaign the *secunda expeditio germanica*. With his army again led by Marcus Valerius Maximianus, the emperor arrived at *Carnuntum* in Pannonia Superior in August AD 178. There the Romans forced a meeting engagement with the Marcomanni who were comprehensively defeated. The Romans then advanced on the Quadi who were almost wiped out at the Battle of Laugaricio in modern Slovakia. Maximianus' own *legio* II *Adiutrix pia fidelis* fought particularly well here. The few German survivors were then chased back north beyond the Danube, where the Praetorian Prefect Tarruntenus Paternus then led a punitive campaign against the Quadi in their homeland which he ravaged.

However, campaigning along the Danube ended dramatically on 17 March AD 180 when Marcus Aurelius died of natural causes in Vienna (Roman *Vindobona*) at the age of 58. He was succeeded by his son Commodus. The new emperor had no interest in continuing his father's campaigns along the Danube. Instead, he was keen to return to Rome to secure his position. Commodus quickly established new peace treaties with the Marcomanni and Quadi, against the advice of his senior military commanders. The terms included that they provide 20,000 warriors to serve in the Roman army, these being distributed to auxiliary units across the Empire. Those remaining were partially disarmed and forbidden from attacking their Iazyges, Buri and Vandal neighbours without permission from Rome. Finally, the Germans were also forbidden from settling along a narrow strip on their own northern bank of the Danube, and also on the various large islands along the river's length. Accompanied by Paternus, Commodus then left for the Imperial capital in early September AD 180 where he celebrated a solo triumph on 22 October. Thus ended the Second Marcomannic War, with the so called 'Peace of Commodus'.

Trouble north of the Danube continued though and soon the Iazyges and a German tribe called the Buri whose homeland was to the north of the Marcommani and Quadi near the headwaters of the Vistula River rebelled again. Once more the emperor ordered his legions north of the Danube and victories were quickly celebrated by Maximianus again, and also by the leading Senators Pescennius Niger and Clodius Albinus, both to play key roles in the 'Year of the Five Emperors'. When a lengthy peace finally descended on the region in AD 182 Commodus celebrated by taking the title 'Germanicus Maximus'.

Thus ended the most challenging series of conflicts faced by the Empire for a century, and given the settlement of many Germans within the Empire afterwards one that began a process which was to change the very nature of Imperial identity. Soon, German warriors were not just filling the ranks of auxiliary units but joining the legions, while their leaders eventually came to dominate the officer class in the Roman military. However, one thing is very telling about the above narrative. In this sixteen-year conflict, when the Roman military was stretched to such an extent that gladiators and bandits were recruited to the ranks, there is not one mention anywhere of *legio* IX *Hispana*. Given the legion is also missing from the *nomina legionum* on the Collonetta Maffei pillar in Rome detailed above, this dated to around AD 168, that is very telling indeed.

Closing Discussion

In this chapter I have searched for evidence that, instead of being lost in Britain, *legio* IX *Hispana* left the province for the continent and fought on the northern *limes* along the Rhine and Danube. In this ambition I have failed. Based on stamped CBM evidence, and a stamped *mortarium* rim, we can certainly place a specific vexillation of the IXth legion at the legionary fortress at Nijmegen between AD 104 at the earliest and AD 120 at the latest. Given this vexillation used the unusual legionary numeral form VIIII, I suggest above it may have come from units of the legion based near Carlisle. Once in Nijmegen this formed part of the composite force that replaced the Xth legion, after its travels east, before the force itself was replaced by *legio* XXX *Ulpia Victrix*. We also know of an officer from the legion who set up an altar at the health spa at Aachen-Burtscheid in Germania Inferior, but with no context. Finally, we have the silver-plated bronze pendant found in the region in the 1990s that was originally part of a *phalera* Roman military medal. Once more, however, we have no context. And that is it. There is no other evidence to indicate what happened to the vexillation in Nijmegen, and no evidence at all that the whole IXth legion travelled from Britain to the northern *limes*, despite the 'all hands required' nature of the later Marcomannic Wars. Therefore I have to remove this hypothesis as one of the options regarding the legion's fate.

A final point to consider is the nature of the vexillation deployed to Nijmegen. One suggestion is that it was actually sent there as a remnant unit from the IXth legion if it had been destroyed in the far north of Britain, surviving perhaps because it had remained in the north-west of the province while its fellow *vexillations* marched north to their doom. Another, separate, consideration is what happened to it if the rest of the legion perished after it had left for Nijmegen? In that event the legionaries were most likely integrated into the other legions in the region, perhaps as battle replacements.

If there is no evidence *legio* IX *Hispana* was lost along the continental northern *limes*, then where to look next regarding its fate? I now move to the east, to look specifically at three conflicts which present a much more credible alternative to it being lost along the Rhine or Danube.

Chapter 6

Lost in the East

As detailed above, the initial focus of research into the fate of *legio* IX *Hispana* concentrated on it being lost in the north of Britain in the later AD 110s. This debate was later extended to consider it deploying, at least in part, to the Rhine frontier some time between AD 104 and AD 120. However, more recently some have begun to look much further afield regarding its fate, specifically to the east. To test this latter hypothesis I first examine the eastern provinces and *limes* of the Empire to provide context for what follows. I then detail the Parthian and Jewish opponents the Romans most feared in the region. Moving on, I next set out three specific scenarios in chronological order that could provide an explanation regarding the legion's demise if this occurred in the east. These are Trajans' eastern campaigns (including the Second Jewish Revolt), the later Third 'bar Kokhba' Jewish Revolt, and finally the Roman-Parthian War from AD 161 to AD 166. As usual, a Closing Discussion concludes the chapter where I assess the evidence presented here.

The Eastern Frontier

By the early second century AD the eastern provinces of the Roman Empire had long been integrated into Imperial territory. Starting at the region's western extremity, Anatolia was a thriving economic and cultural powerhouse. The Imperial presence here had its origins in the kingdom of Pergamum, left as a legacy to Rome by its last king Attalus III upon his death in 133 BC. Rome used this as a springboard for the various campaigns of conquest eastwards led by various later Republican warlords including Marius, Sulla, Pompey and Caesar. Sequentially they targeted the various kingdoms of Anatolia, including Bithynia in the north-west, Pontus to the north (fighting no fewer than three wars against Mithridates VI) and Galatia in the centre.

Anatolia eventually featured six provinces. The most westerly was that of Asia. Senatorial in nature, its geography centred on the lands of the old kingdom of Pergamum. The province featured some of the Empire's leading cities, including the provincial capital of Ephesus (with its Temple of Artemis one of the seven wonders of the ancient world), Pergamum itself, Priene, Miletus and Halicarnassus. To its north was the smaller Senatorial province of Bithynia et Pontus, sitting on the Asian side of the Bosporus. Its provincial capital Izmit (Roman *Nicodemia*) was one of a number of major cities there. The province of Galatia to the south was far more agrarian, with its provincial capital at Ankara (Roman *Ancyra*), while the south coast featured two other small provinces. These were Lycia et Pamphylia to the west, and Cilicia in the east. The former was governed from Demre (Roman *Myra*), the latter Roman *Tarsus*.

Roman Anatolia was far more militarized on its most easterly flank, where sat the province of Cappadocia. Aside from a short period from AD 114 to AD 118 when Armenia, Assyria and Mesopotamia were incorporated into the Empire following Trajan's eastern campaigns (see below), the province was the border territory facing some-time friend, some-time enemy Armenia, and further east the Arsacid Parthian Empire which was the nearest to a symmetrical threat faced by the Roman Principate military until the Parthian monarchy itself was usurped by the Sassanid Persians from AD 224.

Cappadocia featured the key crossing points in the upper Tigris and Euphrates valleys and was often the launch point for Roman campaigns eastward against Parthia and later Sassanid Persia (Pollard and Berry, 2012, 162). Its key industry was olive oil production. While the provincial capital was at Kayseri (Roman *Caesarea*), the most important settlements were the two legionary fortresses and their *canabaes* at Sadak (Roman *Satala*) in the north-east and Malatya (Roman *Melitene*) in the south-east. The former was home to *legio* XV *Apollinaris*, the latter to *legio* XII *Fulminata* (note no mention of *legio* IX *Hispana* here). These were the key anchor points of the Cappadocian *limes*, with the Black Sea port of Trabzon the regular home to the *Classis Pontica*. The province's military component was completed by a large number of auxiliaries, including many locally recruited mounted and infantry bowmen.

Moving south to the eastern frontier proper, this featured the key barrier provinces of Syria and Arabia Petraea, Judaea (later Syria Palaestina, see below) on the Mediterranean coast and the island of Cyprus in the western Mediterranean. Syria was the major bulwark against the Parthians to the east for much of the Principate. It was also highly fertile, sitting as it did on the western arc of the Fertile Crescent. The province was governed from the huge metropolis of Antakya (Roman *Antioch on the Orontes*), which by the later second century AD had a population of 250,000.

In addition to the northern section of the *limes Arabicus*, the border territory also featured a sophisticated system of defence-in-depth based on client and allied kingdoms that often formed a buffer between the Empire and the Parthians. These included Palmyra, Osrhoene, Adiabene and Hatra. The principal legionary fortresses in Syria were at *Zeugma* in the north (this named by the Romans after the bridge of boats that crossed the Euphrates there, originally founded as the Hellenistic city of *Seleucia on the Euphrates*), *Raphanaea* near the Mediterranean coast and *Danaba* to the south. These were home to some of the most battle-hardened legions in the Empire, sequentially *legio* IV *Scythica*, *legio* III *Gallica* and *legio* XVI *Flavia Firma* (Pollard and Berry, 2012, 130, and again noting the lack here of any mention of *legio* IX *Hispana*). In addition to the usual auxiliary complement, the military presence in the province was completed by the *Classis Syriaca* regional fleet that operated out of the port of Seleucia Pierra.

A recent addition to the Empire, the province of Arabia Petraea was the opposite of abundant Syria, being largely a desert inhabited by nomadic and transhumant Arabs. For commerce it relied on desert caravans operating through trading centres such as Petra. The latter was annexed by Trajan immediately prior to his campaigns in the east (see below), initiating the creation of the province. From that time one legion was based here, *legio* III *Cyrenaica* at Bosra (Roman *Bostra*), which was also the provincial capital. From here the legionaries and their supporting auxilia (including camel riding *equites Dromedarii*) had the unforgiving task of manning the southern *limes Arabicus*. Defence-in-depth is also evident here, with the Romans frequently making use of their Ghassanid Arab allies to repel the Lakhmid Arabs who were supporters of the Parthians and later the Sassanid Persians (Heather, 2018, 312).

Heading west to Judaea, here was found one of the most troublesome provinces of the Roman Empire, which like Britain featured a disproportionately large military presence. The province incorporated the territories of the former Hasmonean and Herodian kingdoms of Judaea, including Judaea itself, Samaria and Idumaea. The major issue for the Romans here were the native Jewish inhabitants who proved the most recalcitrant adherents to the ways of Rome following the formation of the province in the early AD 40s by Claudius. Three desperate Jewish Revolts were put down by the Romans in the most brutal fashion. All are covered in depth below in the context of *legio* IX *Hispana*. It was after Hadrian crushed the last revolt that the provincial name was changed to Syria Palaestina, with Jerusalem renamed *Aelia Capitolina* (the provincial capital was actually at *Caesarea Maritima* on the coast). Despite the defeat of this last revolt, the province still featured two legions throughout the second century AD, these being *legio* VI *Ferrata fidelis constans* based at Caparcotna near Megiddo and *legio* X *Fretensis* based in *Aelia Capitolina*. Given their proximity to Syria proper and Arabia, these were frequently used as a strategic reserve when the eastern frontier was threatened, and to campaign in the east during Roman incursions into Parthia and later Sassanid Persia.

Across the eastern Mediterranean from Judea, the province of Cyprus was as far within the Empire as it was possible to get. It was originally incorporated into the Republican province of Cilicia, becoming an independent Senatorial province in 22 BC under Augustus. There was little Roman military presence there, with the provincial capital located at Paphos (Roman *Nea Pafos*) famous for its 'Tombs of the Kings' Hellenistic and Roman necropolis.

Heading south once more, Aegyptus was one of the powerhouse provinces of the Empire, established in 30 BC after the then Octavian and his general Marcus Agrippa defeated Mark Antony and Cleopatra VII Philopator. Given its economic might, the province was always a place of difference within the Empire, this based on the abundantly fertile Nile Valley that provided much of the grain supply to Rome and elsewhere across the Mediterranean. Aegyptus was also unique among Roman provinces in being considered the Emperor's own imperial domain where he was styled the successor to the preceding system of Pharaonic rule. Here the governor was titled a *praefectus augustalis*. We have great insight into the life experiences of all levels of society in Roman Egypt thanks to the thousands of surviving papyrus documents that detail every aspect of life there, many found at the key Roman site of *Oxyrhynchus* near modern El-Bahnassa, 160km south-east of Cairo.

The capital of the province was Alexandria, located on the Mediterranean coast of the Nile Delta. This vast city had been founded in 332 BC by Alexander the Great. Given it was also the location of his *Soma* mausoleum, the city was a particular draw for Roman Emperors when touring the east, with many stopping off here to view his body in its glass-covered golden sarcophagus. By the early second century AD the city's population had reached around 600,000, making it the largest urban centre in the Roman world outside of Rome itself. Roman Alexandria was best known for its 130m tall Hellenistic *pharos* lighthouse (one of the seven wonders of the ancient world), and its great library, the largest in the ancient world. Further south, the Great Pyramid of Khufu at the Giza Pharaonic necropolis was another of the seven wonders of the ancient world.

Aegyptus was a favourite destination for Hadrian, and when he visited in AD 130 the province was enjoying a century of prosperity. His visit included the emperor founding the city of Antinopolis to commemorate his lover who drowned in the Nile that year. However, it was also a source of continuing trouble, for example during the Second Jewish Revolt (see below for detail), with a full revolt of native Egyptians breaking out when Antoninus Pius raised taxes in the Middle Nile Valley in AD 139. This conflict, known as the Bucolic War, lasted several years during which Alexandria was besieged. The rebellion was eventually put down by the Syrian *legate* Gaius Avidius Cassius, who later usurped in AD 175 when mistakenly told Marcus Aurelius had died. Initially successful, he was recognised by the regional legions, but was then killed by a centurion when word reached the province that Marcus Aurelius was approaching with a huge army.

Aegyptus featured one legion, *legio* II *Traiana Fortis*, originally founded by Trajan in AD 105 for his Dacian campaigns. This performed with distinction during the Bucoli War, deploying from its legionary base at *Nicopolis* to defend Alexandria during the siege. The region also featured significant auxiliary forces. The provincial capital was also home to the *Classis Alexandrina Augusta* regional fleet that patrolled the south-eastern Mediterranean and River Nile. This was one of the first regional fleets created by Augustus, in this instance in the later 20s BC. It received its Imperial title after supporting Vespasian in AD 69, the 'Year of the Four Emperors'.

In addition to countering the frequent native insurgencies in the province, the military forces here also fought the nomadic Blemmye and Nobatae who lived in the desert between the Nile and Red Sea. Though not a sophisticated opponent in terms of tactics and technology, they often raided Roman Egypt in such numbers that they presented a real danger. The Romans countered this threat with a series of fortifications and watchtowers to protect the rich agricultural land in the Nile Valley. Most Blemmye and Nobatae warriors were unarmoured bowmen, often mounted on mules and donkeys, though they occasionally used elephants trained for war.

Rome's Opponents in the East

Aside from the Blemmye and Nobatae, the two principal foes faced by the Romans in the east in the second century AD were the Parthians beyond the eastern *limes*, and the Jewish rebels in the revolts of AD 115 and AD 132 (sequentially, the Second and Third Jewish Revolts).

The Parthians, always a major threat to Roman power in the east as detailed above, originated in north-eastern Iran. From the third century BC they had expanded westwards at the expense of the various Hellenistic kingdoms in the region and soon encountered the eastward expansion of the Romans. The Parthian army featured a very effective combination of armoured noble lancers (often fully armoured as cataphracts, both rider and horse) and a multitude of lightly armoured horse archers, the latter famous for their 'Parthian Shot' tactic of approaching enemy formations at speed and then loosing arrows over the croup of their mount as they wheeled away. This mixture of shock cavalry and missile troops proved highly effective against the Romans time and again, most famously almost wiping out the Republican army of the triumvir Crassus in 53 BC at the Battle of Carrhae, where he and his son lost their lives. In particular, the infantry-heavy armies of Principate Rome, with their reliance on legionaries and auxilia, often found it difficult to get to grips with their mounted Parthian opponents. To counter this, when campaigning into Parthian territory, the Romans were most successful when they targeted Parthian population centres down the Tigris and Euphrates valleys. In that regard, the most successful Roman campaigns in the region were those of Trajan, Lucius Verus (see below for detail of both) and Septimius Severus, who all sacked the Parthian capital of Ctesiphon.

Meanwhile, Rome's Jewish opponents proved equally difficult to overcome. Though they lacked any level of sophisticated military organization, they often fought with zealous fanaticism. Most Jewish rebels fought unarmoured as guerillas, armed with a variety of types of spear, javelin and bow, they avoided meeting engagements in the open if possible. As with the Parthians, the Romans countered this elusive foe by directly targeting their cities and towns which they methodically besieged, using artillery and starvation to gradually force their surrender, though many rebels in all three Jewish Revolts chose to take their own lives rather than be captured.

Trajan's Parthian War

The first candidate conflict in the east for the loss of *legio* IX *Hispana* is Trajan's invasion of Parthia from AD 114. Here, the ever restless emperor decided to tackle Rome's 'eastern question' head on as he sought more martial glory after his Dacian Wars of AD 101–AD 102 and AD 105–AD 106. Some have argued that his motivations here were actually economic following his annexation of the key desert trading centre of Petra and creation of the province of Arabia Petraea, after which he built an extensive road network in the east called the *Via Traiana Nova* which stretched from Busra al-Sham (Roman *Bostra*) in Syria to Aqaba (Roman *Aila*) on the Red Sea coast. This meant that the only trading route to import spices and silk from India outside of Roman control was the Parthian port city of Charax Spasinou on the Persian Gulf. Capturing this would give the Roman's a monopoly in this lucrative trade.

As so often when the Romans campaigned in the east, Armenia to the south of the Caucasus Mountains was the first focus of their attention. Trajan had already shown an interest in the region when reports arrived that Sarmatian *Alani* were arriving on the kingdom's northern borders in large numbers (Kean and Frey, 2005). The Romans feared this would turn into a flood of migrants who would destabilize their eastern provinces and resolved to use Armenia as a barrier. Trajan began planning the annexation of the kingdom, but the Parthian king Osroes I moved first, placing his nephew Exederes, the son of a favourite brother, on the Armenian throne. Trajan promptly declared war, keen to avoid the humiliation of being outmanoeuvred politically by the Parthians. This gave Osroes pause for thought, he offering to remove Exederes and replace him with another nephew called Parthamasiris. Though Trajan rejected his offer, the Parthian king followed through his suggested plan anyway, hoping it would still placate the Romans. It didn't, and it is unclear why he expected Trajan to respond positively to yet another royal Parthian nephew being placed on the Armenian throne. By now all of the Roman plans were in place and Trajan invaded Armenia in late AD 114. He quickly defeated the Armenian forces sent to confront him, together with their Parthian allies, and then killed Parthamasiris before following through on his plan to annexe Armenia as a Roman province.

Next, in AD 115 Trajan then invaded northern Mesopotamia which he quickly overran, also annexing this as a new province which he called Assyria. This secured Trajan's northern flank and rear, allowing him to campaign far down the Tigris and Euphrates valleys. Here he used these vast rivers to transport much of his force, including a large siege train. The latter allowed him to quickly capture and sack Ctesiphon, before next sailing further downriver all the way to the Persian Gulf where he famously bathed in the warm waters there. To mark his success he then founded a third Roman province in the region which he called Mesopotamia, before following in the footsteps of Alexander the Great back to Babylon where he over-wintered. Writing 250 years later, Eutropius (8.5) says that he then ordered a fleet to be built in the Red Sea with which he intended to 'lay waste' to the western coastline of India.

However, this was not to be. As ever with the Romans in the east total victory proved elusive, and later in AD 115 major revolts broke out in the region. This included the Second Jewish Revolt in Judaea (also called the Kitos War, see below) which led to the Jewish populations in Aegyptus (especially in Alexandria), the twin Senatorial province of Cyrenaica et Creta to its east, Cyprus, and also Assyria and Mesopotamia rebelling. The latter province was particularly badly hit given the large number of Jewish exiles and refugees living there following the Roman defeat of the First Jewish Revolt. Insurrections also broke out in the latter two new provinces among Parthian remnant populations where some of the wealthy former Hellenistic cities had been used to a large degree of autonomy under their former rulers. Soon Roman military resources were stretched to the limit.

Trajan quickly returned to the eastern Mediterranean from Babylon and counter-attacked, with Roman activities in the Second Jewish Revolt detailed below. However, further east he crucially failed to take the key border city of Hatra which had been seized by pro-Parthian rebels. Parthian forces then attacked key Roman positions and garrisons at Seleucia-on-Tigris, Nisibis and Edessa. Trajan eventually subdued the rebels in Assyria and Mesopotamia. He then installed a Parthian prince called Parthamaspates as a Roman client ruler in Ctesiphon, before withdrawing to Syria where early in AD 117 he became seriously ill and decided to return to Rome. His health gradually declined further as he travelled, with contemporary sources saying that by this time he was suffering from poor circulation, indicating a heart problem. Ultimately he had a stroke which paralysed one side of his body. He finally died on 8 August that year at Gazipasa (Roman *Selinus*) in Cilicia from severe edema. His biggest legacy in the region were the establishment of the short-term provinces of Armenia, Assyria and Mesopotamia.

As can be seen, the revolts which were the key feature of the second half of Trajan's eastern campaigns were a true crisis which caught the emperor far to the south-east of a major conflagration which soon spread throughout the eastern Mediterranean and down the Tigris and Euphrates valleys. Such was the danger it presented that some have used it as an argument to suggest that *legio* IX *Hispana* was moved from Britain to the eastern front to bolster Roman forces there. Lawrence Keppie, Emeritus Professor of Roman History and Archaeology at the University of Glasgow, details this as one possible fate of the IXth legion, adding that as 'no inscriptions recording the building activities of the legion or the lives and careers of its members have come from the east' it must have been lost soon after arriving if this was its actual fate (2000, 247). That might indicate a deployment early in the second century AD, for example as part of Trajan's campaigns in the east, rather than later in the century. To be clear, however, there is no hard evidence at all for this specific hypothesis in the context of Trajan's eastern campaigns.

The Third 'bar Kokhba' Jewish Revolt

The peoples of Judaea revolted against direct Roman rule on three occasions. These are called the First Jewish Revolt which lasted from AD 66 to AD 73, the Second Jewish Revolt of AD 115 to AD 117 detailed above in the context of Trajan's eastern campaigns, and the final and apocalyptic (certainly from the point of view of the Jewish peoples) Third 'bar Kokhba' Jewish Revolt of AD 132 to AD 135.

The first, also called the Great Revolt, was defeated by Vespasian and his son Titus after vicious fighting which included the siege of the lofty Herodian fortress of Masada on the eastern fringes of the Judean Desert. However, the most infamous engagement of the war was the Roman siege of Jerusalem where the Jewish rebel defenders put up a fanatical resistance. Once defeated Titus then destroyed the second temple there, a key turning-point in Jewish history, before looting the city and carrying off its royal and religious treasures to be paraded through Rome as part of his triumph. This is the main event recorded in detail of the Arch of Titus in the *Forum Romanum* in Rome, where the huge golden menorah are the most striking images featured.

The second revolt proved even more sanguineous than the first given its much wider geographic spread. It was so serious that it threatened to undo Rome's political settlement along the south-eastern shores of the

Mediterranean. At first, with Trajan in Babylon, the rebels were able to massacre many Roman garrisons, officials and citizens across the region. The Romans, used to running their provinces with a light touch, always responded brutally against rebelling populations, and Trajan decided to make a specific example of the Jewish insurrectionists, slaughtering huge numbers of them. This was on such a scale that he was forced to repopulate areas now devoid of their original populations with Roman citizens to avoid good-quality agricultural land falling out of use.

The rebellion was eventually put down by the Roman general Lusius Quietus whose *nomen*, in corrupted form, later gave the war its contemporary name as the Kitos War. As the conflict came to an end he eventually chased down the Jewish leader Lukuas to Judaea where he then sentenced to death in absentia his two deputies, the brothers Julian and Pappus. These had taken refuge in the Judaean city of Lydda along with a huge number of surviving rebels and refugees. The Romans promptly put this under close siege, eventually capturing it after a vicious assault. Most of the captives, including the two brothers, were executed, bringing the rebellion to an end.

However it is the third revolt that provides the most likely setting for the demise of the *legio* IX *Hispana* under the hypothesis that it was lost in the east during one of the three Jewish Revolts. This rebellion was named after its leader by Simon bar Kokhba, a mysterious figure whose actual family name we may never know given bar Kokhba seems to be an epithet meaning 'son of a star' in Aramaic. This rebellion was more serious than either of its predecessors given that, for the first time, the various Jewish communities in the region closely coordinated their campaigning against the Romans. Led by the charismatic bar Kokhba, who many declared was a heroic messiah who would restore a united Kingdom of Israel, the Romans were soon on the back foot, with many garrisons once more being put to the sword.

In its initial stages the bar Kokhba revolt was surprisingly successful, with one contemporary report saying it resulted in the destruction of an entire Roman legion (see later discussion regarding the IXth legion as a candidate). The rebels may also have actually recaptured the city of Jerusalem, and were certainly able to secure much of the province of Judaea under their control given they eventually announced the actual creation of the Kingdom of Israel.

However, the Romans soon regrouped. Gathering resources from across the Empire, they deployed a massive army featuring six full legions, *vexillations* from six others, and a large number of mounted and foot auxiliary units to settle matters with the Jewish rebels across the region once and for all. Once in theatre they adopted a scorched-earth strategy that ultimately extirpated most of the rebels, laying waste to much of Judeaea. In the final phase of the conflict bar Kokhba fled to his last surviving fortress which was located at Betar, near modern day Battir. The Romans promptly besieged him there, capturing it after a lengthy siege. All inside perished, either in the final assault or in the ensuing massacre of those captured there, excepting one lone rebel who escaped. Among the dead was bar Kokhba himself.

Roman punishment for Judaea and the Jewish rebels was particularly harsh, even by their own extreme standards when stamping out a revolt. Judean society had already been shattered by seventy years of on-off civil war, with a large proportion of the population killed, dead through starvation, enslaved or exiled (note the resettlement needed after the Second Jewish Revolt detailed above). Now Hadrian permanently changed the nature of the province, renaming it Syria Palaestina and turning Jerusalem into a pagan city that he renamed *Aelia Capitolina*, as detailed above. In so doing he set in train a process designed to deliberately erase Jewish history, executing many surviving Jewish religious leaders and scholars, and banning the Torah and the use of the Jewish calendar. Any surviving Jews were banned from living within sight of newly styled *Aelia Capitolina*, with Eusebius quoting Ariston of Pella in describing the impact of this (4.6.4):

> Thus when the city came to be bereft of the nation of the Jews, and its ancient inhabitants had completely perished, it was colonized by foreigners, and the Roman city which afterwards arose changed its name, and in honour of the reigning emperor Aelius Hadrian was called Aelia.

Given the severe dislocation caused by the three failed Jewish Revolts, only small Jewish communities remained in former Judaea, and the demography of the renamed province now shifted in favour of the non-Jewish population. From this point the remaining centres of Jewish cultural and religious life were all to be found outside of the province, particularly in Babylonia, with other minor communities scattered around the Mediterranean.

Turning to a possible role for the IXth legion in the suppression of the bar Kokhba revolt, certainly the deployment of six full legions (plus *vexillations* from six others) was unusual in a single campaign and would have required reinforcements from outside of the region. In fact the extreme nature of this emergency is indicated by the recruitment of marines from the *Classis Misenensis* Tyrrhenian regional fleet into *legio* X *Fretensis* for the campaign to replace battle casualties (Campbell, 2018, 131). Therefore, one could make the case that *legio* IX *Hispana*, if it still existed at the time, was sent to the east as part of a dramatic military redeployment to cope with the crisis. Further, we do know that the Romans suffered large numbers of casualties in this rebellion, with at least one other legion disbanded by Hadrian afterwards. This was most likely *legio* XXII *Deiotariana*, as detailed in Chapter 3. Some have also speculated that the same fate befell the IXth legion, for example classicist G.R. Watson in his 1969 book *The Roman Soldier* wrote that it was lost 'probably during the Jewish War of AD 132 to AD 135' (1969, 23). More recently, Roman military expert Wolff also makes a case for the cashiering or loss of both legions in the revolt, saying (2015, 1041): 'Hadrian disbanded (legio) IX Hispana and (legio) XXII Deiotariana, or they were destroyed in (the) war.'

However, a specific issue here is the sheer scale of such a disaster. If two full legions were destroyed in the bar Kokhba revolt, that would have been of a scale only just short of Varus' annihilation in the Teutoburg Forest in AD 9 when he lost three legions and their auxiliaries. This latter event was much commented on at the time, and later by near contemporary historians, and one would expect that to be the case in this instance too. However, there is no mention of such an event when putting down the bar Kokhba revolt. To my mind this does therefore mitigate against this war being the location of the IXth legion's disappearance, though I don't rule it out. A much better case can be made, however, for the final candidate I now consider in this chapter for *legio* IX *Hispana* being lost in the east. For that we must turn to the Parthians once more, in the AD 160s.

The Roman-Parthian War AD 161 to AD 166

A long peace settled on Rome's eastern frontier with Parthia after Hadrian abandoned Trajan's new provinces in Assyria and Mesopotamia, at the same time returning Armenia to independent rule. This period of relative calm continued through the lengthy reign of Antoninus Pius. However, things quickly changed after his death in AD 161. This prompted the Parthian king Vologases IV, keen to impress his own nobility, to cause trouble in Armenia once more. At the time Armenia remained a Roman ally under a client king called Sohaemus. The Parthians promptly deposed him and replaced him with their own puppet ruler. Dio (71.2) then says a Roman legion sent to intervene was annihilated, with its commander Marcus Sedatius Severianus, the governor of Cappadocia and an experienced military leader who knew the region well, committing suicide. This is considered in more detail later, given the potential implications for the fate of the IXth legion.

Continuing his campaign, Vologases then captured Edessa, capital of the prosperous city-state of Osroene, another key Roman ally on the border. Here he deposed its ruler Ma'nu VIII and replaced him with a supporter called Wa'el who promptly started minting coins featuring an image of Vologases. The Parthians then went on the offensive against the Empire proper, invading Cappadocia and its neighbouring province Syria. They pillaged deep into the interior of both, severely disrupting the regional economy.

Back in Rome the new dyarchy of Marcus Aurelius and Lucius Verus had only just come to power. Neither had much experience of conflict given the lengthy period of peace under Antoninus Pius. Verus was tasked with responding to the Parthian aggression, the joint emperor's *Consilium Principis* advising that he take the best commanders available with him. These were Statius Priscus and Gaius Avidius Cassius, the latter a noted strategist and commander of *legio* III *Gallica* in Syria (and later the victor in the Bucolic War and a usurper against Marcus Aurelius, see above).

In the first instance, in AD 163 Priscus drove the Parthians out of Cappadocia and then Armenia. There he reinstalled a pro-Roman ruler. Next, in AD 164 Cassius gathered a huge army in Syria. To secure his rear the general first besieged Edessa, this falling to him when the population massacred the Parthian garrison. Ma'nu VIII was then reinstalled as the ruler of Osroene, receiving the epithet Philorhomaios ('Friend of the Romans'). Cassius then launched a savage assault down the Tigris valley where he destroyed the city of Seleucia-on-Tigris. Moving on rapidly, he then captured the Parthian capital of Ctesiphon, which he also burned to the ground. The legions continued their advance, reaching the Parthian heartland in Media by early AD 165. At this point Vologases, his kingdom ravaged, sued for peace. This was agreed on the most onerous terms for the Parthians, including the ceding of significant portions of western Mesopotamia to Rome. These lands were incorporated into the provinces of Cappadocia and Syria, though a plague then prevented them being retransformed into Trajan's earlier province of Assyria again. The joint emperors then celebrated their victory over Vologases with a huge joint triumph in AD 166, with Verus being awarded the honorific titles *Armeniacus*, *Parthicus Maximus* and *Medicus*.

Turning to the fate of *legio* IX *Hispana*, we do have a legion here being lost in the early stages of the war when Vologases defeated Severianus in Armenia. Specifically, Dio says (71.2):

> Volegeses, it seems, had begun the war by hemming in on all sides the Roman legion under Severianus (the governor of Cappadocia) that was stationed at Elegeia, a place in Armenia, and then shooting down and destroying the whole force, leaders and all.

Though short, this is actually a very detailed description given it says where the legion was based, and how it was destroyed. Elegeia was a town just beyond the Cappadocian frontier, near the headwaters of the Euphrates. It therefore appears that Severianus' force, which would also have included auxiliary cavalry and foot, was engaged almost as soon as it set foot in Armenia. Further, Dio's reference to the Parthians 'hemming in' and 'shooting down' the Roman troops seems to indicate that they were ambushed while on the march and unable to build their usual marching camp, victims of the famed Parthian horse archers. This event is also referenced in the *Historia Augusta*, this saying (Lucius Verus, 6.9): 'a legate was being slain, while legions were being slaughtered, while Syria meditated revolt, and the East was being devastated.' Note the reference here to 'legions' in the plural. There are certainly strong resemblances here to Crassus' much earlier annihilation by the Parthians at Carrhae in 53 BC.

If at least one legion was lost here at the beginning of the Roman-Parthian War in the AD 160s, then who are the candidates? As detailed earlier, Cappadocia had its own two legions, *legio* XV *Apollinaris* at Sadak in the north-east of the province and *legio* XII *Fulminata* at Malatya in the south-east. Both had lengthy futures after this conflict so almost certainly weren't the legion or legions destroyed. This has led some to speculate that it was actually *legio* IX *Hispana* (and also possibly *legio* XXII *Deiotariana*) who were the unfortunate victims of Parthian aggression. One of the earliest to suggest this fate for the IXth legion was Eric Birley in 1971 (see Chapter 3), his proposal dividing opinion at the time. However, while some clung to the belief *legio* IX *Hispana* was lost in Britain early in Hadrian's reign (including Sheppard Frere), others followed this new lead, supported by suggestions that those who are recorded in epigraphy serving in the IXth legion were actually doing so much later in the second century AD than previously believed. These included Peter Salway in his influential *Roman Britain* published in 1981 which suggested the legion was 'sent to the east, to disappear in the Jewish Wars of the (AD) 130s or against the Parthians in AD 161'. Another leading archaeologist of the time, Malcolm Todd, agreed, saying (1981, 121):

> The continued survival of the unit at least down to the beginning of the reign of Antoninus Pius, however, now seems probable; it may not have met its end until the early years of Marcus Aurelius (and Lucius Verus).

Here, anecdotally, we do have a very good case made that the IXth legion really was that lost in Armenia at the beginning of the Roman-Parthian War. However, as always with regard to its mysterious fate, we lack any hard evidence, so once more have to speculate.

Closing Discussion

In this Chapter I have considered three very specific scenarios regarding *legio* IX *Hispana* being lost in the east. All have merits. First, we have Trajan's eastern campaign against Parthia, and specifically the Second Jewish Revolt and the regional insurrections in his new provinces of Mesopotamia and Assyria that interrupted his triumphant march eastwards in AD 115. These events did stretch Roman military resources to the limit, and could have seen the rapid deployment eastwards of the experienced IXth legion to the region. However, of the three fates considered for the legion in this Chapter I believe this is the least likely, especially because of the probable crisis back in Britannia as Trajan's reign came to a close and Hadrian acceded to the throne, all as detailed in Chapter 3. Next we have the appalling slaughter on all sides during the Third 'bar Kokhba' Jewish Revolt when Roman resources were stretched even further, almost to breaking point. The massive scale of the Roman response to this revolt, with six full legions, *vexillations* from another six and large numbers of auxiliary horse and foot all being deployed, shows how serious this was. Some of these legions and *vexillations* would definitely have been redeployed to the east from out-of-theatre. This alone provides room to speculate that one such unit was *legio* IX *Hispana*. Further, such was the Roman loss of life as they fought the fanatical rebels that certainly a legion so deployed could have been lost and then cashiered, particularly if deemed to have performed badly. Many speculate that this was *legio* XXII *Deiotariana*, though it could also instead have been the IXth legion, or perhaps both. Though again we have no hard evidence here, this to me seems a more likely scenario than the first option. Finally we have the Roman-Parthian War of AD 161 to AD 166 where Dio details a legion being lost early on in Armenia under the Cappadocian governor Severianus, who promptly committed suicide. Clearly he thought at least his own actions and performance, and perhaps that of the legion he was leading, were shameful given his decision to take his own life. Further, we have the *Historia Augusta* speaking specifically about the slaughter of legions (note again the author is specifically plural here) in the same context. To my mind this certainly is a candidate scenario to be taken seriously regarding the fate of legio IX Hispana (and perhaps *legio* XXII *Deiotariana*). However, as ever we have no hard evidence.

For completeness I would note here one argument against a western legion being deployed eastwards during an emergency in the context of the disappearance of the IXth legion. This is the fact that such an eventuality was very rare, and very costly too. Moving a legion from Nijmegen to fight in Dacia as with *legio* X *Gemina* detailed in Chapter 5 was itself a huge logistics exercise, and here much of the legion's equipment and baggage could be moved along the Rhine and Danube (providing the riparian zone either side of these huge continental rivers was under Roman control). Moving *legio* IX *Hispana* from York or Nijmegen to the eastern frontier was a continental move of a different scale entirely. However, despite this I still don't think this argument totally mitigates against any of the three scenarios detailed above of the IXth legion being lost in the east under Trajan, Hadrian or Marcus Aurelius and Lucius Verus. To my mind, all remain viable candidates, however unlikely they seem.

Conclusion

When writing my various works on the Roman world, academic and otherwise, the conclusion can sometimes prove problematic given the often-complex nature of the questions being asked. Here that is definitely not the case, with the subject matter being very specific, namely what really happened to the famous *legio* IX *Hispana*. This is the legion that disappears suddenly from history, uniquely leaving not a trace of its fate.

There are a number of hard facts known about the IXth legion, as opposed to pure speculation (some informed, some not). Noting most of these are balanced heavily in favour of the legion's earlier history, these facts are:

- 90 BC–89 BC. The original IXth legion participates in the year long Siege of Asculum in the Social War when Gnaeus Pompeius Strabo led his Roman army to victory over their former Italian allies.
- 58 BC–45 BC. This earlier IXth legion participates in Julius Caesar's Gallic conquests, including his two British incursions in 55 and 54 BC, and later in the civil wars when Caesar's *populares* supporters fought Pompey's *optimates* supporters in Greece, Egypt, Africa and Spain. It is then disbanded in 45 BC, for unknown reasons.
- 44 BC–43 BC. The actual IXth legion that is the subject of this book is raised by Octavian shortly afterwards, from Caesarean veterans settled in Italy to counter the rebellion of Sextus Pompeius in Sicily.
- 42 BC. The new legion participates at the Battle of Philippi when Octavian and Mark Antony defeat the Caesarean assassins Gaius Cassius Longinus and Marcus Junius Brutus. It performs well and is shortly afterwards awarded a cognomen styling it *legio* IX *Macedonia*.

- 27 BC–19 BC. The IXth legion participates in Augustus' Cantabrian Wars, the final stage of the Roman conquest of the Iberian Peninsula. The legion again fights with great bravery, afterwards staying in Spain long enough for its *cognomen* to change from *Macedonia to Hispaniensis*. This is later shortened to *Hispana*.
- Circa 10 BC. The IXth legion is redeployed to Aquileia in north-eastern Italy.
- Circa AD 14. The IXth legion is redeployed once more, to a legionary fortress in Pannonia on the Danube. It is one of three legions which mutinies over the living conditions there given it is forced to share the fortress with two other legions.
- AD 20. The IXth legion is sent to North Africa to support *legio* III *Augusta* in its campaigns against the Numidian rebel leader Tacfarinas. It participates in a major victory in AD 22.
- AD 22. The IXth legion moves to the legionary fortress at Sisak in modern Croatia, later returning to Pannonia.
- AD 43. Aulus Plautius leads the Claudian invasion of Britain, with four legions including his own *legio* IX *Hispana* (the latter from the province of Pannonia where he had been governor). The legion plays a full role in the early campaigns of conquest, which leads to the establishment of the original province of Britannia.
- AD 44–AD 49. The IXth legion heads north as part of the initial breakout campaigns in Britain, skirting the territory of the Iceni tribe in modern Norfolk (a Roman client kingdom), then reaching the River Nene where it establishes a vexillation fort at Longthorpe. It continues north to found another vexillation fort at Leicester, and then a full legionary fort at Lincoln on the River Witham.
- AD 60–61. A significant component of *legio* IX *Hispana* under its *legate* Quintus Petillius Cerialis is defeated trying to prevent the sack of Colchester during the Boudiccan Revolt. Some surviving *vexillations* of legionaries may have joined the governor Gaius Suetonius Paulinus in the Midlands where he ultimately defeats Boudicca.
- AD 71. Cerialis returns to Britain as governor and targets the Brigantes tribe in the north. He orders *legio* IX *Hispana* from Lincoln into Yorkshire where it constructs a new legionary fortress at York on an easily defendable plateau at the confluence of the Rivers Ouse and Foss, deep in Brigantian territory.

- AD 82. The legion is last mentioned in contemporary history in AD 82 by Tacitus in the context of Agricola's campaigns to conquer the far north of Britain, this in a negative context when its marching camp is almost overrun by native Britons.
- AD 83. The IXth legion is present at the Battle of Mons Graupius in the far north of Scotland, though takes no part given the fighting is carried out by the Roman auxiliaries.
- At some stage between AD 104–AD 120. A vexillation of legionaries from the IXth legion is redeployed to the legionary fortress of Nijmegen in Germania Inferior. This forms part of a composite force from Britain's three legions to replace *legio* X *Gemina* that had redeployed to the Danube frontier to participate in Trajan's Dacian campaigns.
- AD 108. It is last recorded on an inscription referencing the IXth legion in Britain, this found on an inscribed limestone slab that formed the centre section of a monumental inscription referencing the rebuilding of the south-eastern gate at the legionary fortress in York.
- AD 122. Arrival in Britain of *legio* VI *Victrix* in York to replace *legio* IX *Hispana*.
- AD 120s. Hadrian's Wall is built, with no inscriptions suggesting *legio* IX *Hispana* participated.
- Around AD 168. Construction of the Collonetta Maffei pillar in Rome with its *nomina legionum* list of contemporary extant legions. The IXth legion is missing, and never mentioned again.

Of these hard facts five are the most important, namely the IXth legion is last mentioned in literature in 82 BC, in inscription in Britain in AD 108, it was replaced in York by *legio* VI *Victrix* in AD 122, there are no inscriptions referencing it on Hadrian's Wall, and it is missing from the Collonetta Maffei pillar list of legions in Rome from AD 168. The VIIIIth (noting the differential way of numbering the legion) legion tile and brick stamps from Nijmegen are also important, but the dating of between AD 104 and AD 120 isn't tight enough to be especially useful.

From these facts we can finally explore, comparatively, the four hypotheses being tested in this book regarding the legion's fate. Firstly, were Horsley, Mommsen, Sutcliffe (and so many others) correct in arguing that *legio* IX *Hispana* was lost in the north of Britain? Helpful here is the fact that four of the five aforementioned key facts are set in Britain in the late first and early second centuries AD. Additionally, one has the informed speculation, based on contemporary history and the archaeological record, regarding a serious military crisis in the north of Britain around the time of Hadrian's accession in AD 117. This to my mind is the most likely setting for Sabinus' *expeditio Britannica*, needed to stabilize the situation and fill a power vacuum in the north after – under this hypothesis – the loss of *legio* IX *Hispana*. The arrival of *legio* VI *Victrix* in York then returned the northern frontier to a degree of normality. Whether the protagonists behind the IXth legion's disappearance under this hypothesis were the local Brigantes revolting in the north of the province, the unconquered tribes of the far north either invading the province to the south or destroying the legion as it campaigned in their territory, or any combination of these, is unclear.

Next we have the setting of Perring's Hadrianic War in London in the AD 120s as another candidate hypothesis for the disappearance of *legio* IX *Hispana*. Perring makes a very strong case that at this time a major event shattered the peace in the post-Boudiccan provincial capital. His evidence comes in the form of mass beheadings, with hundreds of resulting skulls found in the upper reaches of the Walbrook valley, the Hadrianic fire in London which seems to have been deliberately started, this causing a citywide conflagration, and the building of the Cripplegate fort to put the stamp of Roman authority back on the town after the event. If lost under this hypothesis, the IXth legion was either the victim of the rebellion, perhaps requested by the governor to intervene and dramatically failing, or was the actual vector of rebellion, it then being destroyed as the Empire stamped out the revolt.

Moving on, I then considered the puzzling appearance of Roman brick and tile in the legionary fortress site at Nijmegen in the modern Netherlands that features the stamp of *legio* IX *Hispana*. These date to between AD 104 and AD 120 and, given they use a differential way of numbering the legion to the norm (VIIII as opposed the IX), they appear to come from a specific vexillation of the legion. This has been identified as one originally based near Carlisle in the north-west of the province. In Chapter 5 I use this presence of a unit from the IXth legion here to consider whether it might have disappeared fighting in the second century AD along the Rhine or Danube. Sadly, though intense conflict did occur along the continental northern *limes* of the Empire in this century (especially in the Marcomannic Wars), there is no evidence *legio* IX *Hispana* participated.

The final hypothesis tested in this work is whether the IXth legion transferred from the west at some stage in the second century AD to the east and was then lost fighting along the eastern *limes*. Here we have three conflicts that, in their different ways, were exceptionally sanguineous, costing the lives of thousands of Roman legionaries and auxilia. First I looked at Trajan's eastern campaign against Parthia, and specifically the Second Jewish Revolt and the regional insurrections in his new provinces of Mesopotamia and Assyria. These interrupted his triumphant march eastwards in AD 115, requiring reinforcements from across the Empire to bring the situation under control. I then looked at the Third 'bar Kokhba' Jewish Revolt, lasting from AD 132 to AD 135, when Roman military resources were stretched once more. This required the deployment of a huge force to finally put down the fanatical Jewish resistance, featuring six full legions, *vexillations* from another six and large numbers of auxiliary horse and foot. This would certainly have needed legionary reinforcements from out of theatre, and some speculate that a legion – often detailed as *legio* XXII *Deiotariana* – was lost. Finally, we then have the Roman-Parthian War of AD 161 to AD 166 where, at its outset, Dio says a legion was lost under the Cappadocian governor Severianus. Some have specifically linked *legio* IX *Hispana* to this event.

As I highlighted in the Introduction to this book, seeking out the fate of the IXth legion has been a true detective story. The obvious difficulty is the lack of any hard evidence of what really happened to it. No classical author describes its demise, no epigraphy references a grim fate, and no archaeological site indicates a military disaster where its legionaries were slaughtered. I am therefore left to informed speculation, and think it my duty to present the readers who have patiently accompanied me on this detective journey with what I personally think about the IXth legion, and why.

Based on the hard facts set out above, and my wider knowledge of the Roman world and military, the least likely candidate hypothesis regarding the fate of *legio* IX *Hispana* is that it was lost fighting on the Rhine or Danube. There is simply no evidence that anything other than a very specific vexillation spent some time in Nijmegen, and then the evidence trail goes cold. The next least likely hypothesis to my mind is that the legion was lost in the east, in any of the three scenarios examined. Of these the most likely candidate conflict would be the IXth legion being the one lost under Severianus at the start of the Roman-Parthian War. However, I feel the chronological gap between it last being referenced in epigraphy in AD 108 in York and the massacre in Armenia in AD 161 is just too lengthy for there to be no record of it in the intervening years. Moving on, Perring's Hadrianic War in London has to be considered a serious candidate event in which the IXth legion met its fate, perhaps with a *damnatio memoriae* subsequently wiping it from the official record. However, given the plentiful analogous and anecdotal evidence, I actually think the most likely hypothesis regarding the loss of *legio* IX *Hispana* is where the book began. This is with it being lost in some dramatic event in the north of Britain, either within the province as the victim of a Brigantian revolt, or even further north in unconquered modern Scotland with the native tribes there the protagonists, or with the legion on the receiving end of a region-wide rebellion across the whole far north of the province and beyond. In that regard, very telling is the emergency deployment of Sabinus' *expeditio Britannica* that I date to this period, and the subsequent arrival in the north of *legio* VI *Victrix*.

The reality of course is that unless some fantastical new piece of evidence emerges in some long lost contemporary history, or through the discovery of one of the archaeological finds of the century, we will never actually know the fate of the IXth legion. Until then, based on what we do know, the above is where the available evidence ultimately points. The legion was lost in the north of Britain.

Timeline of the late Roman Republic and Roman Empire

Below I now outline a timeline of key events in the late Roman Republic and Roman Empire (with an emphasis on the Principate phase of the latter) to provide a framework for the study of *legio* IX *Hispana* and its mysterious fate. Given the key role played by the province of Britannia in the legion's story, this province is given particular prominence.

90/89 BC:	The original IXth legion participates in the year long Siege of Asculum in the Social War.
58 BC:	Julius Caesar begins his conquest of Gaul.
57 BC:	The Veneti submits to Caesar.
56 BC:	The rebellion of the Veneti against Rome, Battle of Morbihan.
55 BC:	The first Roman invasion of Britain, Julius Caesar's first incursion.
54 BC:	The second Roman invasion of Britain, Julius Caesar's second incursion.
52 BC:	The Battle of Alesia. Conquest of Gaul completed.
45 BC:	Original IXth legion disbanded.
44 BC:	Julius Caesar assassinated in Rome.
44/43 BC:	The actual IXth legion that is the subject of this book is raised by Octavian.
42 BC:	The new legion participates at the Battle of Philippi, earning the cognomen Macedonia.
27 BC:	The conquest of north-west Spain begins, with the IXth legion participating. The legion fights with bravery, afterwards staying in Spain long enough for its cognomen to change from Macedonia to Hispaniensis. This is later

	shortened to Hispana. Octavian becomes Augustus. Beginning of the Principate Empire.
10 BC:	The IXth legion is redeployed to Aquileia in north-eastern Italy.
AD 9:	Varus' three legions, together with nine auxiliary units, destroyed in Teutoburg Forest, Germany by the Cherusci tribe and others led by Arminius.
AD 14:	The IXth legion is redeployed again, this time to a legionary fortress in Pannonia on the Danube.
AD 20:	The IXth legion is sent to North Africa to support *legio* III *Augusta* in its campaigns against the Numidian rebel leader Tacfarinas.
AD 22:	The IXth legion participates in a major victory over Tacfarinas. It then moves to the legionary fortress at Sisak in modern Croatia, later returning to Pannonia.
AD 40:	Caligula's planned invasion of Britain aborted.
AD 43:	The third, and successful, Roman invasion of Britain under the Emperor Claudius, with the legionaries, auxilia and naval *milites* commanded by Aulus Plautius. The IXth legion plays a full part. Claudius then returns to Rome, with Plautius appointed the first governor of Britain.
AD 44:	The IXth legion heads north as part of the initial breakout campaigns in Britain, skirting the territory of the Iceni tribe in modern Norfolk (a Roman client kingdom), then reaching the River Nene where it establishes a vexillation fort at Longthorpe. It later continues north to found another vexillation fort at Leicester, and then a full legionary fort at Lincoln on the River Witham.
AD 44:	The future Emperor Vespasian successfully campaigns in the south-west of Britain, leading *legio* II *Augusta*.
AD 47:	Vespasian successfully concludes his campaign to conquer the south west of Britain, returning to Rome with Plautius. The new governor of Britain is Publius Ostorius Scapula who puts down an early revolt by the Iceni and campaigns in north Wales.
AD 48:	The first revolt of the Brigantes tribe in northern Britain.
AD 49:	A coloniae for veterans is founded at Colchester in Britain, with *legio* XX *Valeria Victrix* moving to Gloucester. Scapula campaigns in Wales.

AD 50:	Construction begins of first forum in the newly-found city of London.
AD 51:	The leader of the British resistance to Roman rule, Caratacus, is captured by the Romans after being handed over by the Brigantian Queen, Cartimandua.
AD 52:	The Silures tribe in southern Wales is pacified by the governor Didius Gallus.
AD 54:	Claudius dies, with Nero becoming the Emperor.
AD 57:	Quintus Veranius Nepos becomes the governor, dying in office. Rome intervenes in favour of Queen Cartimandua in a dispute over the leadership of the Brigantes.
AD 58:	Gaius Suetonius Paulinus becomes the governor.
AD 59/60:	The initial subjugation of the Druids in the far west, and the initial invasion of Anglesey by the governor Gaius Suetonius Paulinus. This campaign is cut short by the Boudiccan revolt.
AD 60/61:	The Boudiccan revolt takes place, featuring the destruction of Colchester, London and St Albans. The revolt is defeated by Gaius Suetonius Paulinus, followed by the suicide of Boudicca. Early in the insurrection, a significant component of the IXth legion under its legate Quintus Petillius Cerialis is defeated trying to prevent the sack of Colchester.
AD 61/63:	Publius Petronius Turpilianus becomes the governor, followed by Marcus Trebellius Maximus.
AD 66:	First Jewish Revolt begins.
AD 68:	Nero is overthrown, with Galba becoming the Emperor.
AD 69:	The Year of Four Emperors. In Britain Cartimandua, Queen of the Brigantes and ally of Rome, is overthrown by former husband Venutius. Marcus Vettius Bolanus is the governor.
AD 70:	The Classis Britannica regional navy in Britain is named for the first time in the context of the Batavian Revolt of Civilis on the River Rhine.
AD 71:	Vespasian orders the new British governor Cerialis to campaign in the north of Britain. The Brigantes are defeated, with Venutius captured and killed. The IXth legion plays a major role in these campaigns, heading from Lincoln deep into Brigantian territory where it founds York as a legionary fortress.

AD 74:   Sextus Julius Frontinus is appointed as the new governor in Britain. Further campaigning in Wales follows, and Chester is founded.

AD 77:   Gnaeus Julius Agricola becomes the new governor in Britain. Wales and western Britain are finally conquered.

AD 78:   Agricola consolidates the Roman control of Brigantian territory, and then begins planning his campaign in the far north of the islands of Britain.

AD 79:   Agricola begins his campaign to subdue the whole of the north of Britain, including Scotland. The Emperor Vespasian dies and is replaced by his son Titus.

AD 80:   Agricola continues his campaigning in Scotland.

AD 81:   The death of Titus who is succeeded by Domitian.

AD 82:   Agricola continues his campaigning in Scotland. The IXth legion is last mentioned in contemporary history in this campaign by Tactitus, in a negative context when its marching camp is almost overrun by native Britons.

AD 83:   Agricola brings the combined Caledonian tribes to battle at Mons Graupius in the Grampians, south of the Moray Firth (possibly even further north). The IXth legion is present but doesn't participate. After his victory Agricola orders the Classis Britannica to circumnavigate northern Scotland. The conquest of Britain is declared 'complete', with construction then beginning of a monumental arch at Richborough in modern Kent to commemorate the event.

AD 87:   Roman troops are withdrawn from the far north of Britain because of pressures elsewhere in the Empire. The legionary fortress of Inchtuthil in Tayside is abandoned.

AD 90:   Lincoln becomes a colonia settlement.

AD 96:   Domitian is assassinated, this event bringing to an end the Flavian dynasty. He is succeeded by Nerva. Gloucester becomes a colonia settlement

AD 98:   The death of Nerva, who is succeeded by Trajan. In Britain, Publius Metilius Nepos is the new governor, followed by Titus Avidius Quietus.

AD 100:   Trajan orders the full withdrawal of Roman troops from Scotland, and then establishes a new frontier along the Solway Firth–Tyne line. All of the defences north of this line are abandoned by AD 105.

AD 103:   Lucius Neratius Marcellus is the new governor.

AD 104:   Earliest date for the deployment of a vexillation of *legio* IX *Hispana* legionaries to the legionary fortress at Nijmegen.

AD 108:   The IXth legion is last recorded on an inscription in Britain, this found on an inscribed limestone slab that formed the centre section of a monumental inscription referencing the rebuilding of the south-eastern gate at the legionary fortress in York.

AD 115:   Marcus Atilius Bradua is the new governor in Britain.

AD 117:   The death of Trajan, he being succeeded by Hadrian. This coincides with major disturbances in the north of the province of Britannia. Probable date for Sabinus' *expeditio Britannica*.

AD 115:   Second Jewish Revolt (the Kitos War) begins.

AD 120:   Latest date for the deployment of a vexillation of *legio* IX *Hispana* legionaries to the legionary fortress at Nijmegen.

AD 122:   The Emperor Hadrian visits Britain, initiating the construction of Hadrian's Wall on the Solway Firth–Tyne line. Aulus Platorius Nepos is the new governor, arriving with the Emperor and being tasked with the wall's construction. Also arriving is *legio* VI *Victrix* that replaces *legio* IX *Hispana*.

AD 126:   Lucius Trebius Germanus is the new governor in Britain.

AD 131:   Sextus Julius Severus is the new governor in Britain.

AD 132:   Third Jewish 'bar Kokhbar' Revolt begins.

AD 133:   Publius Mummius Sisenna is the new governor in Britain.

AD 138:   The death of Hadrian, he being succeeded by Antoninus Pius. Quintus Lollius Urbicus is the new governor in Britain.

AD 142:   Military engagements north of Hadrian's Wall continue under Urbicus, on the orders of Antoninus Pius, in an attempt to subdue the tribes of northern Britain and southern Scotland, the latter region being conquered again. Construction then begins of the Antonine Wall along Clyde-Forth line as a new northern frontier.

AD 146:   Gnaeus Papirius Aelianus is the new governor of Britain.

AD 155:   Central St Albans is destroyed by a major fire.

AD 157:   Gnaeus Julius Verus is the new governor of Britain.

AD 161:   The Emperor Antoninus Pius dies, and is succeeded by Marcus Aurelius and Lucius Verus. Beginnining of the Roman-Parthian War. A Roman legion is lost under the command of the Cappadocian governor Severianus, who commits suicide.

AD 162:   Marcus Statius Priscus is the new governor of Britain, followed by Sextus Calpurnius Agricola. The Antonine Wall is evacuated, with the northern border once again moving south to the line of Hadrian's Wall.

AD 166:   End of the Roman-Parthian War. Beginning of the Marcommanic Wars.

AD 168:   Construction of the Collonetta Maffei pillar in Rome with its *nomina legionum* list of contemporary extant legions. The IXth legion is missing, and never mentioned again.

AD 169:   More trouble in northern Britain.

AD 174:   Caerellius is the new governor in Britain.

AD 175:   5,500 Sarmatian cavalry are sent to Britain, perhaps because of a military emergency.

AD 178:   Ulpius Marcellus is the new governor in Britain.

AD 180:   Marcus Aurelius dies, he being replaced by Commodus.

AD 182:   The tribes either side of Hadrian's Wall start raiding along and across the border, with Roman troops responding with counter-raids. Towns far to the south of the wall begin constructing the first earth-and-timber defensive circuits, indicating that tribal raiding penetrated far into the province.

AD 184:   Commodus receives his seventh acclamation as Imperator, taking the title Britannicus indicating the defeat of the insurrection in the north of Britain. Revolt of the three legions in Britain against the governor Marcellus. Some 1,500 picked troops from Britain travel to Rome with a petition for the Emperor Commodus. They ask that he dismiss the Praetorian Prefect Perennis.

AD 185:   The new governor in Britain is the future Emperor Publius Helvius Pertinax. He later survives an assassination attempt by one of the British legions.

AD 191/192:   Decimus Clodius Albinus becomes the new governor in Britain.

AD 193:   The 'Year of the Five Emperors', with Septimius Severus emerging as the ultimate victor.

AD 196:	British governor Albinus usurps, invades Gaul and is proclaimed Emperor by the legions from Britain and Spain.
AD 197:	Albinus is defeated by Severus at the closely fought Battle of Lugdunum (modern Lyon) and is killed. Planning begins to divide the Province of Britain into two, Britannia Superior and Britannia Inferior. Virius Lupus is the new governor.
AD 197/198:	Severus sends military commissioners to Britain aiming to quickly suppress the remaining supporters of Albinus. Roman troops rebuild parts of Hadrian's Wall (some of which may have actually been destroyed) and other parts of the northern defences that had been damaged by an increase in tribal raiding after Albinus had travelled to Gaul with his troops. Construction also starts at this time of the land walls of London. Severus begins his reforms of the military, while he himself campaigns in Parthia for two years.
AD 202:	Severus campaigns in North Africa. Gaius Valerius Pudens is the new governor in Britain.
AD 205:	Lucius Alfenus Senecio is the new governor in Britain.
AD 207:	News arrives in Rome from Britain (a letter from Senecio as detailed by Herodian) asking Severus for urgent assistance in the form of the Emperor himself or more troops. He responds with both.
AD 208:	Severus arrives in Britain with the Imperial household and a huge army, he planning a major campaign against the Maeatae and Caledonian tribal confederations north of Hadrian's Wall. St Alban is martyred.
AD 209:	The first Severan campaign in Scotland begins.
AD 210:	The second Severan campaign in Scotland begins, led by Caracalla as the Emperor is too ill to actively participate. A genocide is ordered by Severus there.
AD 211:	Severus dies at York, with his sons Caracalla and Geta becoming joint Emperors. The campaign in the north of Britain is suspended with the brothers returning to Rome. Caracalla murders Geta. Britain is later officially divided into two Provinces, Britannia Superior and Britannia Inferior.
AD 216:	Marcus Antonius Gordianus is the new governor of Britannia Inferior.

AD 222:	Tiberius Julius Pollienus Auspex is the new governor of Britannia Superior.
AD 223:	Claudius Xenophon is the new Governor of Britannia Inferior.
AD 224:	Ardashir I of Persia defeats his Parthian overlords over a two-year period, bringing the Sassanid Persian Empire into being. Rome now has a fully symmetrical threat on her eastern border.
AD 225:	Maximus is the new governor of Britannia Inferior.
AD 226:	Calvisius Rufus becomes the new governor of Britannia Inferior, being followed by Valerius Crescens and then by Claudius Appelinus.
AD 235:	Assassination of Severus Alexander, ending the Severan dynasty and beginning the 'Crisis of the 3rd Century'. Maximinus Thrax becomes Emperor.
AD 237:	Tuccianus becomes the new governor of Britannia Inferior.
AD 238:	Marcus Martiannius Pulcher becomes the new governor of Britannia Superior. Maecilius Fuscus becomes the new governor of Britannia Inferior, quickly followed by Egnatius Lucilianus.
AD 242:	Nonius Philippus becomes the new governor of Britannia Inferior.
AD 244	Aemilianus becomes the new governor of Britannia Inferior.
AD 249:	The last potential mention of the Classis Britannica regional fleet in Britain, on epigraphy in Arles commemorating Saturninus, ex-Captain in the British Fleet.
AD 250:	Irish raiding takes place along the west coast, with Germanic raiding along the east coast.
AD 253:	Desticius Juba becomes the new governor of Britannia Superior.
AD 260:	The 'Gallic Empire' is declared by Postumus, this splitting Britain, Gaul and Spain away from the Empire for fourteen years.
AD 262:	Octavius Sabinus becomes the new governor of Britannia Inferior.
AD 268:	Postumus is murdered by his own troops.
AD 274:	The Emperor Aurelian defeats the 'Gallic Empire', with Britain, Gaul and Spain then rejoining the Empire.

AD 277:	Vandals and Burgundian mercenaries are settled in Britain, with Victorinus defeating a British usurpation.
AD 284:	Diocletian becomes the Emperor, initiating the Diocletianic reformation of the Empire's administration, and his reforms of the military. The end of the 'Crisis of the 3rd Century'.
AD 287:	The usurpation of Carausius, which splits Britain and northern Gaul away from the Empire.
AD 290:	London's wall circuit is completed with the building of the river wall and bastions.
AD 293:	The western Caesar Constantius Chlorus recaptures northern Gaul from Carausius who is then assassinated by Allectus. The latter then takes over control from his former master in Britain.
AD 296:	The fourth Roman invasion of Britain, with Constantius Chlorus invading to defeat Allectus, the western Caesar then returning the two Provinces to the Empire. Around this time Britain is declared a diocese as part of the Diocletianic Reformation, with the four Provinces of Maxima Caesariensis, Britannia Prima, Flavia Caesariensis and Britannia Secunda.
AD 306:	Constantius Chlorus campaigns in the north of Britain, then dies in York. His son Constantine is proclaimed Emperor by the legionaries of *legio* VI *Victrix* there.
AD 312:	Constantine becomes the sole Emperor in the west, with his military reforms beginning around this time.
AD 314:	Constantine and Licinius agree to end the persecution of Christians, while three British bishops attend the Council of Bishops at Arles.
AD 324:	Constantine becomes the sole Emperor of the whole Empire.
AD 325:	The first mention of *comitatenses* field army troops.
AD 337:	Constantine prepares for war with Persia but falls ill in Nicomedia and dies.
AD 343:	The Emperor Constans makes a surprise winter crossing of the English Channel to Britain following the defeat of his brother Constantine II three years earlier, possibly in the context of a military emergency in the north of the diocese.
AD 350:	The military leader Magnentius (born in Britain) usurps power in Gaul, with the provinces in Britain and Spain

quickly supporting him, and ultimately the whole of the Western Empire.

AD 351: Magnentius is defeated by the Eastern Emperor Constantius II at the Battle of Mursa Major, he then retreats to Gaul. Magnentius is defeated again at the Battle of Mons Seleucus, after which he commits suicide. Constantius II sends Paul 'the chain' to Britain to purge the aristocracy after the revolt of Magnentius. The *vicarius* of the diocese, Martinus, commits suicide rather than face trial.

AD 357: The Battle of Strasbourg, where Julian defeats the Alamanni.

AD 358: Alypius becomes the new *vicarius* of the diocese.

AD 359: British bishops attend the Council of Rimini. The Emperor Julian builds 700 ships to transport grain from Britain to feed his Rhine army.

AD 367: Civilis becomes the new *vicarius* of the diocese. The 'Great Conspiracy' of Picts from Scotland, Attecotti from the Western Isles, Irish and Germanic raiders attack Britain, overwhelming the frontier defences.

AD 369: Count Theodosius arrives in Britain to suppress the revolt and restore order, with Magnus Maximus serving under him. The northern frontier is then rebuilt yet again.

AD 378: The Battle of Adrianople takes place where the eastern armies of the Emperor Valens are defeated by the Gothic army of Fritigern. This is a defeat the Empire struggles to recover from.

AD 383: Magnus Maximus (now the British military commander, and possibly the *vicarius* of the diocese) campaigns against Pictish and Irish raiders. He is proclaimed the Emperor by his troops, then invading Gaul that declares its support for him, as does Spain.

AD 387: Magnus Maximus invades Italy where he ousts the Emperor, Valentinian II.

AD 388: Magnus Maximus is defeated and executed by Theodosius 1, Emperor in the East.

AD 391: Theodosius I bans pagan worship, although the practice still continues in Britain.

AD 395: Chrysanthus becomes the new *vicarius* of the diocese.

AD 400: The Western Empire *magister militum* Stilicho campaigns in Britain and defeats Pictish, Irish and Germanic raiders.

He then withdraws many troops from the diocese to help defend Italy against the Goths, with Britain left dangerously exposed to further attack. Victorinus becomes the new *vicarius*.

AD 402:   The last import of base coins into Britain takes place.

AD 405:   Heavy Irish raiding on the south-western coast of Britain occurs, this being a possible date for the capture of St Patrick.

AD 406:   Vandals, Burgundians, Alans, Franks and Suevi overrun the *limes Germanicus* near Mainz and then invade Gaul.

AD 407:   In swift succession the military in Britain declare Marcus, then Gratian and finally Constantine III to be the Emperor. The latter crosses to Gaul with the remaining *comitatenses* field army troops from Britain, setting up his capital at Arles. The diocese now only has the *limitanei* troops to defend its borders.

AD 409:   The British aristocracy throw out their Roman administrators, with the diocese cut adrift from the remaining parts of the Western Empire.

AD 410:   The Western Emperor Honorius allegedly tells the Britons to look to their own defences.

AD 411:   Constantine III is captured and executed on the orders of Honorius.

AD 429:   St Germanus visits Britain to debate with the Pelagian Christians there. Further conflict takes place with Pictish and Irish raiders

AD 430:   The effective end of coin use in Britain.

AD 451:   The *magister militum* in the west, Flavius Aetius, defeats Attila the Hun at the Battle of the Catalaunian Plains.

AD 454:   The Britons appeal to Aetius by letter in 'the groans of the Britons' request for military assistance, but no troops are available to help at this time.

AD 476:   The last western Emperor, Romulus Augustulus, is deposed by his *magister militum* Flavius Odaocer. The end of the Roman Empire in the west.

Bibliography

Ancient Sources

Apuleius, *The Golden Ass*, trans. P.G. Walsh (Oxford: Oxford World's Classics, 2008)

Aurelius, Marcus, *Meditations*, trans. M. Staniforth (London: Penguin Classics, 1964)

Caesar, Julius, *The Conquest of Gaul*, trans. S.A. Handford (London: Penguin Classics, 1951)

Cato, Marcus, *De Agri Cultura*, trans. H.B. Ash and W.D. Hooper (Harvard: Loeb Classical Library, 1934).

Dio, Cassius, *Roman History*, trans. E. Cary (Harvard: Loeb Classical Library, 1925)

Diodorus, Siculus, *Library of History*, trans. C.H. Oldfather (Harvard: Loeb Classical Library, 1939)

Eusebius, *Ecclesiastical History: Complete and Unabridged*, trans. C.F. Cruse (Oregon: Merchant Books, 2011)

Eutropius, Flavius, *Breviarium Historiae Romanae*, trans. H.W. Bird (Liverpool: Liverpool University Press, 1993)

Flaccus, Quintus Horatius (Horace), *The Complete 'Odes' and 'Epodes'*, trans. D. West (Oxford: Oxford Paperbacks, 2008)

Frontinus, Sextus Julius, *Strategemata*, trans. C.E. Bennett (Portsmouth, New Hampshire: Heinemann, 1969)

Gaius, *Institutiones*, trans. F. De Zulueta (Oxford: Oxford University Press, 1946)

Herodian, *History of the Roman Empire*, trans. C.R. Whittaker (Harvard: Loeb Classical Library, 1989)

Historia Augusta: Life of Pertinax, trans. D. Magie (Harvard, Loeb Classical Library, 1921)

Homer, *The Iliad*, trans. E.V. Rieu (London: Penguin Classics, 1950)

Justinian, *The Digest of Justinian*, trans. A. Watson (Philadelphia: University of Pennsylvania Press, 1997)

Livy, *History of Rome*, trans. B.O. Foster (Cambridge, MA: Harvard University Press/Loeb Classical Library, 1989)

Pausanias, *Guide to Greece: Central Greece*, trans. P. Levi (London: Penguin Classics, 1979)

Pliny the Elder, *Natural History*, trans. H. Rackham (Harvard: Harvard University Press, 1940)

Pliny the Younger, *Epistularum Libri Decem*, ed. R.A.B. Mynors (Oxford: Oxford Classical Texts/Clarendon Press, 1963)

Plutarch, *Lives of the Noble Grecians and Romans*, ed. A.H. Clough (Oxford: Benediction Classics, 2013)

Polybius, *The Rise of the Roman Empire*, trans. I. Scott-Kilvert (London: Penguin Classics, 1979)

Quintilian, *Institutes of Oratory*, J. Selby Watson (Scotts Valley, California: Create Space Independent Publishing Platform, 2015)

Strabo, *The Geography of Strabo*, trans. D.W. Roller, D.W. (Cambridge: Cambridge University Press, 2014)

Suetonius, *The Twelve Caesars*, trans. R. Graves (London: Penguin Books, 1957)

Tacitus, Cornelius, *The Agricola and the Germania*, trans. H. Mattingly (London: Penguin Books, 1970)

Tacitus, Cornelius, *The Annals of Imperial Rome*, trans. M. Grant (London: Penguin Classics, 2003)

Tacitus, Cornelius, *The Histories*, trans. W.H. Fyfe (Oxford: Oxford University Press, 2008)

Victor, Aurelius, *De Caesaribus*, trans. H.W. Bird (Liverpool: Liverpool University Press, 1994)

Modern Sources

Avery, A., *The Story of York* (Pickering: Blackthorn Press, 2007)

Barker, P., *The Armies and Enemies of Imperial Rome* (Cambridge: Wargames Research Group, 1981)

Bédoyère, G. de la, *Praetorian: The Rise and Fall of Rome's Imperial Bodyguard* (New Haven: Yale University Press, 2017)

Bédoyère, G. de la, 'The Emperors' Fatal Servants', *History Today* March 2017 Issue, pp.58–62.

Bentley, P., 'A Recently Identified Valley in the City', *London Archaeologist* magazine, Vol. 5, No. 1, pp.13–16, 1984.

Bidwell, P., *Roman Forts in Britain* (Stroud: Tempus, 2007)

Birley, A.R., *The Fasti of Roman Britain* (Oxford: Clarendon Press, 1981)

Birley, A.R., *The Roman Government of Britain* (Oxford: Oxford University Press, 2005)

Birley, A.R., 'The Frontier Zone in Britain: Hadrian to Caracalla', de Blois, L. and Lo Cascio, E. (eds), *The Impact of the Roman Army (200 BC–AD 476)*, pp. 355–370 (Leiden: Brill, 2007)

Birley, E., 'The Fate of the Ninth Legion', Butler, R.M. (ed), *Soldier and Civilian in Roman Yorkshire*, pp.71–80 (Leicester: Leicester University, 1971)

Bishop, M.C., *The Secret History of the Roman Roads of Britain* (Barnsley: Pen & Sword, 2014)

Bishop, M.C., *The Gladius: The Roman Short Sword* (Oxford: Osprey Publishing Ltd, 2016)

Breeze, D.J., *Roman Scotland* (London: Batsford Ltd/ Historic Scotland, 2000)

Breeze, D.J., and Dobson, B., *Hadrian's Wall* (London: Penguin Books, 2000)

Brodribb, G., 'A Survey of Tile at the Roman Bath House at Beauport Park, Battle, East Sussex', *Britannia*, Vol. 10, pp.139–156 (Cambridge University Press, 1979)

Burgess, R.W., 'Principes cum Tyrannis: Two Studies on the *Kaisergeschichte* and its Tradition' in *The Classical Quarterly*, Vol.43, pp.491–500 (Cambridge University Press, 1993)

Campbell, D.B., 'The Fate of the Ninth', *Ancient Warfare* magazine, Vol. 4, No. 5, pp.48–53, 2011.

Campbell, D.B., 'The Fate of the Ninth: The Curious Disappearance of One of Rome's Legions' (Glasgow: Bocca della Verita Publishing, 2018)

Connolly, P., *Greece and Rome at War* (London: Macdonald & Co Ltd, 1988)

Cornell, T.J., 'The End of Roman Imperial Expansion', Rich, J. and Shipley, G. (eds), *War and Society in the Roman World*, pp.139–170 (London: Routledge, 1993)

Cornell, T.J., and Matthews, J., *Atlas of the Roman World* (Oxford: Phaidon Press Ltd, 1982)

Cotton, J., 'A miniature chalk head from the Thames at Battersea and the "Cult of the Head" in Roman London', Bird, J., Hassall, M. and

Sheldon, H. (eds), *Interpreting Roman London: Papers in Memory of Hugh Chapman*, pp.85–96, 1996.

Cowan, R., *Roman Legionary: 58 BC–AD 69* (Oxford: Osprey Publishing, 2003)

Cowan, R., *Imperial Roman Legionary: AD 161–284* (Oxford: Osprey Publishing, 2003)

Cowan, R., *Roman Battle Tactics: 109 BC–AD 313* (Oxford: Osprey Publishing, 2007)

Cunliffe, B., *Greeks, Romans and Barbarians: Spheres of Interaction* (London: Batsford Ltd, 1988)

D'Amato, R., and Sumner, G., *Arms and Armour of the Imperial Roman Soldier* (Barnsley: Frontline Books, 2009)

D'Amato, R., *Imperial Roman Naval Forces 31 BC–AD 500* (Oxford: Osprey Publishing, 2009)

D'Amato, R., *Roman Army Units in the Western Provinces (1): 31 BC–AD 195* (Oxford: Osprey Publishing, 2016)

D'Amato, R., *Roman Heavy Cavalry (1)* (Oxford: Osprey Publishing, 2018)

Davies, M., 'The Evidence of Settlement at Plaxtol in the Late Iron Age and Romano-British Periods', *Archaeologia Cantiana*, Vol. 129, pp. 257–278, 2009.

Elliott, P., *Legions in Crisis: The Transformation of the Roman Soldier AD 192–284* (Stroud: Fonthill Media Ltd, 2014)

Elliott, S., *Sea Eagles of Empire: The Classis Britannica and the Battles for Britain* (Stroud: The History Press, 2016)

Elliott, S., *Empire State: How the Roman Military Built an Empire* (Oxford: Oxbow Books, 2017)

Elliott, S., *Septimius Severus in Scotland: The Northern Campaigns of the First Hammer of the Scots* (Barnsley: Greenhill Books, 2018)

Elliott, S., *Roman Legionaries* (Oxford: Casemate Publishers, 2018)

Elliott, S., 'Clash of the Titans: The Battle of Lugdunum, AD 197' *Ancient Warfare* magazine, Vol. 13, No. 3, pp.27–35, 2020.

Ellis Jones, J., *The Maritime Landscape of Roman Britain* (Oxford: BAR/ Archaeological and Historical Associates Ltd, 2012)

Erdkamp, P. (ed.), *The Cambridge Companion to Ancient Rome* (Cambridge: Cambridge University Press, 2013)

Fields, Nic, 'Headhunters of the Roman Army', *Minerva* magazine, November/ December, pp.9-12, 2006.

Frere, S., *Britannia: A History of Roman Britain* (3rd edn.) (London: Routledge, 1974)

Frere, S., 'M. Maenius Agrippa, the Expeditio Britannica and Maryport', *Britannia* magazine, V.31, pp.23–28, 2000.

Garrison, E.G., *History of Engineering and Technology: Artful Methods* (Boca Raton, Florida: CRC Press, 1998)

Geoffrey of Monmouth, *The History of the Kings of Britain. An Edition and Translation of De gestis Britonum (Historia regum Britanniae)*, trans. N. Wright, Woodbridge (Boydell & Brewer, 2007)

Goldsworthy, A., *Roman Warfare* (London: Cassell, 2000)

Goldsworthy, A., *The Complete Roman Army* (London: Thames & Hudson, 2003)

Graafstaal, E., 'What Happened in the Summer of AD 122: Hadrian on the British Frontier – Archaeology, Epigraphy and Historical Agency', *Britannia* magazine, V.48, pp.76–111, 2018.

Heather, P., *Empires and Barbarians: Migration, Development and the Birth of Empire* (London: Macmillan, 2009)

Heather, P., *Rome Resurgent: War and Empire in the Age of Justinian* (Oxford: Oxford University Press, 2018)

Hingley, R., 'Roman Britain: The structure of Roman imperialism and the consequences of imperialism on the development of a peripheral province' in Miles, D. (ed.), *The Romano-British Countryside: Studies in Rural Settlement and Economy*, pp. 17–52 (Oxford: BAR/ Archaeological and Historical Associates Ltd, 1982)

Hingley, R., *Globalizing Roman Culture: Unity, Diversity and Empire* (London: Routledge, 2005)

Hingley, R., *Londinium: A Biography* (London: Bloomsbury Academic, 2018)

Holder, P., 'Auxiliary Deployment in the Reign of Hadrian', Wilkes, J.J. (ed.), *Documenting the Roman Army: Essays in honour of Margaret Roxan* Bulletin of the Institute of Classical studies Supplements, London, pp. 101–146, 2003.

Holland, T., *Dominion* (London: Little, Brown, 2019)

Hornblower, S., and Spawforth, A., *The Oxford Classical Dictionary* (Oxford: Oxford University Press, 1996)

James, S., *Rome and the Sword* (London: Thames & Hudson, 2011)

Jones, B. and Mattingly, D., *An Atlas of Roman Britain* (Oxford: Oxbow Books, 1990)

Kamm, A., *The Last Frontier: The Roman Invasions of Scotland* (Glasgow: Tempus, 2011)

Kean, R.M. and Frey, O., *The Complete Chronicle of the Emperors of Rome* (Ludlow: Thalamus Publishing, 2005)

Keppie, L., *The Making of the Roman Army from Republic to Empire* (London: Batsford, 1984)

Keppie, L., 'The Fate of the Ninth Legion: A Problem for the Eastern Provinces?' in Keppie, L. (ed.), *Legions and Veterans: Roman Army Papers 1971–2000*, pp. 247 (Stuttgart: Franz Steiner Verlag Wiesbaden GmbH, 2000)

Keppie, L., *The Legacy of Rome: Scotland's Roman Remains* (Edinburgh: Berlin, 2015)

Kiley, K. F., *The Uniforms of the Roman World* (Wigston: Lorenz Books, 2012)

Knusel, C.J. and Carr, G.C., 'On the Significance of the Crania from the River Thames and its Tributaries', *Antiquity* magazine, Vol. 69, pp. 162–9, 1995.

Kolb, A., 'The Cursus Publicus' in Adams, C. and Laurence, R. (eds), *Travel and Geography in the Roman Empire*, pp. 95–106 (London: Routledge, 2001)

Kulikowski, M., *Imperial Triumph: The Roman World from Hadrian to Constantine* (London: Profile Books, 2016)

Lambert, M., *Christians and Pagans* (New Haven: Yale University Press, 2010)

Le Bohec, Y., *The Imperial Roman Army* (London: Routledge, 2000)

McWhirr, A. and Viner, D., 'The Production and Distribution of Tiles in Roman Britain with Particular Reference to the Cirencester Region', *Britannia* magazine, Vol. 9, pp. 359–377, 1978.

Marsh, G. and West, B., 'Skullduggery in Roman London?' Transactions of the London and Middlesex Archaeological Society, Vol. 32, pp. 86–102, 1981.

Mason, D.J.P., *Roman Britain and the Roman Navy* (Stroud: The History Press, 2003)

Mattingly, D., *An Imperial Possession: Britain in the Roman Empire* (London: Penguin Books, 2006)

Mattingly, D., *Imperialism, Power and Identity: Experiencing the Roman Empire* (Princeton: Princeton University Press, 2011)

Matyszak, P., *Roman Conquests: Macedonia and Greece* (Barnsley: Pen & Sword, 2009)

Merrifield, R., *The Roman City of London* (London, Ernest Benn, 1965)

Millett, M., *The Romanization of Britain* (Cambridge: Cambridge University Press, 1990)

Millett, M., *Roman Britain* (London: Batsford, 1995)

Milne, G. and Richardson, B., 'Ships and Barges' in Milne, G. (ed.), *The Port of Roman London*, pp.96–102 (London: B T Batsford, 1985)

Moffat, B., 'A Marvellous Plant: The Place of the Heath Pea in Scottish Ethnobotanical Tradition', *Folio* magazine, Issue 1, pp.13–15, 2000.

Moorhead, S. and Stuttard, D., *The Romans Who Shaped Britain* (London: Thames & Hudson, 2012)

Myers, S.D., 'The River Walbrook and Roman London' PhD thesis (Unpublished: University of Reading, 2016)

Oleson, J.P., *The Oxford Handbook of Engineering and Technology in the Classical World* (Oxford: Oxford University Press, 2008)

Oman, C., *England Before the Norman Conquest* (London: Methuen, 1938)

Oosthuizen, S., *The Emergence of the English* (Leeds: Arc Humanities Press, 2019)

Ottaway, P., *Roman Yorkshire* (Pickering: Blackthorn Press, 2013)

Parker, A., *The Archaeology of Roman York* (Stroud: Amberley Books, 2019)

Parker, P., *The Empire Stops Here* (London: Jonathan Cape, 2009)

Pausche, D., 'Unreliable Narration in the *Historia Augusta*' (Ancient Narrative 8, pp.115–135, 2009)

Perring, D., 'London's Hadrianic War', *Britannia* magazine, Vol.41, pp.127–147, 2017.

Pitassi, M., *The Roman Navy* (Barnsley: Seaforth, 2012)

Pollard, N. and Berry, J., *The Complete Roman Legions* (London: Thames & Hudson, 2012)

Potter, D., *Rome in the Ancient World: From Romulus to Justinian* (London: Thames & Hudson, 2009)

Redfern, R. and Bonney, H., 'Headhunting and amphitheatre combat in Roman London, England: new evidence from the Walbrook valley', *Journal of Archaeological Science*, No. 43, pp.214–26, 2014.

Reid, R., 'Bullets, Ballistas and Burnswark: A Roman Assault on a Hillfort in Scotland', *Current Archaeology*, Vol. 27, Issue 316, pp.20–26, 2016.

Rodgers, N. and Dodge, H., *The History and Conquests of Ancient Rome* (London: Hermes House, 2009)

Ross, S. and Ross, C., 'Recent Roman Discoveries During the A1 Upgrade in North Yorkshire', *Current Archaeology*, Vol. 30, Issue 359, pp.18–22, 2020.

Rowsome, P., 'Mapping Roman London: Identifying its Urban Patterns and Interpreting Their Meaning' in Clark, J., Cotton, J., Hall, J., Sherris, R., Swain, H., (eds), *Londinium and Beyond: Essays on Roman London and its Hinterland for Harvey Sheldon*, Council for British Archaeology Research Report, Vol. 156, pp.25–32 (York, 2008)

Russell, M., 'What Happened to Britain's Lost Roman Legion?' *BBC History Magazine*, May issue, pp.40–45, 2011.

Salway, P., *Roman Britain* (Oxford: Oxford University Press, 1981)

Scarre, C., *The Penguin Historical Atlas of Ancient Rome* (London: Penguin, 1995)

Scarre, C., *Chronicle of the Roman Emperors* (London: Thames & Hudson, 1995)

Southern, P., *Roman Britain* (Stroud: Amberley Publishing, 2013)

Southern, P., *Hadrian's Wall: Everyday Life on a Roman Frontier* (Stroud: Amberley Publishing, 2016)

Starr, C.G., *The Roman Imperial Navy 31 BC–AD 324* (New York: Cornell University Press, 1941).

Todd, M., *Roman Britain 55 BC – AD 400: The Province Beyond Ocean* (Glasgow: Fontana Press, 1981).

Tomlin, R.S.O., *Roman London's First Voices* (London: Museum of London Archaeology, 2016)

Wallace-Hadrill, A., ed., *Patronage in Ancient Society* (Routledge: London, 1989)

Watson, G.R., *The Roman Soldier: Aspects of Greek and Roman Life* (Ithaca, New York: Cornell University Press, 1969)

Weber, W., *Untersuchungen zur Geschichte des Kaisers Hadrianus* (Leipzig: B.G. Teubner, 1907)

Wheeler, R.E.M., *London: Volume 3, Roman London* (Royal Commission on Historical Monuments of England, London, 1928)

Wilcox, P., *Rome's Enemies (3): Parthians and Sassanid Persians* (Oxford: Osprey Publishing, 1986)

Wilkes, J.J., 'Provinces and Frontiers' in Bowman, A. K., Garnsey, P. and Cameron, A. (eds), *The Cambridge Ancient History Vol. XII, The Crisis of Empire, AD 193–337*, pp.212–268 (Cambridge: Cambridge University Press, 2005)

Windrow, M. and McBride, A., *Imperial Rome at War* (Hong Kong: Concord Publications, 1996)

Wolff, C., 'Units: Principate' in le Bohec, Y. (ed) *The Encyclopedia of the Roman Army Vol. 3.*, pp.1037–1049 (Hoboken, New Jersey: Wiley-Blackwell, 2015)

Index